THE GODDESS CELEBRATES

AN ANTHOLOGY OF
WOMEN'S RITUALS

Edited by Diane Stein

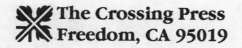

The Crossing Press
Freedom, CA 95019

For Shekhinah Mountainwater, a founder of the Women's Spirituality Movement.

Grateful acknowledgment is made to the following authors for permission to reprint previously published material:

Excerpts from *Miriam's Well, Rituals for Jewish Women Around the Year* by Penina Adelman. Copyright © 1986 by Penina Adelman. Reprinted by permission of Biblio Press, NY.
Excerpt from *The Laughter of Aphrodite* by Carol Christ. Copyright © 1987 by Carol Christ. Reprinted by permission of HarperCollins Publishers.
Excerpt from *The Journey is Home* by Nelle Morton. Copyright © 1985 by Nelle Morton. Reprinted by permission of Beacon Press.
Excerpt from *The Spiral Dance* by Starhawk. Copyright © 1979 by Miriam Simos. Reprinted by permission of HarperCollins Publishers.

Every effort has been made to locate copyright owners and secure permission for material used in this book.

Library of Congress Cataloging-in-Publication Data

The Goddess celebrates : an anthology of women's rituals / edited by
    Diane Stein.
        p.   cm.
    ISBN 0-89594-461-8   ISBN 0-89594-460-X (pbk.)
    1. Women--Religious life. 2. Women and religion. 3. Rites and
    ceremonies.   I. Stein, Diane
    BL625.7.G63 1991
    291.3'8'082--dc20   90-28925
                                                             CIP

Contents

1   **Introduction**
Diane Stein

12   **Teaching Women's Spirituality Rituals**
Z Budapest

22   **Remembering Her**
Marion Weinstein

37   **Ritual Creating and Planning**
Norma Joyce

64   **Exploring Our Goddess Selves Through Stories**
Jay Goldspinner

85   **Writings on Rituals and Spells**

120   **Rites of Kore**
Shekhinah Mountainwater

128   **Creating Sacred Space**
Starhawk

150   **Blood Mysteries**
Antiga

169   **Handfasting Ritual for Mari and Caridwyn**
Caridwyn Aleva

189   **Welcome to the Circle of Women**
Claudia L'Amoreaux

199   **Rituals for Birth**

210   **Healing Cesarean Section Trauma: A Transformational Ritual**
Jeannine Parvati Baker

217   **A Path of Change: Healing from Childhood Sexual Abuse**
Uzuri Amini

232   **Iyyar: A Menopause Ritual**

243   **Tevet: A Ritual for Mourning A Loved One**
Penina Adelman

252   **Eleusinian Mysteries**
Carol Christ

Introduction
Diane Stein

Since the late 1960s and the beginning of the women's liberation movement, Women's Spirituality has grown into the most important activist sub-movement of feminism. Beginning with such thinkers as Mary Daly, Judy Grahn, Ruth and Jean Mountaingrove, Merlin Stone, Starhawk and Z Budapest, Women's Spirituality has expanded into a grassroots movement nationally and internationally, of women and a few men practicing Goddess wicce in ritual groups, with friends or alone. The movement is alive and vital in the United States, Canada, South Africa, Australia, England, Poland, Germany, Mexico and Argentina — to name some of the places I've received letters from — and more. The women involved are also on the front lines for creating peaceful change in the world. They are activists and leaders in the ecology movement, in anti-Apartheid and anti-racism, in disability rights, women's, lesbian and gay rights, in healing, in ending world hunger and in ending the threat of nuclear contamination and nuclear war.

A religion going back to the beginning of time and before the beginnings of history (or herstory), the Goddess movement is highly relevant for women of today. Its foremost idea is that the Earth is alive and a Goddess and that all who live are a part of her. Everything that exists participates in Goddess, in the creation of life on the planet. Each Be-ing on the Earth creates and influences conditions and qualities of all life. Divinity is female, and is birth-giving/creative; all are a part of Goddess and are divinity. Where patriarchal values have submerged the Goddess, abuses to women and people of color and to the earth have created a less than desirable quality of living for too many. Where women's Goddess values are returning, women are validated, all people are honored as equal and free, and the planet begins to heal.

In the Goddess movement, unlike the patriarchal order of the past five thousand years, women have consequence in the world. Every culture's herstory and archeology reveals that this was once universal, but under

1

current political systems and religions (Christianity, Judaism, Islam) it's a new idea. No one in male history has ever told women that they can change the world and can choose their own lives. Women's values can again be validated. The Goddess/Women's Spirituality movement tells women just that and shows them how. It takes the primary political tenets of women's liberation and backs them with spirituality. This is a powerful combination of religion and statecraft which in male hands previously conquered the world. Everyone has a right to be here, and everyone born has the right to live in freedom, safety, health and respect. The Goddess is alive again after five thousand years and her magick is everywhere.

Central to Women's Spirituality is the concept of women's self-empowerment, and this is central in women's Goddess rituals. Rituals in Women's Spirituality create a microcosm, a 'little universe' within which women try out what they want the macrocosm, the 'big universe' or the real world to be. Within the safety and protected space of the cast circle, women create their idea of what the world would be like to live in under matriarchal/Goddess women's values. They enact the herstories of women and Goddesses of other times and make them now, becoming those Goddesses and women. They enact the cycles of the changing earth and thereby become in tune with the Goddess of the planet, become one with her. They celebrate the changing seasons as their own life passages, validating and honoring them. Women create change within the circle, releasing and healing the psychological damage of the patriarchal world and substituting it for a space where women are honored, nurtured, validated and powerful. When the circle is opened, the women take the values, stories, cycles, healing and knowledge of power-within/Goddess-within into the macrocosm of their everyday lives.

Ritual puts women in a position of power-within or Goddess-within. A Women's Spirituality ritual requires a single or shared leadership and requires all women to lead. It creates a safe space where women can develop this skill, and all women are expected to do so. Despite the women's movement controversy over leadership — that everyone leads, that no one should lead, that all are equal, that there are no 'stars' — someone has to take responsibility. As in everything else involving groups, if no one takes charge the group cannot unify to accomplish anything. Women's Spirituality states that all women are Goddess, that everyone is a leader, and ritual provides a place for learning how. Many women who have never taken a leadership role discover and nurture their leadership qualities in Goddess rituals. Many women develop initiative and leadership when working alone simply by creating and enacting their individual rituals. Taking leadership does not mean that one woman in the circle or group is "better" than another; all develop leadership abilities with equal opportunity and as their right. Everyone is Goddess and Goddess-within.

The woman who in the safety of the cast circle designs the world as she would like it to be takes that memory of creation and success out into daily life. A woman who feels Goddess enter her and fill her when she Draws Down the Moon in a Full Moon ritual has a different perspective of who she is after the ritual ends. A woman who has high priestessed a Sabbat for the first time knows something about herself afterwards that is different from what she knew before. A woman who in ritual meditation heals herself and the wrongs of the world, who sees herself whole and the planet clean and free, leaves the circle with a greater idea of what is possible and what it would be like. She has a greater impetus to take that microcosm into daily life and accomplish it on the earth, and a greater realization that her actions have consequence and can cause change. By empowering women through the microcosm of the ritual's cast circle, change becomes possible in the macrocosm real world.

Change begins in the individual. The woman who participates in Women's Spirituality rituals begins with changing herself. She is validated in the circle as the image of Goddess, the all-creating divinity of life on Earth. The validation comes from within and from the others of the circle as a Goddess-given right. Old patriarchal wounds that say she is "not good enough," "not strong enough," "can't do that" or "doesn't matter" are healed and erased forever. When a woman heals her own Goddess-within she is healing a portion of the Goddess and of the planet. First her own individual healing takes place, then she has the courage and strength to help others. Power-within grows exponentially and women together set about to right the wrongs of modern civilization.

A group of five such like-minded women then will set out to clean up a stream bed or a park in their neighborhood; a group of twenty-five will join a protest march for women's reproductive rights; a group of a hundred will set up a peace encampment. The numbers grow, the women elect officials to government who speak for their values and concerns. Apartheid crumbles and totalitarian regimes in Eastern Europe end, disarmament begins, and laws to control polluters are enforced. Homes, food, and jobs are opened to the world's homeless, many of whom are women with children. It all starts with the individual, and often begins in the microcosm of the Women's Spirituality ritual circle. All change begins with a new idea in the individual, and that idea along with "I care" is "I can."

This anthology is a selection of information on how to do ritual, how to change women's ideas to "I can." It is a companion book to *Casting the Circle: A Women's Book of Ritual* (Diane Stein, The Crossing Press, 1990). The writers in *The Goddess Celebrates* include women who are known in the spirituality movement, as well as women whose work may be less known. The topic of ritual was chosen by the writers themselves as an area of major interest to them personally and to the Women's Spirituality movement as a whole. Some of the women include Marion Weinstein, Z Budapest, Shekhinah Mountainwater, Uzuri Amini, Norma Joyce, and Antiga. A sampling of their topics includes the Goddess, teaching rituals, rituals and spells, healing the child within, planning rituals and women's blood mysteries. There is material here to interest every woman involved with Women's Spirituality, the Goddess and the Goddess Craft.

The Goddess Celebrates is a how-to book, based on the sharing of ideas, skills and techniques useful to anyone participating in Women's Spirituality rituals and change. The writers were chosen for their know-how, their contributions to the movement and the activist relevance of their work, as well as their ability to teach others. Most of the women are personal friends, or have become so in the work of writing and editing. There is a multitude of new ideas on ritual to try here and a variety of view-points, all directed to women's self-empowerment and to women's ability to change, transform and have consequence in the progress of the real world.

Ritual has become a central issue among Goddess groups, but very little how-to material is in print that satisfies women's needs. Most women recognize the power and importance of doing ritual, but many are afraid to start. There is an awareness of great power here, the type of inner power women are only beginning to uncover in their lives. The idea of a system of such importance and power-within that is a "create your own" system is a scary one for a population only beginning to learn "I can."

In starting to do ritual, there is a tendency for women to look for someone else to do it. They look for something already written rather than attempting to create their own. While a few books exist that contain already written rituals, little is available on how to create your own. Many groups just beginning to do ritual read from a book and by doing so lose the meaning and spontaneity of ritual-making. Or they elaborately plan a script that is memorized and acted out. The variety of ways to do ritual are barely discovered by this. If the women leave the circle feeling that "nothing has happened," they are less likely to try it again and even less likely to learn freedom of action and movement within the circle. If the group's critique of the ritual afterwards is less than gentle, some women will refuse to participate in or lead rituals again.

When information directed at how to do ritual is available — how a ritual is made, the ways to create it and how to perform it — new choices open up. There is purpose and structure along with content. When the group (or individual) knows that there are several different ways to cast a circle and when and how to do that, and an almost limitless possibility of things to do once the circle is cast, the subject opens up. Why and how come into discussion and the mystique is demystified. Creativity now can enter in, and the spontaneity and humor that makes rituals powerful can manifest. This how and when and why type of information is the purpose of this book.

At every gathering of like-minded women, the topic of ritual arises and becomes the center for many discussions on techniques, topics and skills. Ritual is a central tool for women's self-empowerment and there are many ways to do it. There is no right or wrong but only what works and is effective, important and meaningful for the participants. Women have a wide range of viewpoints and many questions. What makes a good ritual? How are rituals best constructed? What is the role of the high priestess or leader in rituals? Should there be a leader? What besides the obvious Eight Sabbats (calendar holidays) and Full Moons (monthly) make good ritual occasions?

Should rituals be "loud and rowdy" with bells, drums and rattles or should they be quiet and thoughtful? What about women who are uncomfortable with movement or touch or with speaking out loud, or who are disabled or in emotional recovery from incest or abuse? How can so varied a group as women come together in a ritual that gives every woman what she needs? How can everyone with different needs celebrate the Goddess together? What makes a ritual empowering to women, reinforcing the concept of Goddess-within?

The answers to these questions are continually evolving, as the Women's Spirituality movement is evolving, and the topic of ritual is an ongoing one in women's discussions and concerns. The women in this anthology offer a variety of women's movement thoughts on ritual, with the intent to spark new ideas. Their viewpoints are as varied as their own backgrounds and cultures and they offer what works for them so others can try it. These women are highly respected in the Goddess movement and are doing work that is important for women as individuals and for the movement as a whole. They tell the individual woman that she can create her own, and by that experience learn to create change in herself and in the world.

Like everyone else doing ritual, I have my own ideas as to what a Women's Spirituality ritual is. That way is not the only way, but is *one* way for creating successful, change-empowering rituals for women. In this anthology a number of women speak to offer their ideas, and I list my basic outline of ritual structure here as a beginning frame of reference. This is the outline I use for all types of rituals; read *Casting the Circle* for fuller details and much more discussion. The basic ritual outline is as follows:

Ritual Structure
1. Purification
2. Casting the Circle
3. Invoking the Directions/Elements
4. Drawing Down the Moon (on Full Moons)
5. The Charge of the Goddess (on Sabbats and Full Moons)
6. Invocation/Purpose of Ritual
7. Meditation (Most rituals)
8. Body of Ritual
9. Self-Blessing
10. Raising the Cone of Power (Most rituals)
11. Grounding
12. Opening the Circle/Thanking the Elements
13. Endings/Group Hugs/Sharing Food

Drawing Down the Moon is used only for Full Moon rituals and The Charge of the Goddess is read on Sabbats and Full Moons only, with a few exceptions. A *very* brief description of the steps is given below, necessarily incomplete and with little discussion. The steps are used in this order.

1. *Purification* means separating oneself from the cares of the daily world and becoming fully present in the circle of women. It means clearing the mind and getting calm. Most Women's Spirituality rituals use incense smoke, smudging each of the women in the circle with the smoke as the beginning of the ritual. Be aware that some women are allergic to incense; ask before using it. Other methods include sprinkling each woman with salt water, brushing the women's auras with a flower stalk or broom, or the women holding hands and deep breathing together. Sometimes the leader/

high priestess of the ritual or this part of it performs the smudging, sprinkling or stroking, and sometimes the women do it themselves or for each other. Purification does not imply that the women are "impure," but is a means of clearing oneself of the impurities and negativities of the outside world.

2. *Casting the Circle* is done by tracing the circumference of the circle that the women holding hands together creates. This is a symbolic gesture of separating the circle and women from the material world. It is usually done by the leader or another woman tracing the outside of the circle with an athame (ritual knife or sword), wand or flower stalk, walking around it holding a candle or a simply using a sweep of her hand. Once the circle is cast, the women are asked to remain in place and not leave it until it is opened at the end of the ritual. Everyone should be present before the circle is cast. The purpose of casting the circle is to symbolically delineate that within the circle is a safe space for women to be who they really are. Creating safe and sacred space for women is the major prerequisite for doing ritual.

3. *Invoking the Directions/Elements* is to invite into the circle Goddesses of the four directions — North, South, East and West — plus the Center, Above and Below. (Native American traditions use eight directions, some women use only four or five; whatever the group chooses is right.) When I invoke the directions I use a Goddess from each of five cultures for the North, South, East, West and Center. My own choices in this are: North, the earth element, Flora, Roman Goddess of flowers and beauty; East, the air element, Sappho, Greek foremother of poetry and inspiration; South, the fire element, Amaterasu, Japanese Goddess of fire and women's power; West, the element of water, Yemaya, Yoruba African Goddess of birth and healing; and Center, the cauldron of immortality, Spider Woman, Navajo and Hopi Goddess who created the universe and all life. I salute the sky Above and the Earth Below before inviting the elements/directions into the circle. A different woman can invoke each direction. In this invoking, the group invites the Goddesses' qualities into the circle *i.e.,* beauty, inspiration, women's power, healing and immortality. They also invite these qualities into the women's lives. The power of the ritual begins here.

4. *Drawing Down the Moon* is done only at Full Moon rituals, though I also like to do it at Summer Solstice. The high priestess of the ritual, in a gesture of reaching out into the universe and bringing down, invokes the power of the Full Moon Goddess into herself and into the women of the

ritual. This is a symbolic gesture, but the energy felt is immense. In rituals where Drawing Down the Moon is not performed, simply invite the Goddess to enter the circle and be part of it, to participate in and help with whatever the ritual's purpose is.

5. *The Charge of the Goddess* is probably the only written document of Women's Spirituality and was possibly originated by Doreen Valiente. Versions of it are available in almost any book on Women's Spirituality or women's rituals. The Charge is read on Full Moons and Sabbats, but is not used in women's Rites of Passage rituals or for funerals. It describes in beautiful language the purpose and tenets of the Goddess movement:

> If that which you seek you find not within yourself,
> you shall never find it without.

Shekhinah Mountainwater has created a musical version of The Charge on her tape, *Songs and Chants of the Goddess*.

6. *Invocation/Purpose of the Ritual* very simply states why the circle is gathered, what they are celebrating, what they have come to make ritual about. It can be just a line or two of simple statement or involve a poem, song, dance or short literary piece. Many women in Goddess Spirituality are highly creative; someone in the circle will know what to say. Setting out the purpose of the ritual before beginning the active parts of it makes for clarity and sets the mood and intent.

7. *Meditation* in women's rituals usually involves a guided journey. I like to use them in most rituals, as they both create the ritual atmosphere fully and can be used to envision the world as women would create it in the circle. For example, a meditation on what the world would be like if there were no war, or what women's lives would be like if they were healed from the patriarchy, shows women what is possible in their own terms. Once they can envision such a world, free of war and patriarchal damage, they can begin to create it and make it real. The microcosm displayed in the meditation becomes the goal for creating change in the individual and in the macrocosm outside world. In a Sabbat or Rite of Passage ritual, the meditation can be used to view and to be part of the life cycles of the Earth or of women. Some ritualists don't use meditations at all and some only use them occasionally, but for myself the ritual meditation is important and empowering.

8. *The Body of the Ritual* is the main event, what the women came to do in the circle. If the occasion is a Sabbat, the body of the ritual may be to

enact something important about the Sabbat. At Candlemas, for example, that enactment might be to do group healing or initiation, as those are qualities of the Sabbat. At Hallows it may be to enact death and rebirth; at Spring Equinox it may be to re-experience childhood. In a Rite of Passage ritual, the purpose is to celebrate a milestone in the life of an individual woman. The body of the ritual in a Croning would be designed to validate that woman's achievements as a woman of power. New Moons celebrate beginnings and Full Moons wishes and fulfillments; the body of the ritual would reflect these things. The variety of ways to do this in a ritual is almost endless. It may be best to keep the body of the ritual activity very simple, making its meaning very clear and evident to the participating women. Every woman in the circle should be involved actively here.

9. *Self-Blessing* is another activity that some ritualists use with less frequency and emphasis, but I use it in almost every ritual. With women's self-empowerment central to ritual and to Women's Spirituality, the Self-Blessing is a simple, beautiful and powerful way to do just that. One woman leads this but all participate. There are other versions of the Self-Blessing, but mine uses the chakras, touching each energy center with fragrant oil (or use water, wine, menstrual blood or nothing) and saying:

(*Touching the Crown*): Bless me Mother for I am your child and I am a part of you.
(*Touching the Brow*): Bless me that I may see my way and see you.
(*Touching the Throat*): Bless me that I may speak clearly and speak of you.
(*Touching the Heart*): Bless me that my heart be open and whole with love.
(*Touching the Solar Plexus*): Bless me with energy and health for all my life.
(*Touching the Belly Chakra*): Bless my sexuality with balance and joy.
(*Touching the Root Chakra*): Bless my vagina, the gateway of life and death.
(*Touching the soles of the feet*): Bless my feet that they may walk in your paths and know my way.
(*Touching the palms of the hands*): Bless my hands that they may do your work and my own.
(*Touching the Crown again*): Bless me Mother for I am your

child and I am a part of you.

Use the Self-Blessing either before Raising the Cone of Power or after Grounding, before Opening the Circle.

10. *Raising the Cone of Power* is done in most rituals. The purpose of it is to gather up all of the increasing power of the ritual to this point, focus it, and direct it for the purpose of the ritual. This purpose varies from ritual to ritual; the cone may be used for healing individuals or the planet, for making wishes come true on the Full Moon, for a blessing at a Rite of Passage. The cone is raised by singing, drumming, chanting or humming that increases in intensity and speed to an emotional height. At a signal from the high priestess or whoever is in charge of monitoring it, the music is brought to an abrupt halt and the women are led in a visualization of the energy rising into the universe to do its work. When done at just the right time, which takes practice to learn to monitor, the sensation of power and accomplishment of this is immense. All the intent of the ritual goes into this cone of energy that is directed to the ritual's purpose. It is the culmination of the ritual's power.

11. *Grounding* means releasing any excess energy that may remain in the women after the Cone of Power is released. The women bend down to touch the palms of their hands or their foreheads to the floor or Earth, and/or sit on the ground. Nothing needed will be lost, but to skip Grounding invites nervousness or a sleepless night after the ritual. Grounding also brings the women back from the "other world" of the circle's power, returning them to now and the earthplane. Many rituals pass out food at this point, the wine and cakes of traditional wicce, as eating is also a way of Grounding. The Self-Blessing can be done here, after Grounding and before Opening the Circle.

12. *Opening the Circle/Thanking the Elements* is the formal ending of the ritual, done after the purpose of the evening has been accomplished and the Cone of Power sent out to manifest it in the world. In reverse order of Invoking the Directions, the high priestess or women of the circle thank and release the Goddesses that were invoked at the beginning of the ritual. The ritual ends with the formal declaration:

The circle is now open but unbroken,
May the peace of the Goddess go with you.
Merry meet and merry part and merry meet again.
Blessed be.

13. *Endings/Group Hugs/Sharing Food* finish the evening. The women will not want to leave right away. I like to have a group hug as the ending of circles, with either the women piled together for it or everyone hugging everyone else as the circle opens. A potluck dinner is another good way to end a ritual, turning the evening into a social. Once they have shared ritual together, the women will be open and caring of each other and ready for friendships. Groups that engage in critiquing rituals are asked not to do so at this time. Working together and sharing (including the sharing of food and of the work of cleaning up) are fully a part of the purpose of women's rituals.

With this background and structure in mind, I give you *The Goddess Celebrates: An Anthology of Women's Rituals,* and invite you to participate in one of the beautiful things in life, women coming together to empower themselves and each other and to celebrate the Goddess. Women's rituals are the beginning of a return to sanity for the planet and all who live on Goddess Earth. I deeply thank the women who have participated in the ritual of creating this anthology with me, and thank also the women who will participate by reading it. Together we create a women's world, a world of peace between nations and people, where all are equal, honored and whole, a world of freedom, safety, health and respect for women and the planet/Goddess Earth.

March 25, 1990
Darkest Moon in Pisces

Z Budapest

Zsuzsanna (Z) Budapest is a Hungarian born witch and the mother of the Women's Spirituality movement. For the past twenty years she has been teaching women through ritual, books, classes and lectures about feminism and its unique link to the Goddess. She is the author of *The Holy Book of Women's Mysteries*, Volumes I and II and *The Grandmother of Time*, her 1989 release from Harper and Row. In the earliest days of Women's Spirituality, Z was the first, and for a long time the only, teacher of women and women's mysteries in the Goddess. Many of today's Goddess movement leaders are her spiritual daughters, and all have been touched by her work, thought and teaching. For many women, Z Budapest's books were their introduction and first early lifeline to what now is the Women's Spirituality movement.

In 1986, Z Budapest founded the Women's Spirituality Forum, a non-profit organization which produces lecture series, workshops, spiral dances, classes and consciousness-raising groups in its effort to educate women on the Goddess and feminist spirituality. Twice yearly she publishes *Callisto*, the newsletter of the Women's Spirituality Forum. Presently Z is also starring in her own cable TV show, *13th Heaven*. This monthly half-hour show on the Goddess, her herstory and her many manifestations plays on public access channels throughout the California Bay Area. She is also kept busy traveling around the country empowering women with her insightful wisdom and witchcraft.

Z Budapest is flamboyant and powerful, a portrait of the Goddess herself as we all are. She is full of ideas that make women think, whether they agree with her or not. Besides being an expert ritualist who makes it all look so easy, she is an expert tarot reader and counselor. She is a strong, brave woman who has survived much and risked much to bring Women's Spirituality to the west.

In "Teaching Women's Spirituality Rituals," Zsuzsanna Budapest describes what makes a good ritual and what makes a ritual work. With simplicity, power and beauty the component parts come together in a life-changing experience for women. I deeply appreciate Z's participation and wisdom in this book.

Contact Zsuzsanna Budapest at the Women's Spirituality Forum, P.O. Box 5143, Berkeley, California 94705.

Teaching Women's Spirituality Rituals

Z Budapest

Twenty years ago I embarked on a brand new road towards spiritual liberation which included being a woman as its center point. There was, already, a so-called "new age" movement, which featured a lot of long-bearded, dark-faced middle-aged men from the East. The gurus brought with them vegetarian foods, bayberry/banana incenses, and expensive mantras. They also had an attitude towards women which was infuriating. They ignored us. "It's all the same" they would incant with their eyes rolled upwards, "men . . . women it makes no difference. . . ." Hmm. Seductive but untrue. They said it made no difference but to the women it was the same old patriarchal hierarchy. When you looked at how these new-age gurus ran their business, you could see the women in the kitchen peeling the organic potatoes with babies strapped to their saris and the men teaching yoga and running the show. This kind of new age was actually the proverbial "old hat."

Along came Women's Liberation and the feminist discovery of the Goddess and the women suddenly realized that there is more to spirituality than wild rice and "oooom." Slowly and continuously, but in great numbers, women gathered like a weather front to examine this treasure, our own spiritual heritage, and they found it good.

Now we are twenty years later and we have to make sure the teachers actually pass down the baton, the accumulated knowledge and experience. Thank heavens today a slew of published clever and inspiring books exist about the Goddess and are available to new readers. They range from archeology, theology, invocations, study books, Tarot and astrology, including my own books which center on the practice of Women's Spirituality. But there is a problem. Many important teachings which touch the heart of the Goddess practice depend on nonverbal and experiential teachings, which are difficult to pass down since we have not established any Feminaries where we would teach the theology and practice of the Goddess.

14

Such an establishment is very necessary. The teachers are all here in body, ready to fill in the posts, but where are the Goddess philanthropists, who would use their wealth as a magical tool, to buy a building and set up the finances and administration? The most difficult part of the Goddess curriculum appears to be the successful conducting of a ritual. A ritual cannot be learned from books. A ritual can be explained, and it has been explained many times. Its importance has been emphasized and that, too, has been done often, but when people gather together to experience a transformational ritual, often the circles turn out to be a disappointment, because the "intangible" teaching, the very essence of the ritual and how to do it, is nonverbal. We must teach that in person. This personal teaching happens when I am on tour and visit universities, women's festivals, and larger gatherings of women. The exposure is brief, only one night often, one circle — only so much can be passed down. I will contradict myself now and try, however feebly, to communicate what this nonverbal essence is all about.

Imagine that inside of you there is an ancient being, I call her the Slothwoman, this Cro-Magnon, hairy, tall, ungainly, lumbering creature, who is preverbal. This Slothwoman through nature's wise and quirky mood ended up controlling our slick modern person's health, love life, sexual prowess, vitality, body, racial memories — in short most everything that we consider important. The key to our magic is how we can arouse her interest in our work, the key to our magic is how we can wake up this ancient being within us. I know we talk a lot about the Goddess within, which often makes me think of a small Goddess statue stationed somewhere between our heart and the liver, and I laugh. The truth may be much less glamorous, but even more awesome. In order to own our magic we must reclaim our own animal nature, because we are part of nature even though we type on computers and think of ourselves as "higher beings." So who is she? Who is this Slothwoman within? What does she like?

She is bored with your modern life. It isn't she who goes to work every morning to make money to live on. But if you decided perchance to hunt for your supper and bag a rabbit, cook it, and eat it, it would be her greatest pleasure to wake up from her boredom, get excited, and perform it for you. She may come out when you are on a date, to assess your partner for attractiveness. If she likes your date, you will fall in love. If she doesn't like your date, forget it, no sparks will fly. When you eat she wakes up. She likes the smell of food, especially outdoor cooking, she is the one turning over the hamburgers on the barbeque on the Fourth of July, and she gets happy seeing the fireworks. She also likes outdoor hikes. She understands the power of the moon. Friends gathering in a circle makes her excited enough to get up and lend you her vitality. Your Slothwoman loves her sleep and dreaming time. She also likes to be up at night and sleep in late. She understands candlelight, incense makes her feel a mysterious awe, humming and chanting are her arts, dancing is her passion.

Unless you can make your Slothwoman come to your ritual, get excited about the purpose of your ritual, no magic will happen. Hmm. This part of our selves is older than the modern brain, it is the middle of the brain, without which we cannot survive and certainly cannot do magic. Slothwoman is illiterate. She doesn't like books, she would smell them and maybe bite off the edge of the cover to taste it. You cannot preach to her — she would go right back to sleep. Her attention span is shorter than that of an average TV viewer.

So, keeping this in mind, how do you go about creating a successful ritual? Fortunately it isn't that difficult. You need to incorporate elements into the ritual that make her stay with you — candlelight, food on the altar, pleasant smelling incense, women humming, dancing around the altar, chanting, singing, moonshine, stars, outdoors. A good ritual doesn't take a very long time — for a small group half an hour to 45 minutes is plenty of time. For larger groups, one hour, or an hour and a half should do it fine. The purpose is to have a high quality experience, not a long one. When you feel the energy is fading, it is time to thank the spirits you invoked, and start the party, the informal visiting. Never let a ritual die because you have planned many things to do and are sticking to a script.

Planning a ritual: Plan together what will happen in the circle with everybody involved, not just an appointed committee. You need consensus from all members for the purpose of the ritual because you don't create a ritual without a reason.

For example, it is popular simply to let a few women hold a meeting where they cook up ideas for the rest of the group. This sounds good on the surface, but once it is put in motion, you will find that the group is untouched, their Slothwoman stays asleep, because they are passive — they expect you to do it *to* them, instead of creating the gestalt of the circle together.

I have just been to Hartford University in Connecticut. Women were told to bring candles, and sacred objects for the altar, pillows to sit on, and not much else. About two hundred or so women came and a few kids. Half of the women had never attended any kind of Goddess event before, half of them belonged to covens. I decided to field this information right away so I learned the level of the circle. Next I gave a little talk about what a circle is for. I asked the women present if they had any burning issues they wanted to direct the circle towards. As often happens, the women came forward and named many issues, praying for friends in their communities who were ill, but soon we named more general issues: child abuse, kidnapping, world hunger, drought, and AIDS. Women are very inclusive in their spirituality. It has been consistent in the twenty years I have been a priestess that the women have always brought the world into the circles.

Next, I explained who the Goddess is, for those who thought she was the flipside of the patriarchal god. The flipside of the patriarchal god is the patriarchal devil, not the Goddess. The Goddess is mother nature. Nature is the only reality in the universe, and beyond nature there is more nature. Nature has no beginning and no end.

Then I taught them the chants and songs I was going to utilize as we went along, especially the power raising humming, which we practiced for a short while until it warmed them up. In the middle of this humming practice a young male from the university decided to protest the "women only" event (the first at Hartford) by putting a see-through stocking over his face and running on stage stark naked. Once he was center stage, his penis shrunk into a tiny noodle and the women looked up and broke into laughter. This broke the ice and we were now united more than before. The intended disruption had backfired. There were other males who wanted to disrupt our work but the women escorted them out as soon as they stepped out of the elevators. Hartford males are twenty years behind the rest of the country where women-only events have happened since the seventies.

I asked women to create the altar together, everybody placing their candle on it, sacred objects and flowers, fresh baked bread. Now they understood that they were going to have to cooperate with each other, the women moved easily to the altar, establishing their own space, and blending their energies with each other. Slowly a beautiful altar emerged. From here in their deep minds, the slothwomen were engaged.

We formed arches holding hands, but because the women were 250 strong, it was I who moved through the arches created by their arms, holding sage, blessing them as I moved through. Usually everybody passes through these arches, saying "Through women you have been born into this world, through women you are born into this circle." I had made plans to do otherwise. Often you will find that your idea for a circle planned in a room, doesn't fit. Reasons may be numerous — ideas in a room do not fit the outdoors, plans made without the people being there are not shared with the group. Sometimes the best of ideas for a circle opening will die if it takes too long. I just shared my plans with the group and the group came up with their own version for the opening. It may never happen again quite like that in the universe. That is what is so great about the communal energy, it's creative and more brilliant than any one of the individuals in it. The Hartford gathering made do very well with the impromptu preparation we shared before we started the ritual. It is enough to spend about thirty (don't get them tired) minutes discussing details with the group, adding that all this preparation is subject to change, so the moment can teach.

When the Moment teaches, it's magic time. To create this opportunity for the moment to be born is your job as a priestess. The best advice is know how to step aside. In fact that is my most important skill as a priestess — create the circle, prepare the people, then step aside.

At Hartford, the women hummed very admirably for the first time, they sounded like a gathering of bees, there was tension and expectation in their sound, the brand new women and the experienced ones all created a lovely tapestry of sound, rich and varied. I was pleased. Then the humming wanted to rest. It had flown its course, it had risen and fallen and risen again, then subsided. There was magic power so thick amongst us you could slide your hand against it. This was the Moment.

"Light your candles now," I said softly.

"Tell us what is on your heart."

I lit the first candle to show example.

"I light this candle for the Goddess' return all over the world." After this the women took their turns one by one, and as usual they generously represented diverse goals, inclusive of everybody. I have never attended a circle where women asked the Goddess to grant them things for their own lives only. More common is what happened at Hartford:

"I light this candle for ending hunger in the world." (*white*)

"I light this candle to help the sexes make peace and find balance amongst them." (*rose*).

"I light this candle for lesbian visibility." (*lavender*)

"I light this candle for my mother who is ill and in the hospital." (*orange*)

"I light this candle for my friend who is having a baby." (*white*)

Many many women spoke, and at the end when all the candles were blazing it was a wondrous sight. The images of the Goddess, a Diana with her bows and arrows, a fat earth Goddess giving birth to the future, a small bronze of the Aphrodite appeared to be speaking to us in a familiar language. "You are home now. You have found yourself. Be happy, all will be well!"

This is now time for a dance. We chanted:

We are the weavers, we are the web
We are the flow and we are the ebb.
We are the flow and we are the web
We are the witches back from the dead!
      —Shekhinah Mountainwater

When all our candles were blazing bright, we slowly made a Spiral Dance singing:

Lady lady listen to my heart's song,
Lady, lady listen to my heart's song,
I will never forget you,
I will never forsake you,
I will never forget you,
I will never forsake you.

This song is always accompanied with eye contact (Slothwoman's main source of communication). As we walked by each other we nodded respectfully to each other and our eyes met lovingly. It is very rare for women to feel that the other women are actually loyal to them, that there is no competition, no self-hatred, no defeatist backfighting. Women affirming other women is a healing experience and I have seen eyes misted over with tears.

The dance around the circle soon became its own happening. The younger women started impromptu fast dances, the older ones beat their drums or just walked at their own space. I stepped aside and allowed it to do its own thing, just keeping out an inner ear for energy in case a new chant was needed. When I felt the chant had run its course, I jumped in with a new one, and the group took it on and the energy rose some more. It helps if there are some real dancers amongst you, who could start a step easily imitated by others.

The circle finally felt like winding down. Before it lost its steam, I used my Tibetan Ting-Shaws to draw attention to myself in the crowds, and asked them all to participate in thanking the spirits we invoked. The women gladly added their voices to the many thank yous, and we dismissed the spirits. Nearby our auditorium a place called "Gallows Hill" was remembered. This was a place where they hung witches or tossed them down from the rocky peak to their deaths. We thanked those spirits and sent them peace and love from a new generation. A closing chant grounded the group:

> May Artemis protect you,
> and Hera provide you,
> and the womansoul within you,
> guide your way home.

We broke the fresh baked breads, which were in the shape of a wheel, and fed each other bites, saying, "May you never hunger." As we accepted the bites from each other's hands, we fed the next woman the same way. This meant a lot; it meant we would take responsibility for each other's hunger, be it spiritual or physical. You could imagine the Slothwoman was right with us — she loved this part.

We tossed flowers to the four directions of the universe, to the east/south/west/north as an offering to our special spirits who transformed the ballroom with the chandeliers into a cave of the earth for the Goddess' secret rites next door to Gallows Hill. The women took their candles off the altar to be finished at home on their home altars. Those who didn't have one now knew how to build one and were motivated to do so. The magic we raised was internalized through grounding with breath and song, hugs and food. I don't believe in grounding by banging on the floor and inhaling the dust from our feet. Breath and food will do very nicely and it is more elegant.

The circle was a rousing success. Women came to me afterwards saying how miraculously they were touched by the magic and the beauty. They gave me crystals to remember them by, and other mementos. I was deeply moved by their gratitutde. I told them for a first circle they did very well. We had more refreshments, apples and drinks. The women's center responsible for this event provided graciously the feast foods, as well as a place where the women could form new circles, and use their own imagination to create circles like the one we had that night.

Did I convey the intangible essence, the magical something that makes a good ritual? Let me see, what was it? Sharing comes to mind, sharing as many things as possible in a smooth and non-boring way. A little preparation goes a long way. Don't be nervous. When the Goddess is present, the circle will flow. You must have a good repertoire of songs and chants, that is always a must, and somebody must bring that into the circle. Think of dance steps, but if the group is not into it, be prepared to drop all the good ideas and go with what is possible at the time in the present setting. Women's spirituality depends a great deal on improvisation. Many women don't feel free to improvise, so the group leader must have a contagious inner freedom that will liberate the others by example. Be free to call out the names of the Goddess loudly and impressively like you mean it. Don't act like a ringmaster but rather like a gracious hostess who has all kinds of fun ideas on her mind. Humor is the greatest medicine. Develop a sense of humor in the circle, don't let people get too reverential, except of course when that is appropriate. And only then in the moment will you know if it is. Organize follow-up meetings where women can discuss their shared experience and relate it to the rest of the group. You learn many new things when you hear the treasury of the communal mind.

Rotate the role of the priestess in smaller circles so confidence can grow in women who may become good ritualists in the future. Ohh, the future . . . Women have herstorical amnesia. That's why we progress so slowly. We don't know what our sisters have already figured out for us, we don't have a flow of information where we can catch up and go beyond the daily inventing of the wheel all by ourselves again and again. In the nineties we must remedy this. Read and read as much as you can in Goddess study groups, which are the seeds of future women's congregations for the Goddess. Then practice your slothwoman's awareness, bring her out under the full moon howling with the wolves, bring her out with good company and feasts, and you will see your mental state improve as well as your social life, your immune system will be stronger and the communities you build will last and last like the redwoods.

May the Goddess lead us to this new life, the woman-affirming times, these life-affirming woman times, this fortunate future women built. Blessed be!

Marion Weinstein

Marion Weinstein's *Positive Magic* (Phoenix Publications, 1981) has been many women's first introduction to the Goddess craft and was one of the books that brought me into wicce. Its magick, wit, reverence, common sense, information, and strong ethics are a solid grounding in the Women's Spirituality/Goddess movement. *Positive Magic* makes the craft real by offering real teaching on what witches do while demystifying the stereotypes and presenting wicce as the beautiful and viable religion that it is. The book is a work of joy, and one I recommend heartily to women everywhere. It's a book for beginners and a book for experienced witches. Marion's *Earth Magic: A Dianic Book of Shadows* (Phoenix Publications,

1986) offers further information and insights on practicing the Goddess craft.

A public witch since 1969, Marion Weinstein hosted the regularly scheduled radio program Marion's Cauldron on WBAI-FM from 1969 to 1983. The show featured interviews, music, talk, phone calls, comedy and occult information. Her annual Halloween Special was a New York tradition. Long before today's variety of books and information was available, and long before the New Age, Women's Spirituality or wiccan movements were household words, Marion was presenting wicce in positive ways, and introducing women to the Goddess. Appearing on mainstream radio and television programs nationally and locally, on the lecture circuit and featured in numerous national and international magazines and publications, Marion Weinstein has worked for twenty years to educate women on the Goddess craft.

Also a wonderfully funny stand-up comic, Marion uses gentle feminist wit and magick in her comedy routines. She has appeared in New York City at Town Hall, The Village Gate, Cafe Wow and more, and at the First International Goddess Conference in Sacramento. Her comedy tape, *Marion Weinstein, Stand Up Witch* is available on audio and video tape from Earth Magic Productions. Another audio tape, *Positive Magic: The Music* features two songs and is available from the same source. She co-publishes a wiccan newsletter, *Earth Magic Times*, as well. Everything Marion does is a delight.

In "Remembering Her," Marion Weinstein talks about the Goddess, who she is, why she is, what she means to each of us, what the Women's Spirituality craft means to each of us. Her chapter is derived from a lecture and is also the beginning of Marion's new book, *Remember the Goddess*. Says Marion Weinstein:

In my own life, when I've been through some very hard times, She's helped me incredibly. So experientially, I can say that the answer has always been to never forget Her for a second. To remember Her. How to remember Her? *We can embody Her*. Let us explore some of the ways, now.

Contact Marion Weinstein at Earth Magic Productions, Inc., 2170 Broadway, Suite 16, New York, New York, 10024.

Remembering Her

Marion Weinstein

There are so many things to say about the Goddess, to think about Her. I'm really amazed that I was able to pick one subject. But maybe it isn't just one subject after all — it's one *focus*. It's one choice, one facet of a multi-faceted, infinitely faceted reality, which the Goddess is.

I recently had the realization that the Goddess isn't only a powerful concept and a beautiful idea to inspire us. She's with us every minute, every day — and if She's not, I think we should let Her be. This is not a matter of "making" Her be with us, or forcing ourselves to be aware of Her. It's just a matter of shedding some cultural problems that may have prevented us from knowing that She's with us. The ways in which She is with us are constantly being revealed. It is important to note that this *process* of discovery is itself a source of tremendous power. In fact, the unique process which each one of us experiences in finding Her — is part of Her, too.

This is what I mean by remembering the Goddess.

I recently wrote a song called "Remember the Goddess,"[1] and I'm also using this as the title of my next book. When I say "remember the Goddess," of course I mean, remember Her in the way Merlin Stone tells us on the first page of *When God Was A Woman*, which totally inspired me from the instant I read it — by remembering the time when She was in charge of everything. But now I also mean remember Her *always*. As always around, as always there for us. That's really all we have to do.

And even if you're not a witch — if you choose Her realm, if you choose Her power in whatever style you want (because there are no rules except some very basic ones about not hurting other people) — then She's there for you. And yes, even if you're a man, She's still there for you.

Also, you see, the magic of this is: When we remember Her for ourselves, when we have this daily reminder that She's there and powerful for us — then we are bringing Her back into the world. (Not that She ever left, but we are bringing Her presence into greater awareness.) Because the

old magical saying, "as above so below," is synonymous with the theologi-
cal concept of the microcosm and macrocosm, and our beliefs are echoing
in an ever endless echo. When we allow Her to come back into our lives,
then She comes back into the world.

In my opinion, and many of you may agree: There's only one thing
wrong with the world today. I mean, if you could boil it all down to one
problem — I'd call it *lopsided Deity*. It's just too patriarchal! This is not
news to us. I think if you look at any problem — from a nuclear problem to
a political problem to starvation problems to the worst problems we may
see on the news — you could distill it all down to a vision of Deity which
is just too one-sided. Because it's the shared vision of Deity which inspires
people consciously and which affects society on a subconscious level. All
the qualities that She represents and encourages us to be — nurturing, fair,
just, kind, considerate, letting the Earth flourish — that's all what's
missing. Do you agree with that?

How many of us are witches? A friend of mine has been calling
witchcraft The *W-Word* lately, because of public opinion, but I have been
using the word witch since I was a little girl. To deny the word, I feel, is to
dilute the power of being a real witch and to give power to the wrongful
definitions of the persecutions. Being a witch means being a Goddess
worshipper. Now, Goddess religions can take countless other paths too,
and many Goddess worshippers are not witches. But all witches are Goddess worshippers. The Goddess' realm includes what most people call
magic, which I have defined as transformation — and which the established religions have been afraid of. Afraid, because the established
religions, in this culture, worship a Deity who is hierarchical, who has to be
in charge of the miracles. So, for us to say, "Oh, no, we can do the miracles
ourselves" may seem like a threat. I first began talking about the Goddess
and magic on WBAI, in 1969.

And now my point is, I really want Her to come back. It's enough
already! It's not that She hasn't come back — She's back with us. It's not
even that She ever really left. But Her influence is needed, and people's
awareness of Her, and Her involvement in the culture. How can we help
bring this about? We can all remember how to involve Her ourselves, and
that means when/if we are on the line, when we have a problem, when we
don't feel well, if we feel threatened, or angry — if we don't like something
we see out in the world, if we don't like something we see in the news,
something bad, something ugly, some harm, some hurt — *then we use Her
ways to help it*. And we start by using Her ways to help ourselves. And then

of course when things go well, when it's all got solved, cured, healed — we remember to thank Her.

I think it cannot be overestimated, how powerfully the vision of Deity directly reflects in a culture; because even if you reject a Deity, if you haven't replaced that vision with an alternate vision of Deity — then the old Deity that was rejected *is still affecting the culture*. Like when they were all raving "God is Dead" in the '60s — that same vision of God was still affecting the culture, because most people still didn't know they had a choice. Or maybe the answer seemed to be: bring in a Guru, some authority figure (usually a man) to tell everybody what to do. And how radically different was this from the old Deity?

And as for being told what to do: In a spiritual sense, the whole idea in Goddess religion is that She tells each of us individually or personally — not only what to do — but who we are. *We are Her*. She is us. And so it's a different mode, you see. Not only is it a different set of messages, it's a different set of techniques — *and the techniques are the message also*. As I said earlier, the process of discovery is also the message. And all of this is part of Her. This is radical stuff. I don't know of any other religion which recommends a voyage of self-discovery with practically no guidelines, because the very guidelines are also part of the discovery. No rule books, no leaders, no wrong or right. You really have to trust a Deity to get into this, don't you?

In my own life, when I've been through some very hard times, She's helped me incredibly. So, experientially, I can say that the answer has always been to never forget Her for a second. To remember Her.

And how to remember Her? *We can embody Her*. Let us explore some of the ways, now. And also, we'll look out for some of the pitfalls, some of the moments when we might forget, and could slip into other modes of perception.

Because, let's not kid ourselves. Let us not pretend that it's easy to suddenly switch to an entirely other mode of belief while we're living in the midst of this particular culture. On the other hand, I suspect that we all know that we chose this situation, karmically speaking. (We chose to be born into this lifetime, into this set of cultural circumstances.) That's the whole idea. We chose this. So it's our job to do it right.

This particular culture has come up with two very handy definitions — *right brain and left brain* — meaning the two hemispheres, with two distinctly different modes of thought and function. I actually saw a reference to right brain and left brain in a TV car commercial the other day, if you can believe that. (It didn't say, "Remember the Goddess," but I guess that's next.) And by the way, you can't just say that the brain has two hemispheres, and that's it. I mean that's a little simplistic, because the brain is the only organ that can figure out what it is, anyway. The brain has told us so far — told the people who have officially chosen to look into it (and they're using that old way of dividing everything) — that there's left brain and right brain. Each side of the brain functions with a particular kind of perception. We'll use these terms for now, just bearing in mind that actually, there are infinite brains . . .

All right, the right side of the brain is called *the relational*. Now, that is the side that is holistic. That is the side that is encompassing, enveloping — which means: It includes everything. It has to do with inspiration, creativity, and it has to do with art. And now there are books out: *Drawing with the Right Side of the Brain, Writing with the Right Side of the Brain.*

In the creative process, this side is becoming more valued. And it has to do with *no divisions* — that's very important. And, oh, yes, this is the side of the brain that has been traditionally associated with the minds of women.

The other side, the left side of the brain, is called *the rational*. Now, rational does not mean better. In this culture, the word "rational" has acquired connotations of superiority, but this is not implied in the left brain definition. The rational function was very important in keeping the human race from dying out, because it had to do with defining, labeling, dividing, seeing the difference between this and that: "Me person, God there, rock there." You know, naming. Adam naming the animals and plants in the Garden — that's archetypical, classical, rational function. Labeling: *"There's Russia, here's America"* — see how it can potentially get you into trouble? ". . . and this is separate from that . . . and I'm separate from you . . . and the child is separate from the adult . . . and the animals are separate from the people . . . and the people are separate from the Deity . . . and this tribe is separate from that tribe . . . and this race is separate from that race. . . ." *Separate from, better than, worse than.* Divisions which can get you into trouble. It's terrific when you say, "Oh, this is a fern and that is a tree and this is a rose . . ." And then it can be very nice. But when it gets into "Our guy is better than your guy, our spears are bigger than your spears" — that's when it gets into trouble.

And, oh, yes, the rational side of the brain is considered "male."

Coincidentally, I've realized that the way the left brain functions, has a lot to do with the shape of the male organ, if you stop to think about it, because it's like pointing. Whereas the female organ *envelopes,* see. Now, if one is used to thinking in terms of separation and divisions, and if the right side of the brain is considered opposite the left — then it could seem to left brain thinkers that right brain thinking could just take over the world, right? So, some people have been very, very afraid of it. They may not have known it as right brain, or as relational, but they sure knew it as female! Not only female as in actual women, but female as in female thought, female ideas, intuitions — and, yes, female religion. Female Deity.

So talk about denial! I think the dialogue in those early days must have gone something like this:

There's no Goddess. There is One God, and He is male, and anything else is heresy and a crime to even consider. So, men, never mind that our priests are always going to wear skirts to give us power. (Ever notice that?) And never mind that we're going to secretly use lunar calendars, to hold onto the Moon's power. We're going to put our holidays right on top of the lunar holidays, or at least as close as we can get. When little girls reach the age of 13 and they get their periods and everybody says, "Wow, they're in puberty now, they're going to create, they're going to be *women!"* — we're going to say, "Pay no attention to that. Menstruation is unclean and should be hidden. But what's really important is that little boys when they reach 13 are going to be *men!"* We're going to take everything that was once sacred to that Other Deity, and call it *bad luck:* the number 13, Friday, black cats . . . or we'll call it just plain *bad* magic, sex, children out of wedlock, women clergy, witches, ghosts, spirits, looking into the future, "graven" images, folklore, and (mainly): any personal experiences of or questions about religion. Or the Deity.

Now, when you stop and think about it, the thing that is the most powerful in the whole world is creation. There's nothing more powerful than creation. My cat just had kittens, and really, first they were invisible and then they were visible! There's nothing more powerful than that.

And what's magic? It's creation. And you don't need a middleman to work magic. You may need a middleman to pray, to reach a Deity who's bigger and better, who's somebody's vision of bigger and better than you. But you don't need a middleman — or even a middlewoman — to reach our Deity. Because She's in everybody. So we all have the potential to create as She does. Even women who can't physically have kids, you know — or even men — can create matter (projects, art, etc.) from the invisible to the visible. That's what magic is.

I mean, it is not praying and asking the Deity to *give* you something.

It's *making the thing happen,* and giving it to yourself. This is our role model, which the Goddess provided for us when She gave birth to the world. So, that's why the occult sciences have been so hidden for so long — because they're such a source of personal power.

As I was researching the two parts of the brain, I realized that if you concentrate on the relational side, you automatically develop the rational side — that's almost a secret that no one seems to realize. When I made this point over ten years ago in *Positive Magic,*[2] I was amazed then — and you can just imagine how amazed I am now — that no one else seems to be saying this! So, if we embrace the relational function of the brain — and if we align ourselves with that, and use that, and say we want those qualities to come back into culture, because they are Her qualities — then we also have to realize that the rational part is very important too. For example, if you're going to write a book, it's very important to get the words on the page, to get the pages photocopied . . . believe me, I really know! It's very important to deal with the World of Form, to do things in steps. The rational function does things in steps, it does things in stages. So many of us who are artists — as Jung would say, intuitive types — we have a great idea, we tell it to our friends, we make a few notes and then we feel like we've done it. But that's not enough, you know. You not only have to put it into a book or onto the tape, or the canvas — you have to get it distributed, or shown, you have to get it to the people, you have to do the mailing, the publicity . . . Because this is the World of Form. So, we have to use both sides of our brains. And it's the same thing with whatever your project is. Even if you have a child, you have to care for that child every day. You can't just say, "I performed the ultimate act of creation," and leave it at that. You have to deal with the reality of that child's existence on the Earth Plane every single day. So, we have to use that other side of our brains too. The rational people may have denied "our" side — but we cannot deny "theirs." For one thing, the relational encompasses *all,* and that includes the rational. This is part of its very nature. And its strength. To me, that's the metaphor for dealing with the whole world.

I have been very concerned by a phenomenon I've encountered in the witchcraft community and some other Goddess religion groups. It goes something like this: "The Christians (and/or Jews, Moslems) are terrible, and we are wonderful." That did not sound right to me. Well, even if it could be considered true on some grand historical scale, once you say it — once you even think it — it's no longer true. And then I realized, we as Goddess worshippers, alternate religious believers and witches — we're not *opposite* Patriarchy — we're *different* from it. And that's a very important concept. We're not opposite, because the concept of opposition is a Patriarchal concept! And we're not better than, because the concept of *hierarchy* is Patriarchal as well. On a group level, or on an individual level, if anyone seems to be absolutely antithetical to ourselves — let us try not to perceive that person or group as opposite. Instead, try: "I'm different. They're different from me at this particular moment in linear time. But this is a matter of perception, and we could just as easily perceive ourselves to be more alike, if we choose to." Not opposite. Different. And not even that different when we get down to basics — just perceiving the difference rather than dealing with the inherent "alikeness." And that's a very important point. We must be watchful that our mode of thought isn't a patriarchal mode which perpetuates opposition. I call this "Getting rid of the versus."

I cannot, of course, speak for the Goddess; I can only speak for my interpretation of Her. And in my interpretation of Her ways, there is simply no need for a *versus*.

Of course we shouldn't be foolhardy, or go asking for trouble or oppression. But in many cases, getting rid of the versus is primarily a matter of perception. But "what if—?" you may ask. What if, for example, they — meaning any "others" — try to create the versus, try to involve us in a comparison, or an argument? What to do, how to perceive the situation and respond to it? Ultimately, by transcending and transforming not only the immediate situation, but your entire life as well, into Her realm. And how do you do *that?* Try this: *Affirm your personal power.* Because once you plug into that Universal source, it is so profound, it can really fix anything.

How to?

Well, the techniques are quite specific, and I'm sorry that time does not permit teaching them all here. But they're the entire reason I wrote my first two books. These wonderful techniques were hidden over the centuries (because they threatened patriarchy), but you could find them if you really looked. Or remembered. They all have to do with affirming personal power, embodying personal power, believing you have it, believing you have a right, your own special conduit to the One Universal Power source. This is not *power-over* another, by the way. This is not *power-by-comparison.* This is *inherent personal power* which we all have as our birthright from our Mother.

Here are a few pointers:

First, you turn your focus *back on yourself,* instead of on the other person or the feeling of threat. And just that refocusing reaffirms your own personal power.

You may employ visualization or Words of Power or ritual, or any combination of the above, to do this, but please remember: We would dilute our own power, by following anything that anyone else prescribes for us, unless of course we understand it one hundred percent and agree with it fully. I have heard of Goddess rituals being dictated, photocopied, read and/or memorized — all of which sounds no different from a patriarchal church service. This does not lead us back to Her power; it leads us to the power of whoever is calling the shots.

Always bear in mind the Occult Principles: Microcosm (you) and Macrocosm, For the Good of All and According to Free Will (non-manipulative), The Infinity of Solution, Cause and Effect, Form and Essence, Love and Transformation. (I go into detail about this in *Positive Magic*.)

As Goddess worshippers, we have a special technique: We can align with any aspect(s) of Her which we wish to embody specifically: Isis, Diana, Hecate, etc. . . . And having done so, even on a daily basis, we can then simply call on Her for help, aware that we are also calling on that aspect of ourselves. We can say, "I am Diana Incarnate, and/or Hecate Incarnate, etc." Or simply, "I am Goddess Incarnate." (See *Earth Magic*.)[3]

And you don't need a crisis, by the way, to do this work. You can do it on a regular basis, as a way of dealing with everything. In my opinion, we all should. Because every time we do this — every time we resolve (or avoid) a conflict or a problem in our own personal lives, or help another creature, by surmounting polarity, by getting rid of the versus, by affirming personal power and using Goddess Power — we are remembering Her ways. And every time we do this, this process grows out there in the larger world.

Because it's the mode, it's the technique, it's the thought-process, it's the way things work — all of this as important as the work itself. When you do magic to heal a loved one, or solve a problem, or get a job (whatever you want to do magic for), if you believe that you can use magic to do that, and you follow the basic principles — these principles go out into the world. Their reality gets reinforced, and the world is changed thereby. If you really do the magic right, the magic works, your own situation gets solved — and also, the potential for positive magic as a viable process goes into the world. And changes it.

So you see, when we do Her magic, *it affects everything and everyone*. Even if we do it in our own little room, just for ourselves. Even if we do it in our own family. Even if we do it in our own neighborhood, our own community. We can do it just with other pals of ours who believe in the same reality we believe . . . and still the vibes go out there in a relentlessly powerful, positive way. And those vibrations make everything start to change. This is automatic. It's like pebbles in a stream and petals in the wind: ever-widening circles.

And of course, more directly, Her ways include always doing work for the greater good as well — the planet, all Her creatures. But I suppose that here, this can go without saying. This is something we all know.

Now, to be able to do this — although it may sound so far away from where we are in our culture today, *to be able to think constantly this way is really not that hard because it's not alien to us. It's natural to us.* We just have to remember — not to work at it, but to *allow* ourselves to remember. So, that's why we have our altars, and our candles, and our crystals, and our little rocks — and whatever we need. And we have our animals, and our covens, and our friends — to help us remember the Old Ways. Her Ways. This is a natural process, so we surely don't have to force ourselves to do it. In fact, speaking of forcing, I think that every time we feel we're forcing something, it's a signal to really stop, and think twice, and ask ourselves: *is this right?* Because, if you're really forcing, then there's something wrong. But when you really plug into that universal source (I'm not saying I can always do it, but I'm getting there!), when you plug into Her — life and its activities are organic and natural. Life *flows* when She shows you the way.

And if you ever should feel yourself (Goddess forbid!) so discouraged that you forget — or think you are forgetting — all you have to do is call a dear friend who reminds you, who does some affirmation or magic or prayer (call it what you wish) for you, and then you get back on track, and then your situation works out, if not immediately then surely eventually. And if things are not exactly as you requested, then — without compromise! — remember Form and Essence, or as we now call it, EQOB (equivalent or better).

If things do not work out as quickly or as easily as we wish, I think one big reason is that we're all in the role of pioneers in a difficult terrain. This is really amazing when you stop to think about it: We're not on Wonder Woman's island somewhere, where everyone else is thinking and acting and worshipping as we do, and where the whole culture supports us! We're in this old Patriarchal place. And still we can follow Her ways. If we get discouraged, this is truly understandable. But remember that the antidote is really just to remember. Because in truth, our original culture — Her ways — predate the culture we are currently residing in.

Now, I'm going to give you this list of some of Her attributes that we can remember and embody in our lives. I find these all personally empowering.

She is non-hierarchal. That means no sex is better than the other. No race is better than another. No species is better than another. Have you ever noticed that animals are not allowed in churches and synagogues? Some animals are smarter than the people in those churches and synagogues. They're not allowed in cemeteries, yet they understand death better than we do. Anyway, She's non-hierarchal — in every sense of the word hierarchal, especially in its quality of separation. *Hierarchy separates!* Now, there are people who are more karmically developed than others, and you might say we get separated right there. I consider these people more in the "different from" category, actually; in a temporary sense — with the potential for us all to develop further. You know, I wouldn't doubt that there are people who are more developed than we are — who are more educated, taller, cleaner, more graceful, who knows — but that's not what we're talking about when we say "hierarchy." I mean here the classic, Middle-Ages brand of hierarchy, complete with all the built-in rigidity, and all the suffering it can cause. She is non-hierarchal. And personally, I think we are not better than a mouse. We're not! We're not any *better,* if you stop and think about it.

You don't need a middleman or middlewoman to reach Her. Because, really, all you have to do is look inside yourself, and remember who you are; and remind yourself, lighting a candle, or using anything else you wish. And you don't need a priest and you don't need a nun and you don't need a rabbi and you don't need a guru and you don't need an evangelist with a microphone or a TV camera. You just sit right down and reach Her. Or stand up.

She loves us and accepts us as we are — unconditionally. That's very important. Her love is unconditional. It's really like a mother's love. A good mother loves her kid even when the kid is wetting the floor; why not? It's her kid. And even though She loves us that way, it doesn't mean we should not strive to be more developed or more worthy of being a child of the Goddess. It just means: She already loves you, so you can relax, and you don't have to base your whole life on expiating your sins, you don't have to base your whole life on apologizing and groveling. It's just amazing how patriarchal religions are constantly reminding people that they're lower than the Deity; so pathetic, and, I think, so unnecessary. She loves us as we are. We should always try to be better and wiser and help everybody and do good, and all that — because that's Her image too. But She loves us as we are, so we can really relax. That's our starting point — relax. It's OK. If I make a mistake, It's OK! She loves us. She's *nonjudgmental*. That means "no blame." That doesn't mean go make that mistake again. It just means there's no blame if you slipped and you did make a mistake. And there's also no guilt; blame and guilt are close relatives. Instead, the thing to have is *personal responsibility* — that's different from blame or guiilt. Taking responsibility for your own actions means taking responsibility to change them, and knowing you can. Creating your own causes and experiencing their effects is what karma means.

There's a real misunderstanding about karma these days among certain people, and I'm sure it will straighten out eventually, but meanwhile — whew! When I used to be on radio I would explain karma and say, "We all create and perpetuate our own karma," and listeners would call in and say, "Ah ha! Do you mean it's all right to let other people suffer since they are responsible for creating that suffering? Are you saying just leave them to their karma?" And I'd say, "No, it's *not* all right. We're supposed to help them. It's our karma to help them." I mean, that's the whole thing about karma. Yes, they may have created or allowed their terrible circumstance to happen. They may have (and who could prove this, anyway?) over many lifetimes, maybe by being frightened, or by not knowing they had a choice, or for any number of reasons, come to experience some terrible circumstance. Especially people who suffer in wars; very often these are the most defenseless people in ravaged countries. They're the children, or the elderly, they're the oppressed women. Not traditionally "evil" people at all seem to be the ones who get the worst of it. Yes, it may be considered to be their karma, meaning that in that some way they allowed this thing to happen. But that doesn't mean *leave them there*. That means *help them*. Teach them. Show them. Feed them. Heal them. Save them. I don't understand why people think that karma means stop in your tracks. Karma is just an explanation for how somebody may have gotten to that stage. It doesn't mean stop in your tracks or walk away from others' suffering. The idea of taking responsibility is just the opposite.

There are no exceptions to Her rule. A really interesting point. There are *no* exceptions. She is everywhere and that's it! Everywhere. It's not like, "She's everywhere except where the Devil is." That's a nice cop-out isn't it? "Burn everybody who worships the Devil, or wants to worship the Devil, or even thinks about it, or *we think* is thinking about the Devil." That could be very handy. No, there are *no* exceptions to Her rule. None. That's it. (And witches don't believe in a devil, by the way, who is a Christian invention.) This entire Universe is Her creation and we're all part of it.

She wants us to be happy. Happiness is the naturally occurring, optimum state. In my tradition we make a point of giving thanks whenever something positive works out. We stop for a moment and give thanks, either out loud or we write it down. We do this not only when things manifest which we have worked for, but also we believe in making assessments from time to time — even lists — of our blessings. We believe that it is upon our enjoyment of our blessings that She builds future blessings. *She puts no premium on suffering.* Suffering is not a good thing, definitely not a state to aspire to. This includes martyrdom. Goddess religion is life-affirming and celebratory, and does not promise heavenly rewards instead of earthly happiness. If you think about it, this has always been a concept with political overtones.

Her realm has no boundaries. Her realm includes the magic arts, the occult traditions and the occult sciences, ESP, and contact with other dimensions — including people who have moved on to other planes. So, with no boundaries, just because a person has died doesn't mean that we can't still be in touch with them . . . and just because entities may be in another dimension doesn't mean that we can't contact them. And also, by the way, I don't believe that this kind of contact is very exclusive. I believe that we can all do it for ourselves. Again, we don't have to consult or hire somebody. We can sometimes *choose* to consult somebody — a psychic, perhaps — to do it for us, or to help us. But really, we can do it for ourselves. (And instructions are in my book, *Earth Magic*.) Making contact with invisible beings — or just being open to the possibility — is one pathway, and I'm not necessarily advocating it, because it takes careful practice and technique. But really there are many ways to conceptualize and practice the idea of "no boundaries." Another good example is the witchcraft principle of the "Infinity of Solution" which is an infinitely comforting concept when you're doing magic to change things, and things may look bleak or impossible. Nothing's impossible! No boundaries. Remember that.

So when we remember these marvelous attributes and embody them in our own lives, we are affirming our personal power, intensifying and nourishing our personal power, helping others (because we are all linked after all), and living as Goddess. You know that lovely old pagan saying, "Thou art Goddess." I think that's what it means. Let us also constantly rediscover Her and ourselves in the process. Let us trust Her enough to each of us find our own way back to Her. . . . These are just some of the ways to Remember Her.

Notes

1. Marion Weinstein, "Remember the Goddess," on *Marion Weinstein's Positive Magic: The Music — Halloween City/Remember the Goddess,* Audio Tape. New York: Earth Magic Productions (2170 Broadway, Suite 16, New York, NY 10024), 1989. Also, *Marion Weinstein Stand Up Witch,* Audio and Video, as above.

2. Marion Weinstein, *Positive Magic, Occult Self-Help* (Custer, WA: Phoenix Publishing Co., 1981).

3. Marion Weinstein, *Earth Magic: A Dianic Book of Shadows* (Custer, WA: Phoenix Publishing Co., 1980 and 1986).

Ritual Creating and Planning

Norma Joyce

The word ritual can be used in a multitude of ways. Or, rather, the understanding of the word can have many meanings in our heads, depending on our experiences and teachings. Before we talk about ritual then, we must come to common agreement about the word. It wouldn't hurt us to have common understandings about a lot of words that we throw around, but we will come to agreement here only about five. Before we start discussing ritual, I would like to clarify my usage of the other four. They are joyousness, happy, serious, and seriousness.

Happiness is fairly easy to achieve; it is one emotion that most of us have felt at some time or another in our lives. When we are asked what makes us happy, we can come up with at least one situation when we feel happy. Swimming in tepid water makes me feel happy; I'm sure that there are things that make you happy. They are usually something that we feel happy doing, an action or behavior that is contained in an action/behavior. Many actions do not have to combine for us to feel happy, one will do it. When we are in the child mode we can feel it most easily. What is happier than a child who is doing what she wants to do at that very moment?

The feeling of joyousness, in contrast, is a more complete emotion and takes more component parts for us to have it. It is not only that joyousness needs more component parts to have us feel it, but the feeling of it is more complete. It touches more body parts, and we feel a sense of completion when we are joyous. Neither of these emotions are done to us, of course, they are emotions that we choose or not to feel. They can both have other people in the picture/situation that add to our feelings by their actions, but we are still the ones choosing to feel or not to feel.

A ritual that has achieved its purpose leaves us feeling joyous. We feel fulfilled in body, mind and soul. We have that warm glow of knowing that we have achieved what we set out to do. We want to stay connected with the people that we shared the circle with and find it hard to part from them. If we are *happy* with what has happened in the ritual we feel smiley, but find that we have a tendency to reach out and seek contact. We feel that we need other experiences to change our happiness to joyousness. A ritual that has fulfilled part of its purpose gives us the opportunity to feel happy, but only a ritual that has had completion, has fulfilled us, can leave us feeling joyous.

Being serious and being seriously involved with something are two very different degrees of behavior, too. Being serious about something can have an element of gloominess about it. Being serious is often what we do as a "duty," or what we "have to" do. When we take something seriously it means that we are really commited to our involvement with it.

For example, I am not serious about my religion, but I take my religion very seriously. In other words, if I can't laugh and have a good time at a ritual, I'm missing the point of why I'm involved in it. If I do not take what I am doing in a ritual seriously, with care and concern, then I have no business being involved with a ritual. I have no business being involved, because I do not respect the potential of the energy I am working with. I take it very seriously, but do not have to have a serious demeanor about it. I do not let the uptightness of seriousness control the situation.

Our understanding of ritual does not depend on the comparing of two words, but more on the many different ways we use the words. As with many words that have more than one usage, we can get ourselves into trouble by thinking that everyone we are communicating with uses them in the same way. I hope you will bear with me and the way I define the words, for the sake of this article.

Some people use the word ritual as a celebration or ceremony whereas others are talking about a religious service, or a rite of passage, or the use of ritual magic. Or then again, they could be talking about a repeated act or acting on a habit. It can also be said, when someone is doing something in a formal way, that they are ritualizing it.

A ritual, I believe, must have purpose and a focal point for the energy raising to be effective and to have meaning. It is sacred work, and we focus ourselves within a framework to have that work take place. It is not a conglomeration of anything and everything that can be thought of all jumbled together. It has to focus us, not scatter us.

For most of us, a ritual is something we have done before. This is true, and at the same time it is not the same as a habit. It is not like brushing our teeth, where we put the toothpaste on the same way each time. It is not that we have done it before, only that we have a structure built by our agreeing to the purpose, that gives us the "has been done before" feeling.

What a ritual does have is emotional satisfaction and the use of symbolism to help us achieve it. A ritual, to be effective and serve its purpose, needs to trigger the subconscious. It needs to make the subconscious know that something important, something that the subconscious needs to pay attention to, is happening. With all the parts of the ritual we are using mind power; all of us have it and it is all we need to create a ritual, to build the emotional "staging" that helps us go beyond the boundaries we set for ourselves. We all have these boundaries and each of us is in a different place with them. We can change them, moving them further and further out, allowing ourselves to grow, if we use ritual to set the stage. Setting the stage in certain ways helps to tell our subconscious that we are in a safe place to change. It helps us tell our subconscious that we are ready to change and welcome growth.

We need to keep telling ourselves, as we plan and participate in ritual, that when the ritual becomes more important than the purpose of the ritual, we have dogma and are counteracting what we are setting up for the ritual to achieve. If ritual is the only way we can effect change in our lives, then we also need to look at the dependency we are having on ritual. If we use ritual to help ourselves, to set the stage, to give ourselves the emotional "kick start" to effect change, then we are finding the true purpose of it.

The raising or building of energy during ritual helps us to change, and when the raised energy is sent to those who want to receive it, it can help them to change also. The energy helps us to change because it is raised in a circle with that purpose in mind — we want the change to happen.

In *Emmanuel's Book,* by Pat Rodegast and Judith Stanton, Emmanuel says, "Rituals are not the path. They are a reminder that there is a path.[1] In Women's Spirituality, that path leads us to the knowledge that we are all divine, that we are all the Goddess within, we are the Goddess. It leads us along the path that tells us we are all High Priestesses, serving Her in all Her aspects. It teaches us that some of us enjoy planning and leading ritual more than others, but we all can do it. By opening to the collective energy, the energy that produces the Goddess, we learn that we have direct access to the energy. We learn to use it and not fear it.

In some of the older Pagan traditions we were taught that there were a chosen few who could direct energy. We were taught that only by following tried and true formats could we raise the energy and have the work of change accomplished. Now, we know that we are building a new Herstory, and by working with the energy seriously we have direct access to the Goddess. We also know that we are in need of knowledge, some of it from the past to be built on, and some from trial and error to understand what we are dealing with.

There is an old saying, "God watches out for drunks and fools." I have changed that and say, "The Goddess watches out for fools and women involved in Women's Spirituality rituals." She knows our intent. If our intent is pure we will not mess it up. She is patient with us as we learn. There are some points, an outline, a structure that makes it easier for us to work within. This is what we deal with next, and I hope that even though we are dealing with the outline seriously, we want to make it joyous and She will help us.

There are some people who feel a lack of meaningful rites of passage in their lives and seek to ritualize important milestones. They are doing more celebrations and ceremonies than true rituals. This does not mean that ceremonies/celebrations are not of consequence to our spiritual/emotional well-being, but they are not true rituals. They may contain within their form a ritual, but there are certain steps that make a ritual, and a celebration or ceremony does not always have these steps. Smudging, for example, is not a ritual. It can be a part of a ritual or it can be a cleansing without being in a ritual. A guided awareness or guided visualization is not a ritual, but can be part of a ritual.

A ritual can have a select purpose in which to address an issue. Maybe a woman has applied for a job and wishes to clarify her abilities and desires before going for an interview. She also wants to form the energy, to bring it together so she feels less scattered, and she can do that within a ritual context. The select issue ritual can be anything from a personal need, as in the example of the job, to a global issue that we want to address and deal with in a constructive way by focusing ourselves and the energy.

A ritual that I call full blown is one in which we are working out a psychological need. These rituals usually have more component parts and go through particular stages to reach fulfillment/completion. Many times they start with the problem to be dealt with and work through the stages. One of the stages in this type of ritual is to let go of what has been holding us back. It is through letting go that we come to a resolution and are able to effect change in our lives. Other ways of using a full blown ritual would be at a rites of passage ritual, and of course at any of the Sabbats. A full blown ritual is appropriate since it takes a person through the stages of the passage. It starts with the beginning of the awakening and takes the initiate through the passage to the beginning of a new growth potential.

Winter Solstice is a good time to have one of these rituals where you deal with going "underground," the facing of your own darkness and coming through, by acceptance and letting go, into the illumination of understanding and self-love. Any of the other Sabbats have their own focus for using this type of ritual to help us work through our stages of growth.

Personal rituals can be as simple as lighting a candle before meditating to help us be aware of the sacred space created for the meditative process, or going through all the steps of a more elaborate ritual. I define a personal ritual as one in which a woman has a desire that she wants to have wo/manifest and she either goes about it by creating the ritual alone or seeking others to join her. Some rite of passage rituals cross over the line and become personal ones when they are not part of the regular rituals of the community.

Where there is no clear-cut purpose for a ritual, just a felt need, they more often become celebrations than true rituals; or they cross lines and become, after they have started, full blown personal rituals. There is nothing wrong in having celebrations or ceremonies, it is just important to know that a ritual always raises the energy and uses the energy that has been raised. A celebration or ceremony can be very fulfilling and satisfying, depending on the people involved and the reason it is being held. A ritual is sacred work and is not always what would be appropriate for a given situation.

When we start to plan a ritual, our foremost step is to decide why we are planning the ritual. Know the reason, have clarity of intent, and the pieces fall into place as we use the following steps. When we start planning, and know the purpose, we then know if we want children to attend, or if at this particular ritual it would not serve to have them there. We also know what else we need to tell the other women who are attending. Perhaps this is a ritual that we feel is important for the women to be skyclad (nude). This is something that we want to tell the women so they have a choice about attending. Knowing what to expect, the women come to it in a mood that contributes to the energy raising. If we are having a political ritual and some of the women, for instance, do not agree that spirituality and politics are compatible, they have a right to be told before they arrive at the ritual. I, for one, do not believe that we can separate spirituality and politics, but I honor the feelings of the women who do.

On the other hand, when we have been working with women who have been together for some time, as I have been with my Wing[2] for four years, most of the time we don't need to tell each other what is happening. We know each other well enough, and know that if we have a Hallowmas ritual, for instance, it will center on going between the worlds and contacting loved ones who have passed over. It will also be a time to send off any loved ones who have died in the past year. If there is anything that is out of our usual purpose in doing a ritual, then of course we would tell the women who might not find that ritual to their liking. I would rather have a woman stay home than add negative energy to the circle because she is uncomfortable.

Talking about the whys brings up the next step, the who. Who plans a particular ritual for a circle? This deciding is usually done by group consensus, is on a regular group schedule, or just seems to fall into place. Other times there is a special need a woman might have, or she has channeled that she is to do one. One word about channeling here. I think that channeling is valid. I do it myself, but I have seen abuses. This is when someone will not allow any disagreement about an idea because she has channeled it. It also means that one person is not permitted to get into the only-high-priestess-there-is mode because she has channeled a ritual each week.

One of my experiences with channeled rituals happened this way. I was traveling Interstate 5, which runs North/South on the Pacific coast, when I heard a voice say to me, "You are to arrange to hold the same ritual, all over the world, next Spring Equinox." My response was to say, "Oh yeah, how is that to happen?" I never take channeling without questioning it, and myself, as to the "cleanness" of it. Well, it just so "happens" that WICCA was publishing the *We' Moon Almanac* that year, and I was able to put a little notice in the back about the ritual. It was right after that, that a woman called and told me about some women who were planning a conference on Women's Spirituality for the following spring, and she thought I needed to be in the planning meeting. I traveled the sixty miles to the meeting and found that it just so happened that the conference was being planned for the next Spring Equinox, and it just so happened that I was asked to be in charge of the rituals. We ended up having 23 rituals at the same time, all the same ritual, all over the planet. The form of the ritual was also given to me later, and I sent it off to the other women holding them. When someone is told to do a ritual and it is a true sending, usually the means will happen and the ritual will be held.

The one-person type of planning can be for a rite of passage ritual where a woman wants to share a milestone growth point. Rite of passage rituals can also be planned by a group, where someone asks her circle to share with her and help her plan the ritual. With handfasting, of course, we want to have more than one person planning the ritual. Both parties add their creativity to the planning. If it is a "legal" marriage, the person performing the legal aspects might also be involved. It is starting to be obvious that I do not agree with written-out rituals that are always used for a particular occasion. The one that the Christian Church has, for example, for handfasting that starts out "dearly beloved," or any other "always the same" rituals — whether out of Christianity, Judaism or Paganism — to me have not the emotional depth of a personally planned ritual. That doesn't mean that we can't incorporate parts that we like into a ritual we plan. We are moving into a new time/Age and it is for us to develop the words and form for our time and needs. Not only our needs, but for the future of our world, the Mother Earth's needs.

For the last few years, WICCA has held classes in ritual planning before each of the quarter days. At these classes we plan a ritual that will be shared with the women in the different regions, all over the country, as our suggestion for the ritual. Some of them use these rituals and some plan their own. It makes for a strong feeling of connectiveness when you know that women all over are having the same ritual, and that it has been planned for that time and place. When I say the same ritual, of course, the form might be the same, but the energy and the personal touches of the women in the circle change the ritual and make it theirs.

Part of the deciding of who plans the ritual for a circle also goes to the woman who will monitor the energy for it. We call this woman the HPD, the High Priestess of the Day. This is an important function, and one that a woman who has had experience in circles usually fulfills better than a woman who has never raised energy. This does not mean that we think she is better or different, only that she has had more experience. Using the HPD takes some of the potential for an ego trip away and makes us constantly aware that all of us are Priestesses of the Mother, and that it is only at times that She calls on us to stretch our growth potential by being in charge.

I have also been in groups where a spontaneous need has arisen and we have put together a ritual then and there. One time comes to mind when a few of us were sitting around grousing about money, or rather our lack of it. I started feeling uncomfortable, as I felt that we were all feeding into each other's depression and negativity. I suggested we turn the energy around and make a ritual stating our needs and desires. We had a noisy, wonderful ritual making our needs known to the Universe, and we changed our depression to constructive anger.

The "what" of planning starts with creating a way in which we form sacred space. Remember that all we are doing is being done with the power of the mind, so everything we plan is to get our minds to accept that we have created something, and that something is out of "normal" time and space. Once we get the mind to accept that, and we have put out that belief, we find that each of us is able to feel the circle of protection we have created. We are there.

Most of us start with defining that space, in the area that is the circle, and to do that we call the directions or quarters. Once again we are creating something that makes no sense, but that makes perfect sense. We create a circle by defining four quarters, the four directions in a square that becomes a circle.

The four directions are usually associated with the four elements, with Spirit at the center, or the central altar making the fifth. Earth is associated with North, East with Air and then for most, South with Fire and West with Water. If in a ritual we feel that we want to call it differently, using another tradition, and we all agree, the elements will understand and hear. We are the ones creating this sacred space, and we are the ones who make it happen by our agreeing that it does. A way of calling the elements that makes them easier to grasp and gives them form, is to find out goddesses associated with that element and use them in the calling. Another way is to think about the attributes of the elements and to call on them. A third way is to say what those elements remind us of psychologically. Anger, passion, and transformation, the coming through a difficult time and knowing we have been honed and made stronger, are some of the ways we can relate to fire. So with the other elements we find attributes we can relate to.

The use of salt and water to sprinkle around the circle also is a powerful way to help our minds know that we are creating a sacred space. This can be done separately or combined to make the same saline solution that our tears are, and the same solution that is the life blood within us. It then becomes the life blood of the Mother and helps us to *know* that we have created a protected place/space. Once the circle is formed, and we know that our minds feel it, it is time to cleanse the air inside of it, make the air ready for us to breathe while doing sacred work. Cleansing each woman as the air is cleansed is also done at this time.

When we do some rituals, it is more appropriate to cleanse the women as they come into the circle. This is usually done when the circle has been cast, before they are in it, and a door is opened into the circle for them to enter. Honor the creation of the circle, and make it more powerful by not allowing anyone to enter or leave without someone opening a door for them. If women are allowed to come and go, they negate what we have created and our minds will register the fact. It makes the work harder to do when the mind is negating that we are indeed in sacred space, ready to do sacred work. Animals don't count, with their comings and goings through the circle; they are always in sacred space within themselves.

Up to a point, the more dramatic we are in the cleansing, the more the subconscious mind will accept that it is no longer functioning in the mundane world. There is a different feeling and we know that we are ready to work. We know that we have created that sacred space, and we feel the cares and concerns of the day, the garbage we all carry with us, leave us as the incense smoke moves across our bodies. If there are women in the circle who are bothered in their breathing by the smell of incense, then experiment with natural herbs. Cedar, sage, rosemary or lavender, and many other plants that are not mixed with chemicals will oftentimes not bother women who have breathing problems.

After the sacred space has been created and cleansed, we are ready to start the work of the ritual. This is the purpose for which the women have gathered. They have made an agreement, by their coming together, to join their energy for the sacred work. To do this, the woman who is HPD reminds the women why they have gathered. She does this inside the circle after it has been created, but she can also do it before by giving the format of the ritual, so they feel more comfortable knowing what will take place and when. There are times when the energy takes over and no matter what is planned the work goes in another direction. In those times it is best to flow with the energy and do the work in that other way. The HPD takes the energy and focuses it, the women's mind power, with her words. This can be done in many creative ways by the HPD, or by using what has been planned in a group planning.

The HPD could call into the circle a Goddess that by Her personality/ aspects gives the focusing wanted to increase the potential of raising stronger energy. The focusing could also be done by a guided awareness/ imagery, grounding the women deep into the Earth so that they feel secure as they leave this realm of consciousness. Once the HPD has been able to focus all the women, they start raising the energy. This can be done with mind power alone, holding hands and having the energy flow through each woman as it builds in intensity. Of course, there needs to be a decision as to the direction the energy will flow before starting to raise it. The traditional Pagan way, and I agree with it, is to send the energy clockwise, in the right hand and out the left, for any creation work. The opposite, or widdershins, is for the undoing of energy, banishing or cleansing before rebuilding in a positive manner.

Other ways of raising energy include chanting, drumming and dancing. It is important to remember that percussion instruments, the drum for one, are related to the first three chakras. It serves us well to know that the second chakra is the center of creativity, which means it is also the center of sexuality. Our sexuality is an important part of who we are and we want to honor it, but it can get in the way if we are focusing on something else. Experimenting with different drum beats, listening to rock music, helps us to learn what effect they have on our gonads. This is a good group project, listening together, to help the group understand how they each react to different stimuli.

The HPD or energy monitor has to be able to keep her mind in two places at the same time. She has to keep in constant touch with the energy movement to know when it peaks, and at the same time she is guiding the awareness, using her creativity to know whether to say more, how to increase the depth, or whatever is needed to allow the energy to build even stronger.

When the energy has peaked, it is time to send it out. The sending is the "throwing off" of the energy and is usually done with everyone putting their arms up at the same time, allowing the energy that has built in the arms and body to release. At the same time that the energy is being sent, the HPD reminds the women where it is being sent and for what purpose. Energy is never sent without the knowledge that it has gone only to those who wish to receive it. There have been times that it was sent to someone who has not requested it, say a political figure, and it is sent with the words, "If he/she wishes to receive it, otherwise it goes to the healing of the Planet." If energy is sent out without being directed or is raised without a focus, it can be used by anyone for any purpose who chooses to tap into it.

When the energy has been sent, most times, we feel a sense of emptiness. This is not a "bad" emptiness, but we might want to bend down and touch the Earth, or call up Earth energy through the floor if in a building. Another way of grounding is to eat, and at a powerful ritual we find that the women are hungry afterward. We bring snacks to a ritual for that purpose, and for the companionship that eating together brings.

Going into the planning is the naming of the women who are going to clean up the space after the ritual is over. Don't make it the HPD, she has expended enough energy. Most times she wants to eat and be at the edge of the women, as she regroups her energy and comes back from her total involvement of monitoring the ritual. There have been times when the "homey" tasks of cleaning up have helped me, as HPD, to ground again. Have someone ready anyway for the cleaning up.

Personal preparation is usually done before arriving at the site where the ritual will take place. There are sites where there is a hot tub or some other factor. Preparation can include taking a salt bath, meditating or just spending time to gather ourselves together after a busy day. Whatever feels right for the individual woman to put her in the mood for the ritual is what she does. For each ritual I have found that my preparation has been different, depending on where I've been and what my mood is. Whatever makes us feel ready is right to do, with one exception. That exception is when we have agreed to gather at a time and one woman decides that with fifteen minutes left she wants to take fifty minutes to meditate. This is when we need to weigh our priorities and see if we owe a commitment to the rest of the group. If it is more important to meditate than to be fairly on time, I would call and say that it is impossible to attend.

A special piece of clothing that is only used for rituals also helps us to get into the mood and make our subconscious know that this is a special time. A robe that is made in a natural fiber helps to hold the Earth energy that is raised, around and under the robe. This bringing up of energy under a robe helps the energy to raise even higher, as it is contained around the body. Decorating the robe with symbols that have meaning for the woman also adds to the specialness and gives the subconscious more of a boost. As she is decorating it, she is thinking of the reason why she is doing it, and triggers off the same feeling every time she puts it on. I have found that when functioning as HPD, I really appreciate having pockets for matches and the cowrie shells we give each woman at our rituals.

Let's go back over the reasons we want to gather together and plan a ritual. Do we want to celebrate something, have a ceremony? There are many happenings in our lives that are worthy of our taking time to celebrate. Did a woman in our circle exceed even her own expectations in her grades in school this term? Is someone having a birthday that seems more important than most, maybe because there are places she has moved from and is no longer stuck? These and many more reasons deserve to have us take note and to share it with friends. But what can be done to make a celebration into a ritual? It is in planning and knowing the purpose of the gathering. It means taking the purpose, the reason for the gathering, and finding a desire to raise energy within that purpose.

Let's use the example of a woman's grades in school. We could call in the Goddess energy of creativity and intelligence, and use the symbols of wisdom. What are they to the group? Maybe we would want to call in the Crone as the Spirit energy. We would then raise the energy in joyousness of women's intelligence, of our own. We could start a chant about how wonderful each woman is, all clever and bright women. We would then raise the energy and send it out to all the women in the world who want to use it to open their intelligence for social change, for making all of humankind free. The difference then, between a celebration and a ritual, is that in a ritual we raise energy and use it for a purpose. In a celebration we share our times of change and happiness.

Another purpose for a ritual, besides sending the energy, is for cleansing or banishing negative energy. This can be done either from a place or a person. Starting again with the basic outline of ritual planning, we would then use actions that impress on the women what they are doing. If the circle is working on cleansing for a building, for instance, the women gather, create sacred space, and then use a psychological tool for a cleansing that might be stronger than incense alone would be. We could draw our circle out further than usual, including the whole building if necessary. One way to do this is to create sacred space as we normally do, and as the energy is being raised, visualize that it is spreading out, further and further, until the total space to be cleansed is included in the sacred place.

If there is the need to impress the situation even more, all the women or one woman could walk the boundaries with a candle, salt and water and then cleanse the inner space. This could be done with brooms made of cedar, or pulling the energy from all corners of the room and putting it into pails of water, When all the negativity is pulled from the space and placed in the pail, add salt, then pour it down the drain. Flush water after it, knowing that the salt has cleaned the energy in the pail. Raise the energy and replace what was taken: each woman could add her verbal blessing to the space.

Using creative energy, abilities to make dramatic flair, and elegance to touch every part of a woman's emotional make-up and psychological integration, add to the potential of ritual energy being raised even higher. Not only do we want to use the sense of dramatic flair that all of us have, some more buried than others, in the banishing rituals, but for all rituals. Using staging for energy work increases the potential of it working. Using it in healing is a good example. What better place to use flair than in the healing of the body? So many of our dis-eases and illnesses are caused by our psychological state that using the dramatic to heal is well within the potential of using ritual drama and having it work.

Dramatic flair can also set the stage for the conscious control of our mind and allow us to go between the worlds. To go out (or in) to another way of perceiving the environment is a way for us to gain new knowledge about ourselves and the world. It is a state where we give up ego and surrender to ourself, to gain the connection with totality. Since this state happens when we are in alpha, we are able to make deep psychological changes and also to connect with the psyches of other living beings. Allowing ourselves to surrender to self then, serves two purposes depending on what we want from it. We can do work to change ourselves or allow ourselves to become at-one. We can do both in the same ritual if it is structured so and we allow ourselves to let go.

I have known women who have been disappointed that they did not go between the worlds at their first ritual, or their first ritual with a new group of women. This is unrealistic to expect to happen. I'm not saying that it can't happen, but to expect it to happen when they have never been involved with a ritual is to expect the unusual. To go between the worlds you have to let go of ego. When we are with a new group or in our first ritual, we are usually too aware of ourselves to let go. Most times the woman who has this expectation thinks that all she has to do is be good in the drumming and the chants. Not so. It is a case of studying hard and doing all the work so that you can let go of it all and be. It is a case of being prepared so that when the energy is right, all moods and vibrations lined up, we can let go and become one.

Reading the book, *Tarot Therapy*, by Jan Woudhuysen[3] gave me a new perspective on the pentagram, the five-pointed star with the circle around it. I have always thought that it symbolized the four elements/ directions and spirit, which becomes human form. It does, but along with this Woudhuysen says that it is the "symbol of human will." This explains why its use has been so widespread as a symbol of the energy/action of ritual. We are dealing with human wills joined together in agreement, the power of the group mind to first create the sacred space and then to form the energy into a usable construct. We give it life by using our minds, by using all our senses to help our minds create, and we join together in the ritual to create an even more potent energy form than we each could on our own.

Within the ritual all is symbolism, and allowing ourselves to immerse totally into that symbolism, we can then allow ourselves to let go. We need to be able to see the world with different eyes. Jamake Highwater says in *The Ritual of the Wind*:[4]

> First you must learn to look at the world twice, Indian elders advise. First you must bring your eyes together in front of you so you can see each droplet of rain on the grass, so you can see the smoke rising from an ant hill in the sunshine. Nothing should escape your notice. But you must learn to look again, with eyes at the very edge of what is visible. . . . The ability to envision a second world is a major source of an Indian knowledge so deeply felt, so primal, that it is neither word nor outcry, neither sign nor symbol, but the ineffable thing itself, that which preceded speech and thought, that which is the raw experience itself without evaluation and moralities. It is the ineffable structured into an event — that which we call ritual. . . .
>
> Ritual requires us to really see. What we are able to see if we use our eyes without censorship and prejudgements is a virtual image. It is real, for when we are confronted by it, it really does exist, but it is not actually there. The reflection in the mirror is such a virtual image; so is a rainbow. It seems to stand on earth or in the clouds, but it is not tangible. It is the unspeakable, the ineffable made visible, made audible, made experiential.

This is what we are striving for in ritual, to make the ineffable into form, a configuration that we can share with others and help ourselves. At the same time, what we are feeling and perceiving is the ineffable. We are striving for it and yet if we strive we will not find it. We must study and practice and then let go of everything we have ever learned. It must come to us without our thinking about it as we do the sacred work. That is why planning is so important. We can allow ourselves to let go if what we are doing is second nature to us, if it is there ready for us to feel it.

We strive to use symbolism in our rituals that signal all our senses, all of our emotions to build the energy, to effect change within our beings and in the Universe. Any prop that helps us is ours to use. Candles of different colors, incense of different scents, help us to symbolize to ourselves and others what we are striving to communicate about the ineffable.

When I first started going around speaking about Women's Spirituality I felt frustrated; it was as if I had lost my ability to communicate. There just weren't the words, and there were not many women who had a recognition of what they were experiencing to have yet brought it to their left brain. Once I started talking, stumbling with the words, I would get looks of recognition, then the nods of the head and then a smile with the words, "I know, I know." We were all, we are all, looking for ways to communicate what we are feeling. We are looking for ways to communicate, and be in touch with the changes in the energy, the Universal vibration, the ineffable. We know that our purpose as women in this life is changing. We feel it and want to express it, but have not had a way. We didn't, that is, until we found ritual. Now that we have found the potential in ritual we are able to do the sacred work and at the same time to communicate our feelings about the ineffable. We are able to connect with all living and know that each ritual we do brings us closer to creating a world that is safe for all life forms. It is through our belief in the Goddess within — and bringing her into being, connecting with others that are expressing their Goddess within — that we create a Goddess mentality for us all to live with.

During this time of change-over we will not find it easy, but the more we do ritual and become comfortable with the whys and hows of it, the more we are able to create Her way of being. She becomes a model of world interaction. Don't think that the good old boys will give up without a kick and a scream, but they can't go against the energy once we have built it strong. As the Ethiopian proverb says, "When spider webs unite, they can halt a lion." Our rituals asking for, working for world justice change the very fabric of the Universal consciousness. It is happening.

The elements, the directions we call in, also relate to our body and the body of the Mother Earth. Water symbolizes our blood, and the waters of the Earth are Her life blood. Add salt and we have the sea womb that we all come from. Earth symbolizes our physical body and is also Her body. We honor Us when we call in Earth, and we share our space with all the creatures that live here with us. We think of all the images that it conjures up in us, and we ask for that energy to fill us, to give us stability, change and life.

We call in Air and feel the cleansing energy of the wind and the mental clarity to see; it is the force of Spirit but it is not Spirit. Spirit is our soul, our essence, the us that is there when we surrender to self and allow the ego to leave. Fire is the life force, the force that keeps us going even when we think for a short time, that it would be better if this life were finished. It keeps us going and burns us, to hone us, to transform the ego into pure Spirit.

We call in all five elements and know that we are not using them lightly, but we feel light-hearted about their coming. We are able to treat them as good friends, and sometimes we just say, "Come on in, the teapot is on the stove," while other times we call them with full regalia. They know we know our intent. When we have clarity of intent, our purpose in holding a ritual, it happens and we feel it happen. We *know* it is more than a personal satisfaction of having a good time, it is more than being happy, it is a joyousness, a connectiveness with all life, and we experience it.

When we "act" in a ritual and not "be," we do not feel the sense of connectiveness. A lot of women put on the trappings of other cultures and think that will make them feel/be spiritual in the way of that culture. It is like putting on a costume and acting out the part. We can learn from other cultures and then find our own way of using sacred objects — sacred because they have meaning for us, not because another culture uses them. Laurens Vander Post talks about Carl Jung in his book, *Jung and the Story of Our Time*.[5] He says,

> Africa had thus given him final confirmation of the universality of his theory of the collective unconscious of man . . . how he stressed that his and everyone's first duty was to his own culture, place and moment in time, and the material on which he had to work always was nearest and came most naturally to hand. . . . The task of modern man was not to go primitive the African way but to discover and confront and live out his own first and primitive self in a truly twentieth-century way.

We are able in our Women's Spirituality rituals to "discover and *confront* and live" out our changes and our own lives. I have always had an affinity with feathers, collected them long before I ever did a "formal" ritual. When someone asked me why, I would answer, "Because when I have enough I am going to make wings and fly away." I didn't at the time know what double meaning my words had. It would have helped me if I had listened to my own words. My answer said I was not where I "should" have been, but was where I thought I "should" be. The other part alludes to my involvement with Women In Constant Creative Action where we call our local groups Wings. I still collect feathers, but now they are a symbol to me of my freedom of mind/spirit/intellect, and they are also a symbol of my connection with all living creatures. I do not have stories of my own built around the attributes of the animals yet. That is not a part of the heritage I have reclaimed. So I build them into my future and what I want to be/feel. I take from the past what works, and only because it works, not because I am trying to be the people of the past that I am not, and I look to the future where we will create new forms in which to do our work.

Visualization or guided awareness is one of the most powerful tools in creating our new concepts of the Universal design. It can help us to ground or center ourselves, and to be ready for the work we will do in the ritual. Joan Borysenko says the following about meditation, but it applies in the same way to the kind of guided awareness we do in a ritual:[6]

> To develop a state of inner awareness, to witness and let go of the old dialogues, you need an observation point. If you went out in a boat to view the offshore tides but neglected to put down an anchor, you would soon be carried off to sea. So it is with the mind. Without an anchor to keep the mind in place, it will be carried away in the torrent of thoughts. Your ability to watch what is happening will be lost. The practice of meditation, which calms the body through the relaxation response and fixes the mind through dropping the anchor of attention, is the most important tool of self-healing and self-regulation.

The use of guided awareness is that anchor. With the use of soft tones of voice and a careful choice of words, the guider of the awareness can provide a place to keep the mind in while the other women go off into a meditative state as they raise energy. Going into a meditative state, going between the worlds, increases the chance that sacred work will take place. It is in the meditative state also, that important changes in behavior happen.

It is during this time, the anchoring, that the invoking of the deity occurs. If the women planning the ritual choose to do so, the invoking can be used as the centering. Since I believe that deity is our collective divineness, I do not often call in a deity at this time when I am HPD. I do call in the Goddess aspect energy when creating the circle. There are times when we plan a ritual where it seems to work best, as a grounding, to call in the energy form that has been given the name of a Goddess, or a god.

After being grounded/centered, and the energy has been raised to a point that it is almost ready to be sent, the HPD/guider of awareness/ monitor of energy can help again by using a soft voice to guide the energy and focus it. She talks about building the cone of power, or if there are a lot of new women who would not understand the term, she can talk about a funnel being over our heads, with the large part on our heads and the tube end up. The energy then starts by going around the circle and raising up into the funnel. The HPD guides it up, as it becomes more contained, formed into usable substance. Once the energy has been raised and is in the "neck of the funnel," *use it*. Send it out to your designated receiver.

It is not our intention to send energy to those who do not want it. That is control, and is what Fundamentalists do when they pray for someone to do such and so. We have different words for what we do. We call it ritual and they call it church service. We call it raising and sending energy, and they call it prayer. I hope there is more than word differences in what we do, though. I hope that our concern for the Mother Earth goes beyond lip service, and that we bring life and living into an order that reflects our words. I hope that we are not into control and telling other people how they should live. I hope that our use of the energy will create a new way for the world's peoples, but I hope we are always able to keep in mind when we send the energy that we are sending it as an option to use or not to use. If we want freedom we have to give it to all peoples, to make their own choices.

Using the following outline can help in the planning of the next ritual. May we find joyousness and be seriously involved in our spirituality.

1. Why — What is the reason for the ritual?
2. Who — Who is planning this one?
3. What — Creating sacred space
   Calling the quarters
   Using salt and water
   Cleansing the air with incense or herbs.

Grounding/centering.
The Work — focusing.
Sending the Energy.
Grounding.
Opening the Circle — Thanking and dismissing elements/
   Goddess aspects.

The following are portions of rituals, parts that can be integrated into a ritual that is planned around them. They are not meant to be used verbatim, but to give some sharing of what a ritual can contain.

Ritual for First Naming of a Child

In a woman's community, an important circle to be held is for the naming of her child. If there is a father in residence the couple may want to have another naming celebration besides this one, or they might, with the agreement of the women's circle, have it with men and women. This can be used with the total community that the child will grow up in. It is our pledge to the child, appropriate from the whole community.

After the circle is cast, the sacred space created, a door is opened and a person comes in carrying the child. This is the person standing in for the child and not either of its parents. The person carrying the child says, as the reader for the child:

I have just been born,
Come share my wonder, my new life.
I am newly come to this.
It's still so new,
Come share my delight.
Feeling my body,
See how I can move my fingers.
The memories are still fresh in me.
I'm in two places,
Wisdom and newness.
I ask all of you to help me.
Give me a circle of love,
Give me a circle of protection.
Shelter with the light
While I learn to adjust and become.
Give me my name
And your promise of love.

Leader/HPD/Energy Monitor:

Who will answer for this child?
Who will give the circle?
Who will pledge the light?
Answer now this child.

Group:

I will. (*And they form a circle around her.*) The Mother now takes the child into her arms and the other person steps into the circle. The Mother (*or Father*) says:

I look with wonder at this child,
At the perfection of the soul,
And know that I will pledge my heart
To keep the tender bud
Alive, growing and searching
For that special place that nurtures,
To reach the stars with mysteries yet untold.
For I look with wonder at this child

And know perfection of the soul.
Let this child be known, with love,
by this name: _____.

Leader:

So mote it be.

The circle continues its work and raises the energy. A good place to send it during a naming is to the children of this world that are in need, those children who do not have the loving community that the child who has had this naming does.

Ritual for First Blood

The time that a young woman has her first menstruation can be either a time of fear and troubling thoughts or a time of joy and wonder. It all depends on how the young woman has been taught to view the event. Our circles can help her to feel that joy and wonder by giving her a special ritual.

To prepare for this ritual there needs to be three extra candles for the young woman to light. Work with her on what colors she likes, explaining what the symbolism of the colors means. Create sacred space and have her come to the center of the circle to say/read her part.

I was born a woman of a woman
And have always felt my womanness.
But today is different,
Special,
And I would like you to join with me,
Share my wonder at my changing world.
Today I felt the promise,
The potential,
The potential within, if I choose,
To start another life
Born of a woman.
As I feel the wonder,
The new knowledge, new understanding
Born of a woman,

The glorious changing, changing within me,
I know and accept the responsibility that from now on I have.
Knowing that a moment's passion and an ongoing life commit-
ment are two different things,
Help me to keep my pledge, with loving teaching.
Join with me in a circle of joy that I now fully feel my
womanness.

HPD/Leader:

Come circle with us and join our energy in full knowledge. We
welcome you and your being and light.

I light this candle of my sister/mother moon
For now we are at one with our cycles.

I light this candle for my mother, the Earth
For now I can feel her roots and ongoingness.

I light this candle for _____
For this is my ruling Planet, my special help.

Continue the ritual with the young woman now inside the circle, one more
woman adding her energy to the work. One of the assumptions in this
portion of a ritual is that the young woman having her first blood is also
aware of the sexual implications of her life now.

A Ritual Before a Handfasting or Marriage

Before an important occasion like a handfasting or a marriage, a
woman gains energy by the women of her group holding a circle for her.
This is a ritual that would be enjoyable to plan.

Create the sacred space, having the special woman stand by the altar
direction of her choice. She then reads:

Bless me my sisters,
I have chosen a mate,
Someone I would like to share my life.
Give me council, give me guidance,

Give me love, give me grace,
Give me understanding.
Listen to my joy, listen to my successes,
Listen to my gripes.
But do not judge, do not blame,
Do not take sides, do not leave me,
Do not snipe.
Help me to laugh, help me to remember,
Help me to feel, help me to grow,
Help me to revel,
And I will not forget you my sisters.
Join now our energy and bless our union,
Then go with me and share my joy at the joining celebration.

The circle members say:

We bless you with the light.
We hear your desire of us.
We give our pledge of support and understanding.
Go now in peace and joy to start a new growing.
Go now with the blessing and wishes from each of us.

Each woman then gives her a gift of a good wish for her future. Continue the ritual and raise energy to be given to the new couple and their home. Open the circle and help get her ready for the rest of her day.

Full Moon Ritual

After the circle is cast, before calling in Spirit, complete the sacred space. To call in Spirit, using the spirit of the moon, use the following to call her in. The HPD says:

I feel the power.
Let it enter us now.
Oh, sister moon
Come join our circle.

At your fullest,
Share your power.

Oh, sister moon
Come join our circle.

Shine on down now,
Point out the path.
Oh, sister moon
Come join our circle.

I light a candle to you,
Share your knowledge.
Oh, sister moon
Come join our circle.

Let us learn now
The way for us,
Oh, sister moon
Come join our circle.

The Full Moon circle is a good time to have her energy fill us, to use that energy to be completely in touch with our psychic abilities, and to use them to read the cards or some other form of divination for our personal paths.

Chant Blessing for a Meal Together

Circle around the table, my sisters
Think of the food that is grown.

Circle around the table my sisters
Think of the food that is grown.

Circle around the table my sisters
Think of the food that is grown.

Come join with us and share,
Come join with us and share,
Come join with us and share,

The abundance is with us.

The abundance goes on and on,
We share the abundance and are the abundance.

Come join with us and share.
Circle around the table, my sisters,
Think of the abundance of life.

We thank you, oh Mother
As we circle around the table.

A Birthday

Today I am _____ (years old)
A child in the cosmos
An adult on the Earth
Reaching for a balance
Wanting to cry for unfinished dreams
Wanting to laugh with found loves
Reaching for a balance
Share my day with me
Share my sadness/joy
Reaching for a balance
Wasted days and hours
Too full hours and days
Reaching for a balance
Retreating in fear
Rejoicing in expectation
Reaching for a balance
Share my day with me
Share my future with me
Learning to balance

The circle answers:

You have reached a good age,
We rejoice with you in the expectations for the coming year.
We will help you in this coming year to balance and share the
energy.
We now fill you with the light of blessings.

You now fill us with the light of blessings.
You have reached a good age.

An Invitation to Share in a Ritual

And she said to us:
Eat of my bread,
Drink of my waters,
Allow my breeze to cool you.
Allow my fire to warm you.
And dance with me in the cosmic dance of life.

Notes

1. Pat Rodegast and Judith Stanton, *Emmanuel's Book* (New York: Bantam Books, 1985), p. 57.

2. A Wing is what the local groups of Women In Constant Creative Action (WICCA) are called. These are support groups based in Women's Spirituality, that have rituals as part of their activities. They all do self-awareness exercises and metaphysical lessons.

3. Jan Woudhuysen, *Tarot Therapy* (Los Angeles: J.P. Tarcher, Inc., 1979), p. 119.

4. Jamake Highwater, *Ritual of the Wind* (New York: Alfred Van der Marck Editions, 1984), p. 73.

5. Laurens Vander Post, *Jung and the Story of Our Time* (New York: Random House, 1977), p. 51.

6. Joan Borysenko, *Minding the Body, Mending the Mind* (New York: Bantam Books, 1988), p. 36.

Jay Goldspinner

Jay Goldspinner is a storyteller and a witch who lives in the hills of western Massachusetts. She has been telling stories and teaching others to tell their stories for eight years in New England and across the country and the world — at festivals, libraries, museums, coffeehouses, story-and-ritual workshops and in people's living rooms.

Seeing storytelling as a way of bringing people together in our communities and the world, Jay's concern for women and for the earth shines through her stories, her art and her life. She loves to tell stories to women because "we don't hear enough of our own woman-strong stories." Her stories in performance and ritual are filled with joy and with women's goddess-within† affirmation and respect. The stories are another way of reclaiming who we are as women and as witches with long herstories that in goddess spirituality are no longer lost.

In her article, "Exploring Our Goddess Selves Through Stories," Jay says:

> We are all storytellers and the stories we tell are our stories — from the most ancient goddess myth to our immediate experience. Like our ancient foremothers all over the world, women gather in circles around the fire, share words and sounds, shake our bellies with laughter and tears, dance and chant our connections with the earth and each other. In telling the stories, we remember our past, create the future, affirm and heal ourselves and the world.

Her stories are rituals in themselves, and from our own and traditional stories women create goddess/Women's Spirituality rituals.

Jay Goldspinner has created audio tapes of several of her goddess and woman-strong stories. *Rootwomen Stories* and *Spinning the Tales of the Goddess* are available from her at RR2, Box 532C, Shelburne Falls, MA 01370 for $8.00 plus $1.50 postage. Her poem, "The Rootwomen," was set to music by Kay Gardner and performed by the Kansas City Women's Chorus. Her writing has appeared in *Sojourner*, *WomanSpirit* and *Cricket Magazine*, and I am very honored to present it here, in *The Goddess Celebrates*.

---

†Editor's note: Jay prefers "goddess" to be uncapitalized.

Exploring Our Goddess Selves Through Stories

Jay Goldspinner

> There was a time when you were not a slave,
> remember that. You walked alone, full of
> laughter, you bathed bare-bellied.
> You say you have lost all recollection of it, remember . . .
> You say there are no words to describe this time,
> you say it does not exist.
> But remember.
> Make an effort to remember.
> Or, failing that, invent.
>
> Monique Wittig, *Les Guerilleres* [1]

E very ritual has a story behind it and any story can become ritual. In our sacred circles we reenact the ancient goddess myths. We tell traditional tales that have been passed down for centuries. We create our own true stories from fact and fantasy. We share our past, present and even future experiences in story, song and dance. In woman circles we speak and we are listened to; in the telling and the hearing we create ourselves anew.

From earliest times peoples everywhere have told stories celebrating the glory of women — stories of the great goddess and powerful heras. We are discovering the ancient truths again: in images and tales, in lore passed down through grandmothers and children, in women gathering together, in the earth itself.

My own journey back to the goddess began with the Amazons. I came upon stories of the Amazons[2] accidentally; they gave me the courage to reinterpret the amputation of my breast for cancer. The Amazons were ancient tribes of women, horsetamers and warriors, worshippers of the goddess Artemis. They were said to ritually remove one of their breasts as a symbol of gynandry — of being both female and male in themselves. I told myself, I am a one-breasted daughter of the Amazons. I will be bold and free, needing no man to complete me.

I began to search through the pages of books for more stories of strong women. I discovered the goddess, symbol of woman-power. I found stories and images in one culture after another: Inanna, Amaterasu, Turtle Grandmother, Lilith, and She who came before names. She is known as Virgin, Mother, Crone, the Moon, the Sun, Giver and Taker of Life, Queen of Heaven and Earth. She is Woman. I brought together fragments from scattered sources, before most current material on women's spirituality was available, and began to write down the stories I found.

I discovered that women were gathering together to celebrate themselves, the goddess and the earth in ritual, dance and chant: they called it witchcraft. At a weekend in Boston in 1976 celebrating woman-spirit I sat in the pew of a staid New England church and watched as women danced bare-breasted down the aisle, chanting, "The goddess is alive, magik is afoot." I learned then what I had always known somewhere inside me, that a witch is a healer, a seer, a lover of women and the earth. I finally understood what Robin Morgan meant when she wrote, "If you say three times you are a witch, you are a witch." I said, "I am a witch. I am a witch. I am a witch."

In June 1981 I went to a storytelling festival for adults in Rockport, Maine. I remarked to my mother, "I don't like the stories they're telling about witches because I am a witch." She answered, "I don't like the stories they're telling about stepmothers because I am a stepmother." I said, "If I were telling those stories, I would tell them differently," and I became a storyteller.

Telling stories in covens and woman-circles is empowering to all. The women cast a circle and sit facing one another — in a candlelit living room, around a bonfire in a meadow, high on a mountaintop — and the storyteller spins a story: a tale of Lilith the first woman or of Spider Grandmother who brings back the sun[3]; a folktale like the Irish "Horned Women"[4] about a woman who discovers her own powers in a contest with the witches; a newspaper story of the old woman in Worcester who challenges the super-discount department store and wins.[5] The women delve into the story, they dance or act it out or they just listen, letting the story sink into them. The story reminds other women of their stories, and they too spin tales of struggle and love, pain and laughter. So the circle goes on.

Storytelling and ritual — both create their own world beyond the bounds of place and time. Both story and ritual need to be experienced to be understood. I will share some experiences of weaving storytelling into woman-centered ritual. I will tell you goddess stories and folktales with their ancient wisdom. I give you the bare bones of stories in ritual. Take these stories and these ideas: mold them, bring them to life, let them grow. The ritual, the story is always happening anew.

Inanna's Descent to the Netherworld

High on a hill in western Massachusetts women gather to hear the story of Inanna, goddess of ancient Sumer.

When Inanna walks the earth, flowers bloom and the grain blows tall. But once Inanna left the earth. From the Great Above she set her face toward the Great Below. She bade farewell to her faithful companion Ninsubar and went alone down to the underworld. Dressed in the adornments of her high office as Queen of Heaven and Earth, Inanna knocked loudly on the doors of death. She demanded of the gatekeeper Neti, "Let me in. I wish to see my sister Erishkegal." Erishkegal, Queen of the Great Below, was furious. She ordered Neti to let Inanna enter. As Inanna walked through each of the seven gates, she was forced to give up her crown, her jewels, her breastplate and finally the royal robe that covered her. At last she stood before Erishkegal, stripped and powerless. Erishkegal ordered the judges of the underworld to smite Inanna. They uttered the cry of death, and she fell to the ground dead. They hung her corpse like meat from a stake.

Three nights passed, the dark of the moon. Back on the earth Ninsubar mourned in the streets for Inanna, and all cried out for Inanna. Then Ninsubar sought help from the gods to bring Inanna back, but Enlil and Nanna refused to help. They said Inanna's plight was her own fault. Finally Ninsubar went to Nammu, goddess of the deep waters. Mother Nammu was distraught at Inanna's death. From the dirt under her fingernails she formed two gynandrous creatures and instructed them how to bring Inanna back. She sent them down to the underworld with the food of life and the water of life. Erishkegal lay there, sick and groaning like a woman in labor. The creatures sympathized with Erishkegal's pain; she offered them a reward for their caring. They asked for the corpse of Inanna. They sprinkled the food and water on the corpse. Inanna rose from death. But she was not allowed to leave the land of the dead without providing a substitute for herself. Demons guarded her as she returned to the land of the living. The demons tried to take Ninsubar and then Inanna's two sons, but each time Inanna stopped them. They came to her husband Dumuzi, who was sitting on his high throne dressed in gorgeous robes and feasting, not mourning her absence. Inanna spoke the cry of death, "Take him away."

When Inanna returns to the earth, flowers bloom and the grain blows tall. All who travel to the Great Below know that Inanna has been there before them.[6]

We discover ourselves in this ancient story of loss and death and rebirth. The women respond to the story; we discuss its history and some of the questions it raises. I tell a contemporary version of the story that happened to me, which I call "The New Jersey Turnpike Story." I tell of my faithful friend, and of the things that were taken from me as I passed through the gates of the underworld — on the New Jersey Turnpike. Then I tell the ancient Sumerian story of Inanna again.

In the evening the women gather at the top of the hill and center themselves on the descent to the underworld. Each woman walks alone down the hill in the coming darkness. Neti the gatekeeper meets her in front of a small conical-shaped cave at the bottom of the hill. She crawls through the narrow opening into the cave. She stands before her own image in the candle-lit mirror. After everyone has entered and left the cave, the women ascend the hill single-file in the darkness. Around the fire in the lodge they talk about the experience. One woman saw her grandmother in the mirror in the cave; then the image dissolved into herself. The women explore the connection between the story, the ritual, and themselves.

On summer solstice, when the sun stands still, another group of women gather to descend to the caves, this time in the hills of western Connecticut. Outdoors in a grassy place they cast the circle. They pass the rattle to share their names and their hopes of the day. They chant, "There's a river of birds in migration, a nation of women with wings." They listen to the story of "Inanna's Descent to the Netherworld." They talk about the story from their own perspectives. They each choose an object — shell, feather, mask, glass ball, stone — from a pile on the ground, to take with them for the rest of the day. They drive and walk in to a place of cliffs and caves. They explore the stony bones of mother earth as the sun descends in the west.

The women eat supper sitting on the cliffs. Just at sunset they hear the story again. To the beat of the drum each woman climbs down the rocky path. She goes to a place in one of the dark caves and stays there alone. The drum calls them back. The women howl and cry in response to the drum as they emerge from the caves. They gather around a bonfire to share their experience and feelings, and to close the circle. One woman has buried a mask in the cave, and with it her feelings of anger and abandonment. Like Inanna, each woman descends into the underworld, then returns to the world she left — but not the same.

Amaterasu, the Sun Goddess

The myth of Amaterasu, the sun goddess in Japan, is another story of the descent into darkness, but in this story the people make a festival, like the Mardi Gras, to bring back the light.

Amaterasu, the Sun, and Susanowo, the Storm Wind, are sister and brother. For a long time these two have been in conflict. All that she nurtured and loved on earth, he destroyed — and laughed uproariously.

One day Amaterasu was sitting in her heavenly palace, weaving with her woman companions. Suddenly there was a terrible crash. Susanowo tore a gaping hole in the roof tiles; he hurled a horse's flayed corpse into the weaving room and roared with laughter. Amaterasu's companion jerked back in terror. She pierced her vulva with the sharp shuttle, and in awful agony she died. Amaterasu screamed and fled from the room to hide away in the Rock Cave of Heaven. The Sun was gone. Darkness came over the earth.

All the people called her to return. She didn't even answer. The gods and goddesses gathered beside the Tranquil River of Heaven, which we call the Milky Way. They discussed how to lure Amaterasu out of the cave. They brought roosters to crow and make her think it was day. From the faraway mountains they dug up the Everliving Tree and planted it in front of the cave. They decorated the tree with curved jewels and shimmering weavings. In the middle of the tree they placed a round bronze mirror.

Uzume, chubby-faced goddess of mirth, built fires to drive away the darkness. She decked herself out with leaves from the Everliving Tree. She climbed on an overturned tub. She began to dance, a lusty comical dance. She tossed off the leaves that covered her, revealing and reveling in her woman-self.

Hiding in the Rock Cave, Amaterasu heard Uzume's pounding feet, the rowdy laughter of the gods and goddesses, the roosters' crowing. She was curious. "How can they be enjoying themselves so much in my absence?" She peeped out of the cave. She came face to face with her own bright image reflected in the round mirror. Dazzled by her own radiance

70

she stood still in the doorway. Tajikarawo was waiting. He took her hand and gently drew her out of the cave. The sun broke forth. Everyone cheered for joy at her return.[7]

Women in this country are rediscovering goddesses like Amaterasu. Japanese people have revered the sun goddess for centuries. In the mountain town of Takachiho in Japan the people perform a sacred dance every night of the year, celebrating the story of Amaterasu. One rainy March night I sat crosslegged with the other dark-kimonoed spectators. I watched the ritual dance unfold on a stage that was bare except for the miniature Rock Cave in the rear. First Tajikarawo, then Uzume, then Tajikarawo dance around the stage in wide circles, wearing bold masks and robes of white and red. They move slowly and then faster to the music of flute and drums, imploring Amaterasu in the Rock Cave to return. At last the triumph — Tajikarawo pulls open the doors of the Rock Cave to reveal a small bright mirror, which is Amaterasu — and the audience cheered. I experienced the power and continuity of ancient goddess rites still alive today.

Back in this country I tell the story of Amaterasu to a circle of women. Then I tell the story again for women to act out with masks and movement and musical instruments. One woman dons a white plaster mask and moves into the center of the circle as Amaterasu, someone puts on another mask to become Susanowo. They dance the struggle between the two, as women sitting around the circle beat drums and ring bells. One woman passes the mask on to someone else and the drama continues. Susanowo creates havoc in the sacred weaving room, Amaterasu's companion dies in agony, Amaterasu runs to hide in the Rock Cave. The circle of women become the deities trying to lure Amaterasu back. They cheer when she emerges from the cave, as they create the story and ritual of the light's return.

The Turtle Story

As evening comes a group of women gather outside the sweat lodge. The sweat lodge ceremony is a Native-American ritual, now used by people of other traditions as well. The sweat lodge is a low round hut of bent saplings covered with blankets; it is the form of Grandmother Turtle, the earth. Women walk around the lodge chanting, "The earth is our mother, we must take care of her." They bend and crawl one by one into the dark enclosed space. They sit close together naked in a circle around a pit filled with burning-hot rocks. The women call on the directions. They sing and cry. They sweat in the steamy heat—let go of fears, let go of angers, let go of impurities. I tell a legend from the Mohawk people.

There is a world in the sky, above this world where we live. The Sky Queen and the Sky King lived up there. Once the Sky King, with his bare hands, tore the Tree of Life out of the ground; it left a gaping hole where the roots had been. He commanded that no one go near the hole. The Sky Queen was curious and she disobeyed. She looked down the hole and saw another world far below. She wanted to explore for herself. She jumped through the hole.

At that time there was only water in the world below. A pair of Canadian geese saw the Sky Queen falling through the air; they caught her on their wings. Other animals gathered in the water below to try to help the Sky Queen. Someone said, "If we could only get mud from under the water, we could make land for the Sky Queen to live on." First, mallard duck dove down, but he couldn't reach the bottom. Next cormorant went; he too failed to bring up mud. Then muskrat tried. He was gone for a long time. Finally he came up with a bit of mud in his mouth. But where to put it? Grandmother Turtle said, "You can put the mud on my back. I will hold up the earth." The mud spread and grew into plains and mountains and valleys. It became the vast continent we live on, which native people call Turtle Island.

The geese brought the Sky Queen down to Turtle Island. She lived there and bore twin sons, the Good-minded Son and the Bad-minded Son. Between them they created all that is on the earth, the good and the bad. The Sky Queen died and was buried in the ground. Out of her head grew pumpkins, out of her sides grew beans and corn and squash, out of her feet grew potatoes. Thus even in death she nurtures us all who are her children.[8]

We sit in the sweat lodge. We think of the Sky Queen, who leapt to unknown worlds, and of Turtle Grandmother, who holds us all on her back.

Lilith, the First Woman

Lilith is the first woman in Jewish tradition, created before Eve. Her name is spoken in whispers. It is said that she kills babies and seduces men. Knowing how patriarchal religion turns the truth upside down, I began to look for the truth about Lilith.

I had been piecing the story together from heresay and fragments in books when I went to a weekend celebrating the Jewish sabbath, led by storyteller and rabbi Lynn Gottlieb. On Friday night as the sabbath began Lynn told, danced, chanted her version of Lilith's story. When she finished, my friend spoke out to me across the room, "Now, you tell your Lilith story." I didn't answer then. But in that moment I saw Lilith as the flaming dragon and the serpent of the Biblical story, and my Lilith story of freedom and defiance was born.

Long long ago, in the time before remembering, there was a beautiful garden. Into that garden came two people; from the dust of the earth they were created. The man was Adam. The woman was Lilith. For a time they lived happily. They laughed and danced and sang. Then Adam began to lord it over Lilith. "You can't build the fires . . . You can't name the animals — only I can do that." Then one day he ordered her, "Lie beneath me." At that she cried out, "Don't you know we were born equal? We were both born of the dust of the earth." She uttered the ineffable name and flew far away to the desert beyond the Red Sea. There she stayed. She danced in the moonlight, swam in the Red Sea, and bore many beautiful children.

Adam said to God, "Did you see what that woman did?" Adam was so annoyed that God sent three messengers to bring Lilith back. They threatened to drown her and destroy her children to try to force her to return. She drew herself up to her full height, as high as the mountain of the moon, Mt. Sinai, and commanded the messengers to leave.

Back in the garden, Adam was lonely. God made another woman from Adam's rib. Adam and Eve lived happily in the garden. They laughed and danced and sang. Then God told Adam that the man and woman were forbidden to eat the fruit of the Tree of Knowledge of Good and Evil. Out in the desert Lilith overheard God's words. She grew angry. She transformed herself into a flaming-haired dragon, with wings that stretched from horizon to horizon. She flew back to the garden of Eden.

Lilith approached the woman. "Eve?" "Who are you?" "I am the first woman." "I thought I was the first woman." "No, you are the second woman. Now, Eve, listen . . ." She convinced Eve to eat the forbidden fruit. Eve convinced Adam to eat also. Then the man and the woman realized they were naked. They knew God would be angry at them and they hid.

Next morning God came into the garden. He saw that Adam and Eve were gone. He guessed what had happened. God was frightened. He thought, "What if they also eat of the Tree of Life and become gods like us?" God cursed Eve to bear children in sorrow and to obey her husband all the days of her life. He cursed Adam to work the land in sweat and pain. And to those who believe those curses, they are true. God cursed Lillith to crawl on her belly and eat the dust of the earth. But she laughed, for she did not fear God.

God ordered the man and woman out of the garden into the world; they had to leave. But Lilith was never conquered. She still stands there in the garden — the flaming sword that turns every way to guard the Tree of Life.[9]

My story of Lilith draws directly from the Biblical account of Adam and Eve found in Genesis 2 and 3. Eve's story has been used to put women down for centuries. We can find goddess and woman-strong stories in the patriarchal religions we grew up in, if we look beyond the interpretations we were taught and seek out the truth. We need to retell the old stories, refute the lies and affirm women's power.

You can build a ritual around a story or you can choose a story that fits a particular ritual, the season, your own or another culture, or just a fancy. Tell stories of Brigid at Candlemas, Demeter and Persephone at the spring equinox, Cerridwen at the fall equinox, Hecate at Halloween. Unlike the God whom many of us knew as distant and forbidding, the goddess in her many forms is quite accessible. In her stories we recognize ourselves.

You can retell a goddess story using the details of your own life, telling your story as a myth — as I told of myself as Inanna in "The New Jersey Turnpike Story." You can tell the story of Demeter and Persephone, identifying with the mother or daughter; tell your own story of loss or discovery in that frame. See yourself as Hecate, crone of the crossroads.

Tales of the goddess are any stories of women — for we are each and all the goddess. One evening I told the ancient stories of Inanna and Amaterasu. After intermission I told the story of "The Nude Dancers' Bar," about an event that occurred not long ago in a central Massachusetts city: six women set out to remove a female image painted outside the nude dancers' bar, an image they agreed was degrading to women. The sign, filling the whole wall, depicted a nude woman lounging in a cocktail glass. In a carefully planned and executed maneuver, the six women arrived in a car at 3 A.M., posted a guard, painted out the image and covered it with a pink shelf-paper sign of their own which read: "This is offensive to women. Worcester Moral Reform Society." The next morning a photo and article in the newspaper told the hera-ic story to the entire city.

Hearing that story reminded women of their own stories and gave them permission to speak out. One woman after another was inspired to tell her story of defacing and defiance, of confronting and changing the powers-that-be, her own goddess story.

You can use folk and fairy tales in ritual. These tales have been handed down by the common folk for centuries and are rich in ancient wisdom. Watch for the ugly old witch, the stepmother, the devil's grandmother, the old wise woman of the village. When these characters appear there is secret information for women: the answer to questions, the journey toward truth.

The old Russian witch Baba Yaga is one of these characters. She lives in a cottage ringed with fiery skulls. She holds the power of life and death in her hands. But her tools are ordinary kitchen implements; she rides through the sky in a mortar, pushing with a pestle, sweeping away her traces with a broom. In the story "Vasalisa the Beautiful" the maiden Vasalisa is sent by her stepmother to bring back the light from Baba Yaga.[10]

Mother of the Waters

The maiden and the crone are two aspects of the goddess. They often meet in folktales. "Mother of the Waters" comes from Haiti but this theme is worldwide.

A young girl, who was an orphan, went to work for a woman who had a daughter just her age. One day the girl was washing silverware in the river. She lost a silver spoon. The woman angrily told her not to return until she found the spoon. The girl searched along the river all that day. In the late afternoon she met an old woman by the river. The old woman asked the girl if she would wash her back. The girl began, but her hands started bleeding from the terrible sores and prickles on the old woman's back. The old woman looked at the girl's hands, then spit on them and they were healed.

The old woman took the young girl home to the mountains. The next morning she showed her how to make a meal from a grain of rice and a single bean. Then she went out, cautioning the girl to drive away the cat if it came. The cat came begging for food. The girl felt sorry for it and fed it. The old woman returned. The girl stayed with the old woman for a long time. As she left to go back the old woman told her, "You will find a pile of eggs at the crossroads. Take the smallest one." The girl came to the crossroads and chose the smallest egg from the pile. Out of the egg came a tiny box which grew into a chest full of silverware. The girl returned to the woman she had worked for, and gave her the silver.

The woman was so excited by the treasure that she immediately sent her own daughter to find the old woman. The girl pretended to lose a spoon and went down the river until she met the old woman. But this girl ridiculed the old woman's hurt back and her way of making dinner, and acted rude and uncaring. The old woman left the house the next day with the admonition to drive the cat away. When the cat came begging, the girl beat it with a stick. The old woman returned, limping and leaning on a cane. She told the girl to leave. But she said to her, "You will find a pile of eggs at the crossroads. Take the smallest one." The girl came to a pile of eggs, big and small. The largest ones were calling out, "Take me, take me." She said, "I'm smart enough to take the one that calls to me," and she picked the largest egg of all. The egg split open. Out came snakes and lizards to chase the girl away.[11]

In wicca ritual we initiate women into the coven. We often mark our passage into a new phase of life with an initiation. This story throws light on the initiation. The meeting of the maiden and the crone is an initiation for the first maiden though she doesn't realize it. By being who she is — kind and open to learn — she passes the test and is rewarded; she moves on to another stage of her life. To underscore the message another maiden (sometimes called the stepsister) meets the old woman and fails the test.

The Buried Moon

In this English folktale the Moon is the goddess. Her ancient power shines through the telling.

Long ago, in my grandmother's time, the Carland was all in bog. When the Moon shone over the bog land, the people could walk about in safety. But when the Moon was gone, out came the Bogles and the Horrors to do harm to the marsh folk. Now the kind and gentle Moon heard about this. Covering her shining self entirely in a black cloak, she came down at month's end to see if it was as bad as she had heard. All was dark everywhere she looked. But she wouldn't go back till she had seen it all. Near a black pool her foot slipped. She grabbed at a crooked snag to steady herself. That snag twined itself around her wrists and held her prisoner. She pulled and fought but she was caught in the bog — with no one to help her.

Then she heard a calling and a wailing. She saw a man running terrified through the bog. As she tugged and pulled to get free and help the poor man, her hood fell back off her face. The light from her shining hair drove away the darkness and the man ran off to safety. The Moon struggled again to get free and follow him, but in vain. She fell to her knees and the hood fell forward over her head. Back came the darkness and all the Bogles and Horrors to mock and torment her. They fought over her all that night. Just before dawn they buried her in the dark pool. Will-o-the-wisps were set on the crooked snag to keep watch that she might not escape.

The time came for the new Moon. But no new Moon came. The marsh folk waited — and they talked. Finally they went to the wise woman in the mill and asked her where the Moon might be. She consulted her book and her pot and her mirror, but she could not tell. One night folks were sitting in the inn, talking of the lost Moon. Suddenly a man from the far side of the bog cried out, "My sakes, I reckon I know where the Moon is!" He told of the night he'd been lost in the marsh and a great light had come to save him.

The people went back to the wise woman. She told them, "Gather at dusk. Go out together into the marsh. Each one put a stone in your mouth, carry a hazel twig in your hand. Speak no word until you return. Look until you find a coffin, a cross and a candle." They gathered that night and, trembling and frighted, they went deep into the dark bog. At last they saw a great stone shaped like a coffin. Over it was a crooked cross of a tree and the flickering light of a will-o-the-wisp. All together the marsh folk lifted the great stone. The next moment the full Moon was up in the sky, shining down on them and smiling, as if she wished she could drive away all the evil things forever.[12]

The wonder of this story is the love the people and the Moon have for one another; in the end the common folk rescue the goddess. As in the story of Amaterasu, the community holds the power to bring back the light.

There are medieval legends in the Arthurian saga where the goddess appears in disguise, notably the story of Lady Ragnelle.[13] In this story the question is asked, "What is it that all women desire most?" The answer to that question brings about Ragnelle's transformation from crone to maiden — the magic renewal of the earth from winter to spring.

Our Own Stories in Ritual

The storyteller is any woman who has a story to tell — and we all have. I moved through patterns of shyness and fear of speaking out to become a storyteller; I know that anyone can tell a story. If the story speaks to you, tell it. Take the story you read or heard. Let it go inside you, then tell it in your own words. It can be simple or elaborate; if it comes from the heart, it doesn't matter.

You do not have to tell the story as you found it. The storytelling tradition is fluid, everchanging with the teller and the listeners. We use our intuition to re-create the way things should be. If you don't like the ending "and she got married and lived happily ever after," tell the story anyway and change the ending. Women in wicca take familiar fairy tales like "Snow White" and "Sleeping Beauty"; they retell or act them out with changes to restore their original woman-power.

We create our own stories out of our fantasies and our life experiences. The experiences of our lives are rich and valuable. A basic part of wicca ritual is the sharing: passing around the circle a word, a sound, a motion, a story. Each woman takes her turn in a round robin, hearing her words reverberate and grow in the magic of the circle. Each woman tells her own separate story or it may be passed around as a continuous story. We may tell stories of our dreams, stories of growth and harvest, stories of spring, stories of the dark. Someone starts and others join in. Sometimes we pass around a rattle or a shell; the woman holding the rattle speaks without interruption while her sisters listen — what a healing process! If there are many women in the circle, we may tell our story in groups of three; then one from each group may share with the whole circle.

In a woman's house in Oakland a woman named Angela challenged me, "I'm not into the goddess. I'm not into anything superior to me." "But she is not superior," I protested, "She is me, I am her." "Then why don't they invoke my name?" Angela asked, "O Angela come to us . . ." she intoned. It sounded funny and we laughed. But later I remembered the many times in womancircles when we sing one by one each woman's name, weaving the sounds into a chant of power.

Name stories are among the simplest and most powerful of stories. Women may tell whatever story comes to mind about any of their names. Or they may begin by thinking of or writing down all the names they can remember ever having been called, then weave a story of their life from them.

In an often-used introduction each woman gives her own name, then her mother's, then *her* mother's, as far back as she can go: "I am Ann, daughter of Maria, daughter of Katrina, daughter of a woman somewhere in Russia." This can be amplified by following back several family lines (adoptive and natural, father's as well as mother's) — through the women. What stories can come out of that!

Anna tells how storytelling can be used to celebrate sacred occasions, passages, major changes in a woman's life. The one who is celebrating her passage asks another woman, a close friend, to lead the storytelling. She talks with the story leader before the ritual so the leader is in tune with what the woman wants. At the storytelling itself, the honored woman is silent. She receives the gift of the story woven by all the women present. In the circle are women of all ages, representing all phases of a woman's life. The story leader asks the group for the story the honored woman is requesting and begins the story. The storytelling can go on for a long time.

Anna arranged this kind of storytelling for herself as a birthday celebration. She wanted a story of her life up to the present that she could live with after she knew the honest truth of her past. It was not to be about the violence that happened. She told Mara, the story leader, what she wanted in the story and a few symbols that were important to her. She asked that the setting not be familiar to the group.

Mara began out in the cosmos "on the edge of all the waters by the edge of all the lands" with the goddesses talking. She took the story to an exciting point and stopped. Another woman wove a piece into the beginning, then passed it on. Each woman present added her part, for as long as the story needed to be complete. At the end Mara took the narrative back to "the edge of all the waters by the edge of all lands." The goddesses were still there, talking and listening to each other.

Hearing her story told by her friends was transforming to Anna. The force of the horror of her early life diminished. She had a herstory of her life that she could live with. She knew the story was true.

Women may simply make up a story. One group created a mother-daughter story featuring a powerful female character named Vagina Dentata ("cunt with teeth") whose adventures ranged from the top of Philadelphia's City Hall to the island of Tahiti. Women in Portland, Oregon made up a story about Portlandia, whose life and attributes came from the Oregon land; for the goddess is indigenous to the land. Magenta of Prodea gave me a story of how the crone invented tortillas in a year of great drought. "How and why" stories satisfy something in us that wants explanation.

Years ago Susan shared with me a dream she had. I created a story called "Susan's Dragon" from the dream. Out of my story another story-teller Louise made a guided fantasy — which is really an open-ended story. Louise encourages the circle of women to close their eyes, relax and center themselves. She tells of a community of women that is a utopia — except for the dragons. The dragons live far away in the mountains but periodically one comes to attack the women's community. Each woman in the community has her own dragon who is All Her Fears. When her dragon comes to attack the community that woman has to deal with All Her Fears, or the community will be devastated. . . . The listening women move into their own version of the story. When the visualization ends, those who wish to, tell the others their story of encountering the dragon.

Children and Stories in Ritual

Children love to hear stories and to tell their own; it works well to include stories in rituals where children are present. Chris tells the story of Demeter and Persephone[14] with double-faced "lollipop" masks (head-sized round cardboard faces held up on sticks). Chris' daughter Morgan plays Persephone, the adolescent girl who wants to go out on her own and who rather likes Hades, though she does miss her mother. Morgan's kindergarten class loves the story; so do I.

Children can do guided visualization, simple stories of going some-where and meeting someone. Younger children especially like meeting an animal as a spirit guide. After the visualization they can tell the story of what happened to them.

When a ritual is based on a story like the Inanna myth, a mother may tell her child that story ahead of time. In an intimate setting at home, the mother can explain more difficult parts and anticipate scary elements of the story and ritual. For instance, some children are afraid of the dark; with encouragement and love they can learn to deal with it and enjoy it. Stories in ritual become doors to new experiences for children, and for women who are sharing ritual with them.

Times and Seasons for Storytelling

Storytelling seems especially appropriate at certain seasons. At times of great awe and inspiration we tell stories to enfold and protect ourselves and the community. Everyone wants stories at Halloween. In that time of confronting darkness and death, stories help us to come to terms with death and the supernatural.

During the twelve days and nights that fall in the midwinter season in December and January — when darkness and cold hold sway and the veils between the worlds are thin — and especially on the Twelfth Night (January 5) we tell stories and sing songs all through the long night to drive away the darkness and bring back the sun. During the dark midwinter season, common folk in many places dress in wild costume and go through the streets acting out the mummer's play.[15] This is a story of death and resurrection, winter turned to spring, told in slapstick buffoonery that we women might reclaim for ourselves. Again we are reminded that in the darkest times revelry and comical celebration bring us through.

Women have recently revived an ancient Jewish tradition of celebrating the New Moon. Celebrated at the dark of the month — the new moon, Rosh Hodesh is a ritual based on storytelling: women tell their own life stories and tales of other women — women from Jewish tradition and women they have known. Each month they light candles when the new moon is first sighted in the western sky. They gather together on Rosh Hodesh for storytelling, singing, dancing and eating special foods. They celebrate women's rites of passage and women's roles in the world.[16]

In the dark of the month, in the dark of the year we spin our stories. All year long, in the cycle of the seasons, we women spin stories. We are all storytellers and the stories we tell are our stories, from the most ancient goddess myth to our own immediate experience. Like our ancient foremothers all over the world, we women gather in circles around the fire, share words and sounds, shake our bellies with laughter and tears, dance and chant our connections with the earth and each other. In telling the stories, we remember our past, create the future, affirm and heal ourselves in the world.[17]

Notes

1. Monique Wittig, *Les Guerilleres,* trans. by David Levay (New York: Viking Press, 1971), p. 89.

2. Helen Diner, Chapter X, "Amazons," in *Mothers and Amazons* (Garden City, NY: Anchor/Doubleday, 1973), pp. 95-111.

3. Alice Marriott and Carol K. Rachlin, eds., "How the Sun Came" (Cherokee), in *American Indian Mythology* (New York: New American Library, 1968), pp. 47-50.

4. W.B. Yeats, ed., "The Horned Women," in *Irish Folk Stories and Fairy Tales* (New York: MacMillan Company, 1973), pp. 153-154.

5. Jay Goldspinner, "The Old Woman and the Dutch Oven," on *Rootwomen Stories* (Jay Goldspinner, Box 459, Ashfield, MA 01330).

6. Jay Goldspinner, "Inanna's Descent to the Netherworld," on *Spinning the Tales of the Goddess I* (Jay Goldspinner, Box 459, Ashfield, MA 01330).

Diane Wolkstein and Samuel N. Kramer, *Inanna, Queen of Heaven and Earth* (New York: Harper and Row, 1983).

Judy Grahn, *The Queen of Swords* (Boston: Beacon Press, 1987).

July Grahm, *The Queen of Wands* (Freedom, CA: The Crossing Press, 1985).

7. Jay Goldspinner, "Amaterasu, the Sun Goddess," on *Spinning the Tales of the Goddess I.* (Jay Goldspinner, Box 459, Ashfield, MA 01330)

Jay Goldspinner, "Amaterasu," on *Story Stone* Issue 3 (Another Place, Rt. 123, Greenville, NH 03048).

Padraic Colum, "The Sun Goddess and the Storm God," in *Myths of the World* (New York: Grosset & Dunlap, 1972), pp. 245-248.

8. Heard orally from Princess Red Wing, Medicine Story and others.

Joseph Bruchac, "The Creation," "The Two Brothers," in *Iroquois Stories* (Freedom, CA: The Crossing Press, 1985), pp. 15-22.

9. Jay Goldspinner, "Lilith," on *Rootwomen Stories*.

Barbara Black Koltuv, *The Book of Lilith* (York Beach, ME: Nicolas-Hays, 1986).

Raphael Patai, *The Hebrew Goddess* (n.p., Ktav Publishing Co., 1967), pp. 207-241.

10. Jane Yolen, ed., "Vasalisa the Beautiful," in *Favorite Folktales from Around the World* (New York: Pantheon Books, 1986), pp. 335-342.

11. Diane Wolkstein, "Mother of the Waters," in *The Magic Orange Tree and Other Haitian Folktales* (New York: Schocken Books, 1980), pp. 151-156.

12. Joseph Jacobs, "The Buried Moon," in *More English Fairy Tales* (New York: G.P. Putnam Sons, n.d.), pp. 110-117.

13. Ethel Johnston Phelps, "Gawain and the Lady Ragnell," in *The Maid of the North* (New York: Holt Rinehart & Winston, 1981), pp. 35-44.

"Sir Gawain," in *Bullfinch's Mythology* (New York: Thomas Y. Crowell, 1970), pp. 414-417.

14. Padraic Colum, "Demeter," in *Myths of the World* (New York: Grosset & Dunlap, 1972), pp. 73-80.

15. Richard Chase, mummer's play, in *Grandfather Tales* (Boston, Houghton Mifflin, 1948, 1976), pp. 9-15.

16. Penina Adelman, "Rosh Hodesh," in *Miriam's Well, Rituals for Jewish Women Around the Year* (Fresh Meadows, NY: Biblio Press, 1986).

17. My appreciation goes to Susan Baylies, Louise Kessel, Antiga, Noel-Anne Brennan, Chris Carol, Jeanette Dennis, Penina Adelman, Princess Red Wing, Katie Green, Cheryl Savageau, Diane Wolkstein, Lynn Gottlieb, Magenta, Meg Heisse, Morgana and many others for ideas and insights shared.

Other Stories to Tell in Ritual

Goddess Stories

"Pele and Hiiaka": Padraic Colum, *Myths of the World* (New York: Grosset & Dunlap, 1972), pp. 261-271.

Cerridwen:

"Taliesin," in *Bullfinch's Mythology* (New York: Thomas Y. Crowell, 1970), pp. 626-633.

"Cerridwen," in *Ancient Mirrors of Womanhood* (New York: New Sibylline books, 1979), pp. 58-60.

"Hippolyta, the Amazon Queen": Jay Goldspinner, *Rootwomen Stories* (Jay Goldspinner, Box 459, Ashfield, MA 01330).

"Isis and the Secret Name of Power": Jay Goldspinner, *Spinning the Tales of the Goddess II* (Jay Goldspinner, Box 459, Ashfield, MA 01330).

"The Lamentation of Isis": Jay Goldspinner, *Spinning the Tales of the Goddess II* (Jay Goldspinner, Box 459, Ashfield, MA 01330).

"The Goddess of the Blue Mountain": Jay Goldspinner, *Spinning the Tales of the Goddess II* (Jay Goldspinner, Box 459, Ashfield, MA 01330).

"Shakti, the One Force": Jay Goldspinner, *Spinning the Tales of the Goddess II* (Jay Goldspinner, Box 459, Ashfield, MA 01330).

"The Dance of Kali": Jay Goldspinner, *Spinning the Tales of the Goddess II* (Jay Goldspinner, Box 459, Ashfield, MA 01330).

"Cupid and Psyche": Padraic Colum, *Myths of the World* (New York: Grosset & Dunlap, 1972), pp. 125-138.

"How the People Came to the Middle Place" (Tewa): Alice Marriott and Carol K. Rachlin, *American Indian Mythology* (New York: New American Library, 1968), pp. 87-95.

"Artemis": Cynthia R. Crossen and Louise Kessel, *Goddess Suite and Stories* (Cynthia R. Crossen, Rt. 2, Box 435, Pittsboro, NC 27312, or Louise Kessel, PO Box 8, Bynum, NC 27228).

"The Queen of the Planets": Sean O'Sullivan, ed. and trans., *Folktales of Ireland* (Chicago: Univ. of Chicago Press, 1966), pp. 205-209.

"The Seven African Powers": Luisah Teish, *Jambalaya* (San Francisco: Harper & Row, 1985), pp. 113-127.

Witch and Other Strong Women Stories

"Strega Nona": Tomie de Paola, *Strega Nona* (New Jersey: Prentice Hall, 1975).

"The Witch's Ride": Lupe de Osma, *The Witche's Ride and Other Tales from Costa Rica* (New York: Morrow, 1957).

"Betty Booker's Bridle": Toni McCarty, *The Skull in the Snow and Other Folktales* (New York: Delacorte Press, 1981), pp. 25-30.

"Befana" (don't be fooled by the Christmas setting): Tomie de Paola, *The Legend of Old Befana* (New York: Harcourt Brace Jovanovich, 1980).

"About the Good American Witch": Helen Hoke, ed., *Witches, Witches, Witches* (New York: Watts, 1958), pp. 101-109.

"Gum Lin and Loy Yi Lung" (China): Merlin Stone, *Ancient Mirrors of Womanhood* (New York: New Sibylline books, 1979), pp. 35-40.

"Songi" (Bantu in Africa): Merlin Stone, *Ancient Mirrors of Womanhood* (New York: New Sibylline books, 1979), pp. 145-149.

"The Strong One" (Mende in Africa): Jay Goldspinner, *Rootwomen Stories* (Jay Goldspinner, Box 459, Ashfield, MA 01330).

Harold Courlander, *A Treasury of African Folklore* (New York: Crown, 1975), pp. 69-70.

"The Woman Who Had No Story": Jay Goldspinner, *Rootwomen Stories* (Jay Goldspinner, Box 459, Ashfield, MA 01330).

"Esther and Vashti": The Book of Esther in *The Bible*.

"Mother Hildegarde": Howard Pyle, *The Wonder Clock* (New York: Dover, 1965), pp. 189-202.

"Why the Tides Ebb and Flow": J.C. Bowden, *Why the Tides Ebb and Flow* (Boston: Houghton Mifflin, 1979).

"The Stars in the Sky": Joseph Jacobs, *More English Fairy Tales* (New York: G.P. Putnam Sons, n.d.), pp. 177-181.

Ethel Johnston Phelps, *The Maid of the North* (New York: Holt Rinehart & Winston, 1981), pp. 135-141.

"The Bird of Seven Colors": Ricardo E. Alegria, *The Three Wishes, A Collection of Puerto Rican Folktales* (New York: Harcourt Brace & World, 1969), pp. 25-30.

"The Lass Who Went Out to Wash Her Face in Dew": Sorche NicLeodhas, *Thistle and Thyme* (London: The Bodley Head, 1965), pp. 82-91.

"Goblin Bread": Dorothy G. Spicer, *13 Witches* (New York: Coward McCann, 1963), pp. 43-48.

"Tatterhood": Ethel Johnston Phelps, *Tatterhood and Other Tales* (Old Westbury, NY: Feminist Press, 1978). pp. 1-6.

"Little Sister and the Month Brothers": Beatrice Schenk de Regniers, *Little Sister and the Month Brothers* (New York: Seabury Press, 1976).

"The Last Panther in Western Kentucky": Jennifer Justice, *Spiderwoman: A Celebration of Woman Heroes* (Yellow Moon Press, PO Box 1316, Cambridge, MA 02238).

"Sister of the Birds": Jerzy Ficowski, *Sister of the Birds and Other Gypsy Tales* (Abingdon-Nashville, 1961), trans. by Lucia M. Borski, 1976.

"The Chicken Woman": Doug Lipman, *Folktales of Strong Women* (Yellow Moon Press, PO Box 1316, Cambridge, MA 02238).

(Called "A Dispute in Sign Language") Dov Noy, ed., *Folktales of Israel* (Chicago: Univ. of Chicago Press, 1963).

"Song of Bear": Anne Cameron, *Daughters of Copper Woman* (Vancouver BC: Press Gang Publishers, 1981), pp. 115-119.

"The Spell of the Mermaid": Davis Pratt, *Magic Animals of Japan* (Boston: Houghton Mifflin, 1967).

"The Old Woman Who Tried to Find God" (Baila): Susan Feldman, ed., *African Myths and Tales* (New York: Dell Publishing Co., 1963), pp. 311-313.

Shekhinah Mountainwater

Shekhinah Mountainwater is a mystical, musical, magical woman who loves the Goddess and the Earth. She has been facilitating Women's Spirituality groups for almost twenty years, from the smallest intimate circles to large public rituals. Working to develop systems that express a female reality, Shekhinah has created new myths and sacred theater, Goddess-based songs and chants, and ideas and ritual methods that are known to women throughout the world. Her music is sung and chanted in every Women's Spirituality ritual.

 She says:

I have always served the Goddess, but did not consciously realize Her until the early '70s, when many people were waking up to Her around the world. I learned that all the things I was doing: ecstatic singing, epic myth-making, mime interpretations of sacred symbolic stories, pursuing a passionate, earthy spirituality . . . were missing pieces of her lost traditions.

Women approached me, asking me to work with them, and so my first women's circles were born. We chanted Ma because it seemed the natural female alternative to Om, and found ourselves intuitively meditating in circles. Old Feminist Consciousness Raising process helped us to learn the power of speaking our hearts in turn, each person being heard, all paying close attention.

Since then I have taken vows to be a full-time priestess and Goddess-worker. I teach classes, make ceremony, develop calendars and culture, write, play music, create art and poetry. I long for a society where women and men are free to be themselves, to be creative and loving and fulfilled in all their great potential.

Shekhinah has created a women's tarot system, called "Shekhinah's Tarot" and been involved in the creation of "Daughters of the Moon" and "Book of Aradia" tarot decks. Her "Womanrunes" is the first women-oriented runeset and system. Several audio tapes are available by Shekhinah Mountainwater, including *Songs and Chants of the Goddess I and II,* and the song, dance and theater cycle, *The Myth of Kore,* which is performed regularly in Santa Cruz, California, Shekhinah's home. She has developed calendars and other grids to express a belief system that is non-linear and flowing. Her thirteen-lesson Women's Spirituality correspondence course is based on Shekhinah's philosophy and work — a lesson from it follows. She is a superb teacher, performer, ritualist, artist, writer and priestess of the Goddess.

In "Writings on Rituals and Spells," Shekhinah describes both the ecstasy and theory of ritual work and suggests rituals and spells for affirming the Goddess and the Goddess-within. In "Rites of Kore" she shares her ritual enactment of the Demeter and Persephone myth. To contact her about her correspondence course or other work, write to her at PO Box 2991, Santa Cruz, CA 95063.

Writings on Rituals and Spells

Shekhinah Mountainwater

Make for yourself a power spot
Bring you a spoon and a cooking pot
Bring air
Bring fire
Bring water
Bring earth
And you a new universe will birth . . .

Spells are directed at circumstance; rituals are directed to the soul. In many ways they are the same, and employ the same basic techniques. Both can be done solo or with others. Both have an orderly progression of events. Both work by trance, visualization, mantra, desire, belief, movement, breath, focus, and ecstasy. Both are enhanced or detrimented by surrounding forces of nature, temperament and circumstance. Both can employ various symbolic tools and power objects, or simply be done with nothing but one's own body, mind and spirit. In fact, the line between them is somewhat arbitrary, as it is between matter and spirit, or the sacred and the mundane. In the tarot these two qualities are represented by the Witch (or the Magician in older decks) and the Priestess. If you examine these cards together you will see that they are similar.

Traditional tarot draws a heavier line between the sacred and the mundane than present-day feminists of the craft. Esther Harding calls the goddess "the connecting principle." The goddess teaches us that all things in the universe interact and are related. The public and the private, the individual and society, the weather and the crops . . . all are interconnected and not split as we have been taught. This same awareness can also be applied to magical systems and the Tarot. Because of it I changed the concepts of Major and Minor Arcana, as seen in traditional decks, naming my suits after the elements; Earth, Water, Fire, Air and Spirit. This approach can be applied to rituals and spells, as it can to the Witch and

Priestess cards. A Priestess *is* a Witch, and vice versa.

Starhawk defines magic as that which changes consciousness. This is a profound thought, for any effect can be seen as a change, and we know that all reality begins in consciousness. Magic can also be defined as a spiritual science which is directed at shaping reality, or making things happen. And we can see it as a religious form, a way of worshipping the divine source of existence through enchantment.

The best spells and rituals are exactly this; enchanting. One feels swept up in a kind of heightened sensibility, inspired, exalted. One's emotions flow freely, the spirit soars, the body moves seemingly of itself. Revelations come to mind, poetry to the lips. Energy is released and spins out into the universe where it gathers momentum and gradually evolves into happenings and things.

Here we can see the link between theatre and magic. We know from high school history books that all theatre began as ritual. The first plays were poetic mimes of the goddess and her many stories. The first poems were prayers in her honor. The essential themes of drama are still Hers; birth, love, beauty, death, separation, rebirth . . . But ancient rituals were more than play-acting. The enactment of birth was an echo of nature's awakening at spring. The growth of food was at once a dance and a reality. The harvest celebrated was actual nourishment. The passion of the goddess for life and the passion between human lovers was literal enactment.

Good spells and rituals have a theatrical touch. One places the flowers so, lights the candles with meaningful attention, times each chant and prayer so, begins, builds power, lets the power die down, ends. Once the energy is begun and the circle cast, everything that happens becomes significant. One reads meaning into everything, whether it was planned or not; even mishaps have messages. One becomes sensitized to details and nuances. The more elegantly, carefully and attentively done, the more powerful the results.

Timing is also an important aspect of all ceremonies. Events should flow effortlessly, as a tree grows, "without haste and without rest." The best metaphor I can think of for a well-timed ritual is an orchestrated concert of music. Music flows like the psyche, and is a perfect model for ritual form. Different movements begin and end with grace, new movements take up the energy and carry it on. A priestess learns to sensitize herself to these peaks and valleys of energy, to know when it is the right moment to begin or end something.

Because all that happens takes on meaning in a ritual, and because flow and timing are so important, it becomes necessary to be well prepared before one begins. All earth-plane or practical matters should be attended to well ahead of time. Matches should be laid, ready for striking, with an ashtray handy. Props and power objects and offerings should be placed conveniently. Nothing breaks trance so easily as the little distractions caused by lack of preparation. My best rituals have been well planned and carefully prepared for, and also had room for the unexpected. There is a delicate balance between this kind of order and spontaneity; too much of one is boring and static, too much of the other and the focus is lost and the intensity dies. One therefore prepares for everything, but in the end one opens oneself to the moment.

Nine Powers of Magic

Focus—The power spot could be interpreted as the spirit element. Though this can be symbolized by a physical spot in a room or on the earth, a power spot is really a focus. Focus creates concentration, which creates all that comes to be. It's like frozen orange juice, so to speak. A focus can be on any topic, with any motive, can be represented in many ways, but you can't do magic without it. Once you have it, energy begins to gather or converge around it. Altars are one of our most familiar tools for helping to create focus. Goals can have the same effect, as can dreams or visions. Anything that holds the attention in a one-pointed and intense way is a focus.

If you think of spell-casting as a planting cycle, focus is the seed. The plant needs nourishment and love (water), encouragement (air), weeding and various other activities (fire), until it finally gives fruit or flowers (earth). A gardener waters her plant again and again, again and again until it grows to fullness. Spells often need the same type of repetition in order to come to be. A lot depends on the surrounding aspects; plant in loose or clay-filled soil and this will affect your odds of success. Plant in a windstorm and you will need to build a shelter. The more optimum your surrounding circumstances, the more likely you will have success. This is why a witch looks to the seasons, the moon phases, the astrology aspects, the social climate, her own moods and inclinations, what has come before and what is happening at the moment. As her experience accumulates, so does her skill.

But focus is step one. You can't create anything without it. I have one friend who comes to me year in and year out, always with the same dilemma; what to do with her life. But when I try to pin her down to a goal or focus, she wavers. It is too much responsibility, perhaps, or she fears success, or she has been trained to believe that she will fail, or that she does not deserve to have a dream come true. The less focus one claims for oneself, the more one is ruled by those of others. We might even be able to make a case for focus being a class problem. In the win/lose set-up of patriarchy, those who are successful develop some sort of focus, those who are termed "losers" tend to be swayed by the focus of others. We could even take this a step further and see it as a male/female problem. Men are encouraged to set goals for themselves, concentrate on them, achieve. Women are trained to be "dumb blondes," to have relatively little focus, to serve the focus or goals of others.

Focus brings power to spells, and group rituals as well. A good group pays attention to everything that is happening, supports each moment of the magic whether it is coming through a priestess, another member, through everyone at once, or from the universe surrounding them. Random focus will create random energy and the magic will dissipate or scatter. Some people will resent being asked to remain focused on the same thing as everyone else. They feel that their free will is being denied. This is a sad loss for everyone, including themselves, because the very freedom they seek lies in the ability to create what they choose. Creating requires the willingness to discipline oneself in order to have this point of concentration.

In patriarchy group focus is achieved most often through coercion, manipulation or strong leadership. People will listen with hushed attention by the thousands to one person singing or talking, if that person has been deemed worthy or advertised sufficiently. Yet they will not notice the chirping of a bird outside their window, or the amazing stories pouring from the lips of small children. Thus focus has been bound up with authoritarian structures. It is no wonder that people rebel and grow restless when they are asked to pay attention.

But going to the other extreme is just as entrapping. This need for disciplined focus is probably an issue for many teachers of the craft. We do not wish to be authoritarian, nor offend anyone's free will, yet we know that it is a basic ingredient for successful magic. This topic has much to do with issues of power and group dynamics.

When we talk about magical focus, we do not mean the hard-driving linear sort such as is required to solve a math equation. Remember, we are in a dreamy, floating, relaxed state. Magical focus is comfortable, flowing, effortless. It is a "letting" rather than a "putting" of the image we choose to work with. This allows for sudden inspirations, often the best magical source.

Trance—This altered state engages the psychic energies. Trance awakens the deep mind, which is slow, nonrational, dreamy, ecstatic, revelatory. In trance we can de-program and program ourselves, behave differently, with different reflexes. For example, the famous fire-walking shamans of Hawaii, who can walk barefoot on blazing heat without being burned. This deep mind controls us in many ways, for it is the part of us that takes on automatic programming belief/response mechanisms. Even our autonomic sensory responses, such as hunger and pain have been attributed to unconscious programming. Witches seek to make contact with the deep mind, to learn how to use and direct it at will.

Trance is achieved by relaxing, breathing deeply, casting off anxiety, making monotonous droning sounds, moving in a simple circle dance (or simply weaving the upper torso), and visualization. When you are in trance you should feel a kind of dreamy floating sensation, pleasant and completely relaxed. A kind of electricity runs through the body and a sense of vibrating and expanding out beyond the body. You might even fall asleep for a while, which is okay. Sometimes we can do an amazing amount of work in a trance-induced sleep. You should feel totally safe and open, able to surrender completely to whatever is happening, confident that all will be well. This is why covens are built on "perfect love and perfect trust." Trance opens one to the core, like making love or giving birth. It requires the utmost vulnerability. It is better to trance by yourself than in the company of people you do not feel safe with; better indoors than out if the only outside space you can find may be intruded upon.

To achieve a trance state it is essential to relax. In our world of daily tensions this may be difficult and can require repeated practice. A commonly used technique is to lie flat (or sit up; straight spine is best) and starting with the toes, clench and release each part of the body. Stubborn areas may need repeated work. Many people find it helpful to have a guide to take them through the areas of the body. Some use taped recordings of someone giving suggestions and guidance. You can also record your own relaxing guidance tapes and play them back for yourself.

Slowing down is another important aspect of trance. The brainwaves of the alpha mind are longer than those of the beta or waking consciousness. This means putting aside your worries for a while, letting go of those fast-moving activities, and most important, breathing slowly and deeply.

Breath—For many of us deep breathing is another natural ability that we have unlearned. Often we are tense or upset, and will find ourselves breathing shallowly. Deep breathing from the diaphragm is natural; watch a child or an animal breathing and you will see full, rhythmic breaths. Breath brings nourishment to every cell of the body, and energy to the aura. Rhythmic breath when slow and even and deep is one of the main ingredients of sustained trance. The yogis say that we control everything with our breath. Rebirthers have discovered astonishing healing techniques through breath. Much of our power is reduced through inhibited or shallow breathing.

The cells of our brain and body carry memories or sensory impression of all past experiences, both pleasant and painful. When we breathe deeply we stir up those memories, giving ourselves an opportunity to erase old recordings and replace them with new ones. Thus we can affect our destinies with simple breathing!

Here is a good exercise to strengthen breathing and breathing awareness:

Take long and rhythmic breaths and chant:

I am the breather (*visualize yourself breathing*)
Breathing in (*breathe in*)
And breathing out (*breathe out*)

Repeat the above four or five times. Then change to:

I am she who watches the breather (*visualize yourself observing yourself*)
Breathing in (*breathe in*)
And breathing out (*breathe out*)

After several repeats, change to:

I am the breath (*visualize yourself as the breath*)
Being breathed in (*breathe in*)
And being breathed out (*breathe out*)
—developed by Andraliria

Sound—Sound vibrations, when they are soothing and peaceful, can help to induce trance. You can hum your own sounds, drum them, or play them on a droning instrument such as a dulcimer or harmonium. Or simple repetitious chants can be sung:

> Maiden mother crone in me
> All three in harmony . . .

The simpler and more repetitious the better. A good trance can last for hours, supported by the same simple chant, and never be boring. People get bored because they are trained to expect something different, a variation. Sameness, we are told, is uninteresting. But it is possible to pass beyond the "boredom barrier" so to speak, where the simplest things become the most fascinating of all. The greatest experiences are based on the most simple factors. We must cast aside our technological programming that directs us to look for dazzling displays of varied feats of perfection to hold our attention.

Droning music can be found in cultures the world over. In India there are the sitar and sarod, with their intricate rhythms and modes. From Spain comes the passionate Flamenco. Our own Appalachian folk music, played on banjo and dulcimer, is full of droning sounds. Irish and Scottish folk music often is built on beautiful droning modes. The effect is enchanting and hypnotic. Coupled with poetic lyrics, this music can touch the soul. There is an ancient and universal wisdom here, coming from the grass roots, from ordinary people.

Eastern mystics have brought us the Aum chant which is having immeasurable effect on consciousness. I remember being amazed at the power of this chant when I first learned it. Whenever I was in a circle, holding hands with other people, closing my eyes and droning the Aum, I would notice that tingling vibration moving through me at the end. Later I changed over to the Ma chant, when I discovered the goddess. Ma is the universal mother cry and an appropriate female alternative to the Aum. Recently I have heard that the Ma chant is used everywhere! There are many goddess names that make wonderful chants, such as Amaterasu, Aradia, Diana. When one chants such names of power, one is invoking the forces that deity represents. Add this to the effects of trance, breath and sound vibration and you have a very potent spell.

Visualization—The making of concrete images is essential to magic. Most of us lose this natural ability as we grow older, because the culture provides us with so many prefabricated ones. We are bombarded by media, architecture, advertising, education and especially TV. And yet as children we usually make images as a natural part of fantasizing. Often it is necessary to work consciously to reclaim and rebuild this ability. Children are often discouraged and told not to "make believe." Gradually they desert this aspect of themselves, thus leaving the creation of reality-making images in the hands of others.

I have found that many of my students come to me with a weakness in this area. Often when we do our meditations and the spell-throwing begins I hear abstract wishes, such as "let peace come to so-and-so," or "let my friend be healed." These are worthy and beautiful sentiments, but they are too abstract to work magically. It is necessary to create a simple visual representation of the end in mind. For example, peace and healing could be represented by an image of the person surrounded in a glowing aura of green light.

Symbols are potent thought-forms that provide impetus for deep-mind programming and universal response. The more inspiring and layered with meaning, the more impact they have. As in casting off other complexities, we also need to rediscover the simple childlike ability to create images that symbolize feelings and events. Sometimes one can simply evoke an image of the event itself. For example, Mary Lou wants a car, and visualizes herself driving one. Some wishes are more complex and involve a variety of feelings, states of being, etc. For example, Aradia wants to see harmony between friends who have been quarreling. She creates an image of them in a fond embrace, with golden cords of love connecting their heart chakras. The more one practices focusing on images, the more potent one's magic grows. Adding the support of group focus can be very powerful indeed.

Belief—This is also a basic ingredient for success in magical workings. As we have said, doubt eats away at your spell. There can be many kinds of doubt: self-doubt, doubt in the realness of magic, doubt about the goddess, doubt about good or evil, doubt about the validity of getting what we want, doubt because social tradition does not necessarily support what we are doing, etc., etc. There are so many forces assailing our psyches, attempting to sway our beliefs. We need to realize that we are human and subject to some extent to such influences. Therefore we need to strengthen our belief or faith in what we are doing. Blind faith is not enough. We need validation, experiences and events to help make it real.

Studying goddess traditions is so helpful in this regard. We *do* have a tradition; this is the irony of it. And it is so ancient, far more ancient than the one we are struggling with! The more we learn about it, the firmer our faith will be. Learning to see the goddess in all things is part of it too. When you slice an apple across, sit under a tree, or watch a moonrise. When you perform simple tasks, such as sweeping, and recall the symbolism of brooms. A goddess view of cooking turns the pot into a cauldron of transformation . . . gardening into godhood, singing into sorcery.

Changing belief programming is not an overnight proposition. We are usually dealing with years and years of repetition and acceptance. Banishings are wonderful for erasing old programs. Remember to replace what you have banished with the new reality you have chosen. A simple rebirthing exercise for re-programming is to breathe out the negative image of that which you wish to eliminate, and breathe in the new positive image into your aura and cells. Evelyn Eaton (a powerful shaman sister who has recently passed over) says that the psychic babble is continuous, and we must "keep our rainbow round our shoulders."

Experience and practice are most effective in affirming belief/reality. Connecting with other people who are involved in alternatives, reading material on the subject, looking at art, joining in with other practitioners to do rituals and spells, spending time practicing by oneself and communing in nature . . . all these help to reinforce belief. The more community and tradition we build, the stronger our faith or "knowing" will be. These are the "taproots" of magic, that give it stability and lastingness.

Devotion—The path of the Goddess is a path of the heart. Unlike the detached meditations of the East, or the sedate Sunday prayer meetings of the Church, pagan ceremony is passionate. The more deeply we feel about the goddess when we pray to her, the more moved we are by the liturgy, the more powerful the experience. The more intensely we desire the fulfillment of our spell, the more life-force there is behind the casting, and the more likelihood of success.

There is a place of truth and love that reaches the heart. People have come through many religious paths to this same center. Their sincerity and dedication shine out, whatever the metaphors or teachings may be. In this sense any religion or psychic practice can be valid when the seeker comes "in good faith." The irony of this is that the potency of devotion is real, yet the metaphors it supports may be questionable. As they say, "the road to hell is paved with good intentions." Atrocities have been committed in the names of many gods and goddesses because of the unquestioning devotion of their worshippers. We need to be passionate about the goddess, but we also need to be discriminating about the forms and metaphors that are used.

If there is violence, hierarchy, manipulation, opportunism or harm, no amount of devotion will make it right.

This is the dilemma we face with the rise of patriarchal religions today. Many people are running back to the fold because of the terrible crises of our time, and because they know of no alternatives. Their devotion may be real and their hearts sincere and their intentions of the best. We must respect this and understand that many are finding some strength and healing from the traditional faiths they embrace. They are also finding tradition and community, and these factors are real and necessary. They bring roots and stability to any belief system.

In the end devotion is a supremely personal matter, found by each of us in our own hearts. There is no doubt that it gives potency and effectiveness to any undertaking or religious pursuit. A religious movement can sweep across nations and change societies like nothing else can, when that gut-level, passionate devotion is aroused in the people.

I therefore encourage you to get as emotional as you like in your ceremonies. It may take practice to allow yourself to open up. Many people are shy in our culture, having been taught all kinds of restraints. It takes years of covening, sometimes, to reach the kind of free expression one reads about in books about "primitive" ritual. The ancients were wiser than we know in their unrestrained demonstrations of appreciation for their deities.

Movement—This can be seen as a fiery aspect of rituals and spells. It brings energy and actualization to any undertaking. It can take the form of dance, swaying, weaving, walking to different parts of the circle, raising one's arms in the air, etc. Or it can be actions that help to realize one's spell. Pagan rituals often include wild free-form dancing. A powerful cone can be raised as each body radiates energy and each mind shapes it.

My favorite way to move during magic-making is in a moon-wise weaving motion. This is done simply by sitting straight and swaying in a circle with the upper torso. I call it "stirring up the cauldron" because I feel the motion sending all my aura energies swirling into orbit. Circular and spiral movements are especially effective, as they create a continuum and are in harmony with universal movements.

Formalized movement can be used to physicalize metaphors and beliefs. The most complete meditations include the body, mind, and spirit. I have often done work with people in this mode, who would dance to my myths and songs. When my children were small they trance-danced instinctively to my music. We found out later that this was an ancient ritual form. When you back up your symbols with your body you are saying, "I am becoming that which I express."

Here is a simple movement ritual that can be used as a meditation for magic:

Say aloud —

Earth witch	*Crouch on the earth*
Ear to the ground	*Put your ear to the ground*
Listening to	*Listen to the sounds of the earth*
Her heartbeat	*Feel them*
Water witch	*Rise to sitting position*
Arms in the stream	*Make undulating, watery movements*
Reflecting on reflection	*with arms and torso*
	Feel watery
Fire witch	*Rise to the knees with the same undu-*
Breath to the flame	*lating energy, only faster, with arms*
Kindles passion	*upraised*
	Feel fiery
Air witch	*Keep flowing upwards to your feet*
Throat full of song	*Move gently*
Spinning sweet spells	*Feel airy and floating*
Spirit witch	*Leap and reach, move out, dance*
Embracing stars	*freely*
Imagining her magic	*Reach upwards*
	"Touch" the stars
Earth witch	*Gradually flow back down to earth*
Ear to the ground	*Crouch and press your ear to the*
Listening to Her heartbeat	*ground once more*

Affirmation—To affirm is to make firm. To speak aloud one's vision is to add the impetus of breath and sound. Finding words to express these visions helps give them focus through the power of naming. Names bring form where there was chaos, understanding where there was confusion. Whether alone or in groups, affirmations give a lot of power to spells or rituals. Phrases such as "so be it," "so mote it be," "together we can do anything," "all that we have seen and said shall come to be," etc., are powerful affirmations. Here are a few more:

As we weave it so doth it be

By all the powers of earth and sea
As I will so mote it be

We are women reclaiming our powers
We are women rebirthing ourselves

I deserve love
I deserve happiness
I deserve abundance
I deserve . . . etc.

I am an endless source of all that I choose to create.

Writing down one's affirmations is also very effective. Affirming one another's visions during group ritual is another way to intensify the energy. Often we need this reflection and support from one another. A simple "So be it, blessed be" is commonly used in most witches' ceremonies to affirm and bless all undertakings. It is also very effective to invent your own affirmations, as your own language and symbol system will resonate best in your own psyche.

Affirmations are actually an aspect of the poetic language of spells. You can do them in and of themselves or blend them with descriptions and requests, such as:

Earth, sea, wind and fire
Bring to me what I desire

Goddesses of darkest night
Send our troubles all to flight
Burn them in thy sacred fires
And replace them with our hearts' desires

Words of Power

May the circle never be broken
May the earth always be whole
May the rattle ever be shaken
May the goddess live in my soul
　　　　—From Circle of Hecate

I shall live
I shall be free
Goddess goddess
I am thee . . .

Mother Goddess, keep me whole
Let thy beauty fill my soul

Maiden Goddess, keep me whole
Let thy power fill my soul

Crone Goddess, keep me whole
Let thy wisdom fill my soul . . .

Blessed be the Maiden within me
For she bringeth courage and freedom
Blessed be the Mother within me
For she bringeth love and life
Blessed be the Crone within me
For she bringeth wisdom and understanding . . .

We are the flow, we are the ebb
We are the weavers, we are the web . . .

I am whole unto myself
Centered in the Kore of me
I shall give and shall receive
Goddess goddess loves me . . .

Let my magic be.

Let all illness
Be cast from me
Cleansed of all impurity
Free from all wrongs
I may have done
'Til goodness
And love
And I
Are one . . .

Goddess Names

Hecate	Kwan Yin
Tiamat	Tanath
Astarte	Chantico
Asherah	Athene
Kore	Nut
Selene	Amaterasu
Sybele	Brigit
Diana	Nimue
Aphrodite	Anu
Themis	Mari
Psyche	Maya
Cerridwen	Queen of Heaven
Hathor	Ix Chel
Isis	Oceana
Bast	Habundia
Persephone	Fortuna
Rhiannon	Afrekete
Arianrhod	Nu Kwa
Ariadne	Kali
Aradia	Lakshmi
Demeter	Sarasvati
Shekhina	Durga
Melissande	Yemanja
Ea	Oshun
Gaia	Mbaba-Mwana-Waresa

Images of Power

flame:
life, energy

rose:
love, beauty

egg:
birth, potential, cosmos

cauldron:
transformation

sun:
happiness, optimism iradiance

cornucopia:
abundance, wealth

pentagram:
magic, goddess, protection, earth element

attraction

moon:
maiden goddess suggestion, subconsciousness

rainbow:
happiness, fulfillment perfection

water:
emotions, sub-conscious, flow, agreement, cleansing, baptism

tree:
life

eye:
wisdom, vision

heart:
love

spiral:
infinity

square:
stability, protection

woman

Colors

There are many color systems that assign a variety of moods and meanings to colors. This can be applied to candle magic, to drawings of power images, clothing, altar draperies, etc. Below is a suggested list of colors and their meanings. Use it if it works for you; if not make up your own color system.

Green	Healing, abundance
Brown	Grounding, stability
Deep Pink	Optimism
Blue	Peace, protection
White	Spirit, purity
Yellow	Expansion, success
Orange	Energy, affection
Red	Love, passion, anger, blood, womb
Grey	Wisdom, union of opposites
Black	Banishment, binding, death, mystery
Purple	Power, psychic power
Silver	Moon, enchantment
Gold	Wealth, power, venerability, sun energy

Many witches use the elements of fire, water, earth and air as a basis for magic. These are represented by wands, cups, pentacles and swords, as in the Tarot. Esoteric traditions say that wands are to summon spirits, cups are to hold power, pentacles (or platters) are to give offerings, and swords are to cut spells. These concepts are powerful and beautiful and I encourage you to try them at your own altar. I am not a strict traditionalist myself, and often find that I work magic in a more improvisational style. Yet no matter how varied my spells and ceremonies may be, I find that the old elements are always there in some form, because everything is made of them.

When dealing with elements I do prefer to think of them in five, however, rather than four. As I have said, odd numbers are more cyclical, even numbers more static and linear. Many witches cast the circle in "four quarters," designating one element to each of the directions, North, West, South and East. I have an ingrained resistance to all four-square structures, as I feel they are signs of a dualistic reality system. I would rather think of time in terms of thirteen moons rather than twelve months, seasons in terms of Maiden Mother and Crone (Spring, Summer and Winter) rather than four, gender in terms of Female, Male and Androgyne instead of Male and Female. Or Female as root form; the center out of which the Male is born. I would rather cast a circle with a five-pointed star on the ground, rather than the four directions. In ancient Rome odd numbers were sacred to the Goddess, and holy days were planned to be held on odd-numbered dates. Even-numbered dates were used for Her consort's celebrations. It seems clear to me that even numbers, four-square structures and gender polarities are all signs of patriarchal ascendance. I can't help feeling that a religious group that boasts of its liberating ideas is contradicting itself when it perpetuates non-cyclical grids or structures.

The Five Senses

In studying techniques of theatre I learned the importance of the five senses for evoking strong emotion. The Stanislavsky method teaches "sense memory," a technique in which one recalls the sensory aspects of an experience. By concentrating carefully on what one has seen, tasted, touched, smelled and heard, one can call up powerful feelings and express them through the role one is playing.

For instance, we would do an exercise, pretending to eat an apple. First holding it in our hands, feeling its texture and weight, seeing its shape and color. Then bringing it close to our noses, smelling its fragrance. Finally sinking our teeth into its flesh, tasting its sweetness and juice. This kind of work deepens one's creative ability and can be invaluable to magic-makers.

One day I was talking about image-making to a former student. She wondered how a blind person, who had never experienced seeing in this life, could make images. That was when I realized that images are not necessarily confined to the visual, but also include the other senses.

For example, I have had great success doing weather work using the senses. In a meditation circle for rain-making I asked each member to describe the rain; how it looks, tastes, sounds, smells, feels. After such workings rain would always come within a few days!

The senses can be seen to correspond with the five elements of the witch's star. I have correlated seeing with spirit, hearing with air, touching with fire, smelling with water, and tasting with earth. You can use this system when casting your pentagram circle and meditating on the object of your spells.

The Witch's Star

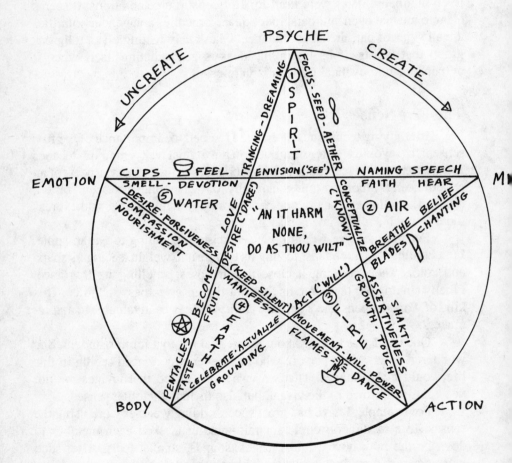

The Directions

Most magical systems include some concept of the directions or dimensions of space. Native Americans talk about four directions, attributing animal symbolism to each. Witches talk about the same four and designate Earth to the North, Air to the East, Fire to the South, and Water to the West. Paul Case, in his book *The Tarot*, describes the occultists' Cube of Space, a representation of all known directions, with various tarot cards and Hebrew letters associated with each plane and corner.

Why be concerned with the directions? I asked my tarot deck about this, and got the Four of Pentacles, "Security." I take this to mean that describing and defining the directions gives us a point of focus, some form of stability in an otherwise random universe. We operate in a multi-dimensioned space and need to be sensitive and aware of its nuances. A case in point: While driving, I was once hit by another car from behind when not paying attention to that direction. Becoming conscious of the directions gives us control. Creating symbols for these gives us choice.

However, as you must realize by now, I have an instinctive resistance to four-square structures, and so have spent much time questioning the concept of four directions or a "cube" of space. I would much prefer to operate in cycles or spheres. A four-directioned universe sets up oppositions, whereas a three- or five- or seven-directioned universe would be more flowing. There are many trends appearing in the world today that would seem to back up this concept. Quantum physics is taking us from linear to clustered forms, architecture from square to round buildings, social changes from meeting in status-defined rows to non-hierarchical circles. Philosophy and science are discovering the connections between things such as time and space, now often called the "time/space continuum." It seems important to apply this expansion to magical systems as well.

Of course we do need linear structures and even numbers for continuity, grounding, and stability. This is one of the messages of the Tarot cards numbered four, such as the Emperor. In Shekhinah's Tarot these powers were given back to the Mother Goddess in keeping with her sustaining and nurturing qualities. I have developd a seven-direction concept which can allow for the four and the three to co-exist. New forms, if they are to last, must contain the old within them.

Thus I operate in terms of seven directions as follows:

North
South

East
West
Above
Below
Within

These words can be chanted and visualized as an effective means of casting the circle. Another way of conceptualizing this is: Above, Below, Before, Behind, To the Left, To the Right, and Within. These words allow us to bring more layers of symbolism into the process. Before and Behind are not only space, they are also time; Future and Past. To the Left and Right are the Present, and they are also Creating/Giving (Right) and Dissolving/Receiving. Above is Goddess and Infinity, Below is the path or premise, the foundation on which we rest, and our connection to the Earth. Within is the Self and can encompass past, present and future. The result is a sphere. Perhaps this will be the accepted way of casting circles in the future.

Visualizing the Pentagram for five directions is perhaps more radical, placing an odd-numbered figure on the ground. I usually set it up this way:

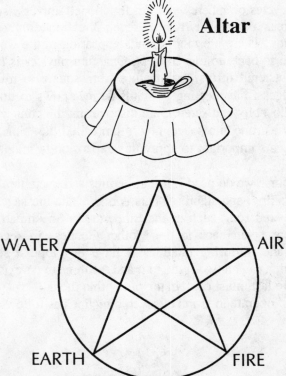

Altar

WATER   AIR

EARTH   FIRE

With the altar as guide to the five elements, as the guardians, one can bypass North, East, etc. This works well for people who may have difficulty telling which way is west, etc. You can still add Above, Below and Within.

Other simpler ways to cast circles are:

Breathe and weave your upper body
Take hands if you are in a group
Close eyes
See energy swirling as you continue to breathe and weave together
See this energy as light, forming a cone that encloses all present and comes to a point above the circle's center

Affirmation:

The circle is cast
The spell is made fast
Only the good can enter herein
The magick is made
So let it begin . . .

Or:

Goddess in the sky! (*Reach up*)
Goddess in the ground! (*Touch earth*)
Goddess all around! (*Spin*)
Goddess within! (*Hands on heart*)

Or:

Free Ticket to Heaven
Let the path be clear before me
Let all go as I will
And the past be clean behind me
Let all go as I will
And the ones I love beside me
Let all go as I will
And the Goddess light above me
Let all go as I will

And the solid earth beneath me
Let all go as I will
And my own true self within me
Let all go as I will . . .

Psychic Self-Defense

There are varying attitudes among magic-makers regarding the need for protection from the presence of destructive or hostile forces. Some are so frightened, they hesitate to practice. Others feel that any attention paid to such possibilities creates them, and therefore it is best to erase all such thoughts from one's mind. I am into sensible prevention myself, with a minimum amount of attention. Those that are frightened make victims of themselves by not risking at all, therefore denying their power. Those who choose to ignore all evil, I feel, are naive and have probably led compara- tively sheltered lives. When we open up the psychic powers we must realize that there are risks involved, as with the use of any force. It is also true that attention creates, and so we must find a healthy middle ground where we can create freely but safely.

There are beings on all planes, as well as forces, and some of them are not always nice. As women who have been trained to be nice and open to everyone, we may need to develop some Amazon energy. Just as women are learning aikido and karate and other earth-plane self-defense tech- niques, we also need psychic-plane techniques. This does not mean we need to become belligerent or start seeing threats at every turn. We can learn from the example of Israel in this century. They went over the line of self-defense and became offensive to those beyond their boundaries. Knowing where that line is requires delicate balance and understanding. Those who have been victims tend to be weak in self-protection. Often when they realize this they go to the other extreme and become violent in their attempt to compensate. This unfortunately serves to create more violence, and so the vicious cycle continues round the world.

True strength resides in firm but gentle guardianship. A good mother knows the difference between loving discipline and revenge. A good image of protection: place a pentagram around oneself and the environ- ment, with a mighty Amazon goddess posted at each point, facing outward towards the world. Each has a shield with the snake-haired Medusa's face, and a labyris at her side. These weapons are there for use in need, and stand as a warning to those who would violate. But they will be used only to protect and otherwise not at all.

Athene is a traditional image of balanced protection, and she can be found in most tarot decks under the name of Justice. In her ancient representation she had the Medusa on her breast to show protection of the mysteries. She also represents karmic protection, or the principle of return; that which we send out will come back around.

In a natural state most of us are equipped with an instinct for self-preservation. But in patriarchy many women have lost this and become prey to the predators. We are taught that men and institutions will protect us, and that we must be open and kindly to all who come our way. The guardian in us can get blocked and often turns inward and destructive. Starhawk calls this the Self-Hater. Because of this conditioning we may have to work to build up what should have been instinctive behavior. As in all healing, it begins inwardly, with an attitude of self worth. We are precious, we are wonderful, we are sacred, we deserve to be, etc. We therefore have a natural right to protect ourselves from any destruction.

A simple self-protection is done by imagining a sphere of light around ourselves and declaring that only good energies can exit or enter. Many magicians suggest white light. Another method is to imagine a many-faceted sphere of mirrors facing outwards and surrounding. Each surface deflects any negative thought-forms which may be directed at it, bouncing them back to the sender. They must then take responsibility for their own creations. Some witches suggest we wrap ourselves in rainbows or place ourselves in a rainbow bubble or sphere. Starhawk places a sphere of porous energy so that only good can get through.

There are also many herbs that are considered protecting, such as rosemary and sandlewood. Often when I am preparing to enter a situation that may be risky or difficult I pluck a sprig of rosemary and put it in my pocket. Witches traditionally have rosemary growing by their doors. It can also be placed over doors and windows, as can pentagrams. And then there is the old reliable burning of sage which is said to cleanse, purify and protect. Bell-ringing throughout your environment is also good protection. But in the end one's inner attitude is the most important. If you believe that you are precious and well-defended, you will be. If you create safe and loving energy, it will come back to you in kind.

Protecting Magic

Salt—Witches have used salt for protection for many ages. Throw some over your left shoulder, wear some in a pouch, sprinkle it everywhere in your space, pour a circle of salt for rituals.

Garlic—Another ancient protection; often a clove or two are placed in an amulet pouch. Garlic also can be hung in bunches around the house.

Incantations—Invoking the names of protective deities such as Demeter, Ceres, Isis, etc. Or create affirming chants, such as: "I am perfectly safe," and repeat them with visualization.

Stones—Certain stones have protective qualities, such as amethysts. Crystals can be invested with protecting energy and worn or kept nearby.

Candle-Lighting—Blue and white candles are often used for protection. These can be anointed with rosemary or sandlewood oil, or rolled in protecting herbs.

Mother Goddesses—Protection is a motherly act in that it preserves and nurtures; therefore any Mother Goddess can be called upon in this regard. Imagine a circle of mothers surrounding you, or see yourself cradled in Her arms.

Sigils—These are drawn symbols, used to represent many things. A pentagram is commonly used. A simple circle can also be used, or a square. Write your name in runes in the center along with the name of a protecting deity. Fold up the paper and place it under a stone on your altar. Create a number of sigils and fold them up; tuck them into secret places around the house. Draw them with visible or invisible ink over doors and windows. Carve them on lintels and doorposts.

Talismans—These are symbolic objects, usually worn or carried on the person. Special jewelry, pentacles, ankhs, the Eye of Maat, etc. You can create your own talismans, using objects that represent protection to you.

Oils and Incenses—Anoint yourself with protecting oils like rosemary and sandlewood. Burn these incenses; also sage, laurel and myrrh.

Spell for Grounding

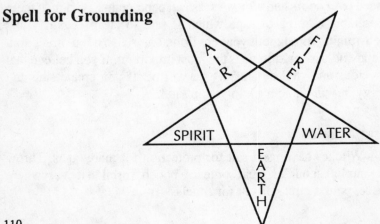

Ingredients:

Pentacle, as shown	Protection oil
A few sage seeds	Journal
A piece of sage root	Pen
A large stone	Parchment
Two brown candles	Sage and Rosemary, for burning

Grounding is an essential tool for survival and magic. Many of us have lost this ability, due to patriarchal conditioning. Our lifestyles tend to take us away from the earth and our connections to nature, leaving us psychically uprooted from our Mother-source. In a natural state, our auras are connected to the Earth's aura at all times, so there is a natural flow between us and we can be continually replenished by her vast energies. If you find that you tend to be ungrounded most of the time, you need to do spells occasionally, and also to incorporate these techniques on a regular basis, until they become habitual. Also, be sure to ground thoroughly after all magical workings.

The first step to any grounding is to *slow down*. So, set aside a special day for yourself, when you can be completely alone and quiet. In preparation for your Grounding Day (!), prepare a pot or a spot in your garden for planting your sage seeds. Keep the seeds on your altar in the meantime, to charge them up. Also place your large rock beneath your altar, affirming its stabilizing energy as you do so.

Set up your altar the night before, so that you will see it first thing upon waking. Stand the pentacle at the center, with its earth arm pointing downwards. Prepare a cauldron with the sage and rosemary, ready for burning. Anoint the two brown candles with Protection Oil and arrange them on either side of the pentacle. Place all spell ingredients aesthetically and symmetrically.

Before going to sleep, anoint yourself with some of the oil. Take your dream journal and pen to bed with you. As you are awaiting sleep, ask the Goddess to send you a healing dream to help give insight on what you need for grounding, and what might be preventing this. Sleep as late as you like. When you awaken, lie around in bed for awhile and enjoy. Write down any dreams or insights you may have had. Move to the altar only when you feel completely rested. Take your journal and pen with you. Anoint yourself once more, placing a protective bubble of golden light around yourself as you do so. Light the candles, saying:

As these flames burn
So grounding returns
When they are gone
This spell will be done.

Next light the herbs in your cauldron, letting the smoke surround and purify your aura. On the parchment write your dream messages; the obstacles and solutions to your grounding needs. Refold it and place it beneath the large stone under your altar.

Take the sage root and hold it as you meditate. Relax and center, breathe deeply for awhile, letting your eyes rest on the pentacle, particularly the Earth arm, sensing its downward energy.

Keep breathing deeply as you close your eyes, letting the pentacle appear in your mind's eye. See it grow and expand until you are at its center, with the earth arm beneath you, pointing downwards. Now see the pentacle change into the roots and branches of a tree, with yourself as the trunk. See the roots connecting you with our Mother, growing down and down into the center of the earth. Chant:

The roots of me go down and down
O Mother Earth in thee I ground

Repeat this chant again and again, visualizing its meanings. Keep chanting as you take the sage root and arrange it in such as way that you can carry or wear it for some time. Then take your seeds and plant them as previously arranged. Chant the above chant throughout.

Return to your altar and sit in silence for awhile, continuing to breathe and visualize your roots connecting to the earth's center. When you feel complete, snuff out the candles. Repeat this spell every now and then, until the candles are burned down. If you still need to repeat it, you can replace the candles but be sure to light the new ones from the old flames.

Spend the day peacefully, doing simple things that allow you to move slowly. In general it is a good idea to give yourself one day a week like this, especially when you are learning to work magic. As you return to your regular routine keep the sage with you. Visit your sage plant from time to time, watering it with chanting as well as liquid. As she matures, you can use her leaves for future grounding spells, and wear them in a pouch as well. Whenever you tend her, affirm your roots and centeredness; talk to her and thank her for being your ally.

Repeat the chant wherever you may be, whenever you feel the need.

Ritual for Lovers

To be done in a safe, secluded place, at the full of the moon.

Before sundown create a love bower. The bed is your altar. Dress it with clean sweet-smelling pillows and coverings, scented with rose. Adorn it with red roses for passion, and laurel for purity and protection. Hang an image of Aphrodite. Place red candles and rose incense, ready for lighting. Place a bowl of red wine at the foot of the bed.

As the full moon ascends, draw a ritual bath and scatter petals of roses on the water, also add a few drops of rose oil. If possible, let the water catch the light of the full moon.

Put on some gentle and passionate music. Approach the altar bed together. Light the candles and incense, saying:

We ignite the spirit of Aphrodite.
Hail to thee, Goddess of Love!

Undress one another slowly, by candlelight and moonlight. Enter the bath and bathe each other in turn. As you wash each part of your lover's body, proclaim its beauty and sacredness:

Blessed be thy hair that caresses my face
Blessed be thine eyes that look upon me with love
Blessed be thine ears that hear my words of love
Blessed be thy lips that kiss, thy mouth that speaks to me of love
Blessed be thine arms that embrace me in love
Blessed be thy heart that throbs in the heat of love
Blessed be thy hands that touch me
Blessed be thy breast that contains all sweetness
Blessed be thy belly that holds the womb of life (for a woman)
Blessed be thy back that gladly bears love's burdens
Blessed be thy genitals that are the gateway to mystery and ecstasy
Blessed be thy legs that carry thee to me
Blessed be thy feet that take thee on love's journey . . .

Kiss and wash each place as you name it.
As you emerge from the water, chant together,

We are love rebirthing.

Dry each other gently and place flowing robes upon each other. Anoint one another's brow with rose oil, saying:

Aphrodite bless you

Walk hand-in-hand to the altar bed and kneel before it. Raise up the bowl of wine towards Aphrodite, saying:

Hail, Goddess of Love, who brought us together
We thank thee for thy wondrous gift of true desire
Bless our union tonight
Give us openness that we may flow into one another
Strength to return to our separate selves
And flexibility to dance and merge and re-emerge again . . .
May our love never be bound, but fly in freedom
May our hearts never be cold, but overflowing
With the heat of Thy love . . .

So be it!

Blessed Be!

Offer each other the wine. Rise and embrace. Disrobe one another slowly. Take hands and move to the bed.

The rest is beyond words.

Spell to Strengthen the Witch Within

This is a time of the rebirth of the root cultures of many peoples. Ancient wisdoms that were lost or obscured by the power shifts of history are now coming to light through many channels. Native people are discovering their rituals, their myths, their shamans. Scientists are discovering the cyclical behavior of nature, the consciousness of matter and the connectedness of all things. Psychologists are discovering rites of passage in the human psyche, dream power, archetypes and the importance of ritual. Even the advances of technology are adding to this wave of discovery in many ways, such as through media and communication.

The image of the witch is at the root of our own cultural past. To embrace and affirm this aspect of ourselves is to tap the power of tradition, longevity and cellular memory. Though there is bound to be some resistance in these transitory times, I believe that the wave of change is on our side. We are moving into a wonderful renaissance that will effect the entire planet. The crises we see around us in the world are the result of a need to change our perception of reality, for reality has already skipped ahead of us. Once we understand, harmony sets in.

In preparing for your spell, first do some serious thinking about just what the image of the witch means to you. Make a list of all her qualities, her powers, her names, how she looks, what she wears, thinks, feels, etc. See her in your mind's eye with as much clarity and detail as possible.

This spell should be cast three times, at the new, full and dark of the moon.

Ingredients:
Large piece of parchment paper
Pen
Two purple candles
Moon Oil
Power incense
A small moonstone

Arrange your altar. Carve moons into your candles and anoint them with oil. Anoint yourself as well, on brow, heart, and hands. Seat yourself comfortably and light the candles, saying:

With this flame I awaken the Witch within me.

Light the incense. Close your eyes and breathe deeply for awhile, relax and let go. Bathe yourself and your aura in white light. Keep breathing deeply and slowly as you begin to sway and weave, letting your body move into a circular motion. Empty yourself of all distractions and anxieties. When you feel flowing and peaceful, let your imagination fill up with images of your inner Witch. Take up the parchment and pen and make a sketch of her, or you can use the Witch tarot image provided. (Don't worry about style or quality; the simpler the better.) Write your impressions and ideas beneath the drawing. Set this up between the candles so that it is facing you. Take the moonstone and clasp it to your heart. Keep

Qualities of the Witch Tarot Card

Community ritual
Communion with the Goddess
A sudden conversion
Unity with all beings and things
Spiritual evaluation
Life after death
Spiritual transformation
Replaces "The Last Judgment"

Qualities of the Celebration Tarot Card

Creating with the Powers of Earth
Air, fire, water and spirit
Casting spells
Creating reality
Concentration
The cauldron is the cup-water — emotions
The spoon and flames are will — fire
The pentacle is the body — earth
The athame (knife) is mind — air
The spiral is psychic energy — spirit
Replaces "The Magician"

breathing and weaving as you fill yourself with the image on the parchment.

Draw the Witch image into yourself, see her multiplied a thousandfold, vibrating in every cell of your body. Repeat the following incantation three times:

I am willing to be different and strong
I am willing to be different and beautiful
I am willing to be different and free
I am willing to be different from patriarchy
For this difference
Is the same
Sameness
With the Non-Linear
World of Magic
The Goddess
Her forces
My dreams
The moon
My feelings
My creativity
My passion
My deep love
Of all creation . . .

And the only con-forming
I need to do
Is Forming Creation
For I am form
And I am forming
To universal law
And therefore
Must survive . . .

And even though
I may at times
Feel alone
And misunderstood
I will remember

That I have sisters out there
Who are learning to be free
Like me
And that I am not alone
But all One
And one with the all . . .

And that once free women
Were respected
And loved
And will be again
And will be again
And will be
I will to be
I will it to be
And so doth it be
Forever
And ever
So be it
Blessed be . . .

As you repeat this chant let your words flow rhythmically as you weave and sway, let your voice create melody. Improvise, make new words if you feel inspired.

When you feel complete, slip your parchment beneath the altar cloth. Give thanks to the Goddess and snuff out the candles.

The moonstone is to carry at all times. Keep it in your pocket, under your pillow, or wear it in a pouch. Whenever you feel the need, hold the stone and rub it with your thumb in a circular motion. Think or say:

I am safe
I am me
All is well
Blessed be.

Tell no one of this spell until it has come to fullness. Even as you feel your powers strengthen, it may be best to maintain silence. Be discreet about sharing your magic.

May the Goddess give wings to the Witch within you! So be it.

Rites of Kore

Shekhinah Mountainwater

"Ritual is the Enactment of Myth"
—Joseph Campbell

The woods are soft and fresh with spring. Gentle drops of sunlight kiss the new-grown green. The earth is springy underfoot, welcoming. Mother Nature stretches vast and thick, throbbing with birth, with re-connection. And the women come. We come with tents and pots and plans. We come with blankets and bells and magic. We come to sleep and wake and sing, we come to adore, to bless and receive blessing.

We sit on the earth and circle to speak and listen. "We need a ritual space." "And sleeping places." "And a fire . . ." Together we build. First a trip down into the dark belly of the woods to the magic clearing below. We tie bells and ribbons to the branches as we go, to mark the way, and sing a blessing song:

Oh thank you Mother for this beauty
Thanks to you for being so near
Oh thank you for the green and golden
Thanks to you for being here . . .

Oh thank you Mother for the beauty
Thank you for the gold and green
For sending us your Maiden daughter
For birthing the unseen and seen . . .

We find the altar place, two tall thin trees with a great many-terraced stumps at their feet. We hang the mystic veil between them and place our sacred things . . . Mara brings a great round candle of gleaming yellow-gold, like the sun; Selene a crystal moon. Yoko's candle is silver, to everyone's amazement. Ariel places her tarot deck for later. Yemanja has her big beautiful conch shell. She blows a deep and solemn note before placing it lovingly on the altar. The twins, Ivy and Madrone, bring armfuls of flowers and little Ngame places all the bells. They chime and twinkle in the waning sun, echoing their sisters on the branches above. The whispering leaves and soft voices of women mingle with the ringing sounds.

We stand back together, arms round each other, and contemplate our handiwork. "It's beautiful." "It makes me want to start right away," Ngame squirms impatiently. "We have," laughs Yemanja, and everyone laughs and nods. Someone starts a chant to bless the altar:

> Come goddesses of fire and water
> Goddesses of earth and air
> Give your blessings to this altar
> Give a listen to our prayers . . .

We wind our ways, still singing, back up the path to fire and food. Sasha is stirring up her famous gypsy stew in the cauldron. The smells reach out enticingly; everyone is hungry. We find our bowls and cups and gather round. First a thank you song for the cook:

> Great are the life forms that let us eat them
> Some day our bodies too will be food
> Great is the goddess who makes things so yummy
> Great is the woman who cooks it so good!

Yay Sasha! Yay Sasha!

Sasha beams. For a moment there are only bird sounds. We are swept up in good feelings and the sacredness of the moment. And then we are spooning the delicious steaming chunks of sensuous stew into our bowls...

The young moon sails across the sky and the distant "hoo-hoo" of an owl comes moaning through the trees. Tonight we will sleep in a dream wheel in the temple space below. Flashlights and lanterns bob through the dark like fireflies as women wind their way back down the bell-rung path. We set our bedding in a circle, heads at the periphery, feet to the center. Mara lights the silver candle on the altar and asks the goddess to bless our dreams. The murmur of sleepy conversation dies down bit by bit, finally supplanted by crickets and stars . . .

We waken with the dawn. Lucina is dancing playfully and low, her golden arms come slanting through the dappling leaves, fingers tugging at our eyelids. The air breathes on our faces, wafting sweet piney smells and morning birdcalls.

> O sisters wake up, wake up
> Night has emptied her cup

sings Ngame who is seven, and always the first one up. Women wake up slowly, stretching and blinking, sitting up amidst the bedding. We tell each other our dreams, "I dreamed that a woman came to the ritual, and she was pregnant." "I dreamed that my friend, who died, came back to life." "I dreamed that my sister came." "I dreamed that we were priestesses in an ancient temple cave. . . ." Our dreams weave a tapestry of symbols and reality. We share and lend counsel, find the connections . . .

The ritual time approaches. We robe ourselves for the ceremony, painting each other's brows with blue crescent moons, twining leaves and flowers in our hair. Everyone looks so beautiful, transformed into magnificent beings of fantasy. Ngame dresses as the young child Kore who will be born. Selene as the Maiden who will grow. Yemanja will dance the Mother and Mara the Crone, and Ariel the swift-footed Diana . . . everyone else will be Hours or Seasons, except for Sasha in her many-colored robe, who will be the Muse.

We practice the chanting as we dress:

Kooooraaaaaay . . . Maaaaaaaaa . . . Hecaaataaaay . . .

We try to contain our excitement. Miraculously we are ready when the first sounds of voices come from above; our friends have arrived on the land and are approaching — Ivy and Madrone run half-flying to greet them and form a procession down to the temple. Everyone takes their places round the circle with Yoko and Willow standing, hands upraised to make a living gateway. Selene is poised beside the altar, ready to light the candles and perform the invocation.

Our friends are closer now; we hear them singing and see them appear one by one upon the path. Like us they have bedecked themselves in garlands and flowing robes. The air is electric and we are filled with wonder. As they file in slow procession through the trees we feel transported to another time. How often through the eons have we stood like this with our sisters, to come and praise the Goddess and welcome the Kore....

Sasha starts beating on her drum, a slow steady rhythm. One by one the women pass beneath Yoko and Willow's upraised arms. They exchange kisses and blessing:

> From women you were born into this world
> From women you are born into this circle
> (I learned this chant from Fiona — don't know who wrote it.)

Gradually the circle is formed by the bodies of women. As the last one takes her place the drumming ceases. Yemanja raises her conch shell and blows a long and vibrant note. We all join hands, gazing upon one another with reverence. The robes, the flowers, the colors and shining faces make us into a vision of beauty. The energy throbs and we sense the majesty of this moment.

Someone starts the Ma, low and steady at first. Our voices blend and swell, gradually rising to a crescendo of sounding power. We close our eyes and pour ourselves out, playing now with harmonies and chords, flying into a oneness of vibrating tones. The energy pulses, undulates, thrilling through our bodies and spirits, filling the forest with magic.

Now the sounds wane and gradually die, until we are left standing in a silence that is loud with intensity. We open our eyes again and gaze into one another's eyes, feeling the love and divinity in every woman. "You are goddess." "Hail to thee sweet goddess." "Blessed be my sister," and other acknowledgements are murmured round the circle as eyes meet and hearts connect. And we sink to the earth, taking seats and readying ourselves for the play. Selene turns to the altar and lights a match.

> With this flame we ignite the spirit of the Maiden.
> Welcome Persephone!

Everyone stares into the tiny flame, investing it with Maiden visions, and crying out, "Welcome Persephone!" It seems that even the birds have become hushed with expectancy.

One and two at a time the women rise to make their offerings to the goddess. "I bring buds of birth for the maiden." We twine the delicate baby flowers in our hair. "We bring sprouts for new life." Everyone eats the tiny sweet sprouts. "I bring a red candle for the flame of love between the Mother and the Daughter." She lights it from the flames of the gold and silver candles. "I bring a shell from Mother Sea." Elf brings a poem and a Penny a dance. Willow has a chant to teach us all. When the circle of offerings is complete the drum's heartbeat stirs again, slow and deep.

Yemanja and Ngame move to the center before the altar. Ngame crouches, Yemanja stands and closes her eyes, listening to the drum. Her body starts to undulate and sway. Sasha begins to speak the sacred words:

> Come to pass
> Yea
> In the beginning of things
> That She Mother Goddess
> Is a giving . . .
> Of birth unto her own Self
> (This and all ensuing verses are from *The Myth of Kore* by
> Shekinah Mountainwater.)

The drumming gathers, throbs, Yemanja moves more fully now, her pelvis swimming, heaving, her face suffused with ecstasy. Ngame comes forward to be "born" through Yemanja's wide open legs:

". . . and a Maiden is born!"

The two women, Maiden and Mother, hold one another tenderly as everyone chants:

KOOORAAAAAAAY . . .

Like a musical tapestry the story weaves. The Maiden grows and dances to meet her lover Diana in the forest. Out of their swooning embrace Kore sinks to the earth and down, down to the dark realm of the Crone. The women's voices twine among the drumbeats, chanting droning the holy names:

DIANAAAAAAA . . . HECAATAAAAAY . . .

The moods of love and death unite as Sasha's voice soars, spilling poetry like jewels into the air:

When She touches me
Sweet-honey-lightning
Sets my limbs a-quiver . . ."

and

I am the petals of the trembling rose
Awaiting the kiss
of thy breath . . .

The Hours and Seasons whirl around the periphery of the circle, spinning out the dizzying dance of life and love and death. Everyone is draped in black, moaning and wailing the griefs of separation. We all join with our screams for the pain we have known. It is as though we are dying together, knowing that we will be reborn, that spring will always come again.

Let grey Wisdom's arms enfold thee now
Thou art here because thy time has come
To learn the secrets of the soul
Let go of life and earthly love for now
And I will show to thee they greatest lover . . .

Mara as the Crone is majestic and mysterious in her gray hooded cloak. She sways and spins around the Kore, wipes away her tears and fears, enfolding her in velvet gray, leading her around and down, around and down the spiral dance of trance-formation . . . and we are crying out the great Crone names:

CERRIDWEN
KALI
ARACHNE
BABA YAGA
WISE WOMAN
HECATE

Entranced, we watch as Kore learns the mysteries of immortality, manifestation and dissolution. We learn them with her once again, celebrate with her the initiations. The Hours crown her with a garland of many-colored feathers to show the freedom of her eternal spirit, hang a gleaming crystal at her throat for her new-found powers of creativity, a belt of fragrant herbs at her hips for healing. And we sing with her the joy of knowing truth once more, invoking goddesses of wisdom:

> AAAAARAAAAADIAAAAA
> SOOOPHIAAAAAA
> AATHEEEENAAAA . . .

The drumbeat swells to the full once more and Kore is alone in the center of the circle, swaying, heaving and rising up, birthing herself into the upper world. Sasha sings:

> She
> Laughing Maiden
> Is a-rising
> Song a-singing
> Up a-flying . . .

Mother, Lover and Grandmother are there to welcome her, joining with the Hours and Seasons to circle dance and chant the name of her transformed self:

PERSEPHONE! PERSEPHONE!

. . . and all our voices soar together through the trees to touch the sky in jubilation. A jaybird in a nearby tree joins in with raucous tones, feeling the change of energy. Our song is spiced with laughter.

Now the drum slows to the throbbing rhythm of birth and Persephone is in the center, moving, swaying, undulating as her Mother did for her. Mara casts off her gray crone robes and crawls to roll out from between Persephone's widespread legs. Demeter is there to midwife and catch the baby, and the three women hold and rock one another as the story begins again:

> Comes to pass
> Yea
> In the beginning of things
> That She Mother Goddess

Is a giving
Is a-giving
Is a giving of birth
Unto her own self she
Flex
She heave
And the mountains moan
And a great opening
Opens
Up to the world
And a Maiden is born . . .

As the last KORAAAAAY swells, we all dance together, helping those who are seated to their feet. The dancers throw leaves and petals up into the air, showering us all with their fragrance. We dance and hug and laugh and cry, feeling the love and the joy of spring and the beauty of life's mysteries.

Starhawk

No anthology of women and ritual could be complete without writings in it from Starhawk. This San Francisco witch, ritualist and political activist is a primary theorist in the Women's Spirituality and wiccan movements, as well as in the anti-nuclear and peace movements. Her work is known worldwide through her books, articles, rituals, workshops and her activism for a saner planet. Starhawk's writing brought me into the Craft in 1982; reading *The Spiral Dance* changed my life joyfully, completely and irrevocably, as it has done for so many others before and since. There may have been a Women's Spirituality movement without Starhawk, but it could not have been as profound or fun a movement had her influence not helped shape it.

Starhawk's three books are required reading for Women's Spirituality. Her book *The Spiral Dance: A Rebirth of the Ancient Religion of the Great Goddess*, originally published in 1979, and revised and updated in 1989 (Harper & Row), focuses wiccan rituals and the Craft as a process of inner change and celebrated personal growth. This was many women's first introduction to wicce and remains the primary sourcebook on ritual and the Craft today. *Dreaming the Dark: Magic, Sex and Politics*, published by Beacon Press in 1982, presents a further vision, that of creating a power-within society based on group dynamics of cooperation and peace. It uses the model of the coven to delineate the possibilities of societal political change. Starhawk's latest book, *Truth or Dare: Encounters with Power, Authority, and Mystery* (Harper & Row, 1987), builds upon the models of the individual and the group to create a new world. She designs a utopian new planet, based on power-with values and the influence each individual has in creating world change and world peace. Starhawk's books are three of the most vital documents of our times.

In "Creating Sacred Space," from *The Spiral Dance*, Starhawk describes the basic technique of how to cast a circle, how to create sacred space. This is the beginning of ritual—of the magick that evolves in women's space between the worlds—to create positive change in women, society and the planet.

Creating Sacred Space

Starhawk

Between the Worlds

The Casting of the Circle

The room is lit only by flickering candles at each of the cardinal points. The coveners stand in a circle, their hands linked. With her athame, *her consecrated knife, unsheathed, the Priestess*† *steps to the altar and salutes sky and earth. She turns and walks to the Eastern corner, followed by two coveners, one bearing the chalice of salt water, the other the smoldering incense. They face the East. The priestess raises her knife and calls out:*

> Hail, Guardians of the Watchtowers of the East,
> Powers of Air!
> We invoke you and call you,
> Golden Eagle of the Dawn,
> Star-seeker,
> Whirlwind,
> Rising Sun,
> Come!
> By the air that is Her breath,
> Send forth your light,
> Be here now![1]

As she speaks, she traces the invoking pentagram in the air with her knife. She sees it, glowing with a pale blue flame, and through it feels a great onrush of wind, sweeping across a high plain lit by the first rays of dawn. She breathes deeply, drawing in the power, then earths it through

---

†For literary convenience, I have designated the Priestess as casting the circle. But any qualified covener, female or male, may take her role.

her knife, which she points to the ground.

As she sprinkles water three times, the first covener cries out, "With salt and water, I purify the East!" The second covener draws the invoking pentagram with incense, saying,

"With fire and air, I charge the East!"

The Priestess, knife held outward, traces the boundaries of the circle. She sees it take shape in her mind's eye as they continue to each of the four directions, repeating the invocation, the purification, and the charging:

Hail, Guardians of the Watchtowers of the South,
Powers of Fire!
We invoke you and call you,
Red Lion of the noon heat,
Flaming One!
Summer's warmth,
Spark of life,
Come!
By the fire that is Her spirit,
Send forth your flame,
Be here now!

Hail, Guardians of the Watchtowers of the West,
Powers of Water!
We invoke you and call you,
Serpent of the watery abyss,
Rainmaker,
Gray-robed Twilight,
Evening Star!
By the waters of Her living womb,
Send forth your flow,
Be here now!

Hail, Guardians of the Watchtowers of the North,
Powers of Earth,
Cornerstone of all Power.
We invoke you and call you,
Lady of the Outer Darkness,
Black Bull of Midnight,

North Star,
Center of the whirling sky.
Stone,
Mountain,
Fertile Field,
Come!
By the earth that is her body,
Send forth your strength,
Be here now!

The Priestess traces the last link of the circle, ending in the East. Again she salutes sky and earth, turns and touches the tip of her athame *to the central cauldron, and says,*

The circle is cast.
We are between the worlds,
Beyond the bounds of time,
Where night and day,
Birth and death,
Joy and sorrow,
Meet as one.

The second covener takes a taper to the South point candle and with it lights candles in the central cauldron and on the altar, saying,

The fire is lit,
The ritual is begun.

They return to the circle. The first covener smiles at the person on her left, and kisses her or him, saying,

"In perfect love and perfect trust."
The kiss is passed around the circle.

> The unfolding of God . . . involves the creation of new space, in which women are free to become who we are. . . . Its center is on the boundary of patriarchal institutions . . . its center is the lives of women who begin to liberate themselves toward wholeness.[2]
> Entry into the new space . . . also involves entry into new time. . . . The center of the new time is on the boundary of patriarchal time. . . . It is our life-

time. It *is* whenever we are living out of our own sense of reality, refusing to be possessed, conquered, and alienated by the linear, measured-out, quantitative time of the patriarchal system.[3]

Mary Daly

In Witchcraft, we define a new space and a new time whenever we cast a circle to begin a ritual. The circle exists on the boundaries of ordinary space and time; it is "between the worlds" of the seen and unseen, of flashlight and starlight consciousness, a space in which alternate realities meet, in which the past and future are open to us. Time is no longer measured out; it becomes elastic, fluid, a swirling pool in which we dive and swim. The restrictions and distinctions of our socially defined roles no longer apply; only the rule of nature holds sway, the rule of Isis who says, "What I have made law can be dissolved by no man."[4] Within the circle, the powers within us, the Goddess and the Old Gods, are revealed.

Casting the circle is an enacted meditation. Each gesture we make, each tool we use, each power we invoke, resonates through layers of meaning to awaken an aspect of ourselves. The outer forms are a cloak for inner visualizations, so that the circle becomes a living mandala, in which we are centered.

When we cast a circle, we create an energy form, a boundary that limits and contains the movements of subtle forces. In Witchcraft, the function of the circle is not so much to keep *out* negative energies as to keep *in* power so that it can rise to a peak. You cannot boil water without putting it in a pot, and you can't raise power effectively unless it is also contained. Leaving the circle during the ritual is discouraged because it tends to dissipate the energy, although cats and very small children seem to pass across without disturbing the force field. Adults usually cut a "gate" in pantomine with an *athame,* should they need to leave the circle before the ritual is ended.

The casting of the circle is the formal beginning of the ritual, the complex "cue" that tells us to switch our awareness into a deeper mode. In ritual, we "suspend disbelief" just as we do when watching a play: We allow the critical and analytical functions of Talking Self to relax so that Younger Self may respond fully and emotionally to what happens. Younger Self, as we have seen, responds best to actions, symbols, tangibles — so this change in consciousness is acted out, using a rich array of tools and symbols.

In the permanent stone circles of the Megalithic era, where rituals were enacted for hundreds of years, great reservoirs of power were built up. Because the stones defined the sacred space, there was no need to draw out the circle as we do. The form of circle casting most Witches use today probably originated during the Burning Times, when meetings were held secretly, indoors, and it became necessary to create a temple in a simple hut. Witches may have taken over some forms from Cabalists. It is said that Witches often harbored Jews from Christian persecution and that they exchanged knowledge. (I must admit that, while Witches in general like to believe this is true, Jews don't seem to have heard of it — or, if they have, aren't advertising the fact.)

Before any ritual there is always a period of purification, during which participants can clear away worries, concerns, and anxieties that may hamper their concentration. Some covens simply aspurge (sprinkle) each member with salt water while casting the circle. At very large rituals, this is the only practical method. But for small groups and important workings, we use a more intense meditative exercise called the Salt-Water Purification.

Salt and water are both cleansing elements. Water, of course, washes clean. Salt preserves from decay and is a natural disinfectant. The ocean, the womb of life, is salt water, and so are tears, which help us purify the heart of sorrow.

Salt-Water Purification

(This is one of the basic individual meditations that should be practiced regularly. During periods of high anxiety or depression or when undertaking heavy responsibilities, it is helpful to practice this daily.)

Fill a cup with water. (Use your ritual chalice, if you have one.) With your *athame* (or other implement), add three mounds of salt, and stir counterclockwise.

Sit with the cup in your lap. Let your fears, worries, doubts, hatreds, and disappointments surface in your mind. See them as a muddy stream, which flows out of you as you breathe and is dissolved by the salt water in the cup. Allow yourself time to feel deeply cleansed.

Now hold up the cup. Breathe deeply, and feel yourself drawing up power from the earth (as in the Tree of Life exercise). Let the power flow into the salt water, until you can visualize it glowing with light.

Sip the water. As you feel it on your tongue, know that you have taken in the power of cleansing, of healing. Fear and unhappiness have become transformed into the power of change. Empty the leftover water into a running stream. (Alas, in these decadent times the nearest stream is usually running out of the kitchen faucet and down the drain.)

Group Salt-Water Purification

Coveners assemble in a circle, with incense and point candles lit. The Priestess goes to the altar, grounds and centers herself. She takes the cup of water in her right hand, saying, "Blessed be, thou creature of water." She takes the dish of salt in her left hand, and says, "Blessed be, thou creature of earth." She holds them both up to the sky with arms outstretched, and lets power flow into them, saying,

> Salt and water,
> Inner and outer,
> Soul and body,
> Be cleansed!
> Cast out all that is harmful!
> Take in all that is good and healing!
> By the powers of life, death, and rebirth
> So mote it be!

("So mote it be" means "So must it be" and is traditional for ending a spell or magical working in the Craft.)

She sets them down on the altar, and takes her athame *in her strongest hand, saying, "Blessed be, thou creature of art." She spills three mounds of salt into the water and stirs it counterclockwise, saying,*

> May this *athame* be purified,
> And may these tools and this altar be purified,

as she shakes a few drops over the altar, then salutes sky and earth:

> In the names of Life and Death, so mote it be!

She then holds the cup to her heart and charges the water with power. When she can feel it glowing, she returns to the circle. The cup is sent around, and each person performs her or his private purification. Others may sing softly as the cup goes around. In a large group, three or four cups of water are charged at the same time; otherwise the cup may take hours to go around the circle.

When the cup returns to the Priestess, she sends a kiss around the circle. Then she begins the casting of the circle. If the meeting space is felt to need special cleansing, the following Banishing can be performed.

Banishing

After the purification, the Priestess takes the sword or athame *and goes to the center of the circle. She points the blade to earth and sky, and says, forcefully,*

> Spirits of evil,
> Unfriendly beings,
> Unwanted guests,
> Begone!
> Leave us, leave this place, leave this circle,
> That the Gods may enter.
> Go, or be cast into the outer darkness!
> Go, or be drowned in the watery abyss!
> Go, or be burned in the flames!
> Go, or be torn by the whirlwind!
> By the powers of life, death, and rebirth,

All the coven together shouts:

> We banish you! We banish you! We banish you!
> Begone!

All scream, shout, clap hands, ring bells, and make noise to frighten away negative forces.

Bath water can be "charged," and a few salt crystals added, and coveners can take a ritual bath before entering the circle. Due to the limitations of time and hot water, it is best done at home.(To magically "charge" an object means to imbue it with energy.)

The concept of the quartered circle is basic to Witchcraft, as it is to many cultures and religions. The four directions and the fifth, the center, each correspond and resonate to a quality of the self, to an element, a time of day and year, to tools of the Craft, symbolic animals, and forms of personal power. Constant visualization of these connections creates deep internal links, so that physical actions trigger inner states. The action of casting the circle then awakens all parts of the self, and puts us in touch with mind, energy, emotions, body, and spirit, so that we are constantly made whole.

The "Guardians of the Watchtowers" are energy forms, the *raiths* or spirits of the four elements. They bring the elemental energy of earth, air, fire, and water into the circle, to augment our human power. The vortex of power created when we invoke the four directions guards the circle from intrusions, and draws in the higher powers of the Goddess and God.

Each movement in a ritual has meaning. When we move "sunwise" or clockwise, "deosil," we follow the direction the sun appears to move in the Northern Hemisphere, and draw in power. Deosil is the direction of increase, of fortune, favor, and blessing. When we move "widdershins" or counterclockwise, we are going against the sun, and this direction is used for decrease and banishings.

The tools, the physical objects we use in Witchcraft, are the tangible representatives of unseen forces. The mind works magic, and no elaborately forged knife or elegant wand can do any more than augment the power of a trained mind. The tools are simply aids in communicating with Younger Self, who responds much better to tangibles than to abstracts.

There are two basic schools of thought about tools in the Craft: the Ceremonial Magic school and what I call the kitchen magic school. Ceremonialists are purists, who feel that magical tools should never be handled by others or used for any but ritual purposes. Objects can become reservoirs of psychic power, which may be dissipated by, for example, slicing fruit with your *athame*. Kitchen magic Witches, on the other hand, feel that the Goddess is manifest in ordinary tasks as well as magic circles. When you slice fruit with your *athame,* you consecrate the fruit, and a kitchen chore becomes a sacred task. Whichever school of thought you follow, it is a breach of manners to handle another Witch's tools without asking permission.

Tools may be bought, handmade yourself, given as gifts, or found, sometimes in unusual circumstances. Mother Moth of Compost found her *athame* lying on the white line in the middle of the freeway when she was driving home late one night. A set of tools are sometimes given to a new initiate by the coven. When buying magical tools, never haggle over the price.

Correspondences may differ in varying traditions, and interpretations of symbolism may not always agree. The following are the correspondences used in the Faery tradition.

The East

The East corresponds to the element Air, to the mind, dawn, spring, to pale, airy colors, white and violet, to the eagle and high-flying birds, and the power to *know*. Its tools are the *athame* and the sword, which are used interchangeably. The *athame* is traditionally a double-bladed, black-handled knife, but people use anything from kitchen knives to Swiss Army knives complete with corkscrew, so indispensable for opening ritual wine. Many Witches do not own a sword; they are dramatic at large, open rituals but awkward in close quarters.

Air Meditation

Face East. Ground and center. Breathe deep, and be conscious of the air as it flows in and out of your lungs. Feel it as the breath of the Goddess, and take in the life force, the inspiration, of the universe. Let your own breath merge with the winds, the clouds, the great currents that sweep over land and ocean with the turning of the earth. Say, "Hail, Arida, Bright Lady of the Air!"

Athame or Sword Meditation

Ground and center. Hold your *athame* or sword in your strongest hand. Breathe deeply and take in the power of Air, the power of the mind. The power of this tool is that of discrimination, of drawing lines, setting limits, making choices, and carrying them out. Remember choices you have made and carried through in spite of difficulties. Feel the power of your mind to influence others and the strength of your responsibility not to misuse that power. You have the force to act ethically, in accord with what you believe is right. Let the power of your intelligence, your knowledge, your moral courage, flow into your tool.

The South

The South corresponds to the element Fire, to energy or spirit, to noon, summer, fiery reds and oranges, to the solar lion and the quality of *will*. Its tool is the wand, which may be a slender branch of hazel, a stout oak staff, or a magically shaped piece of driftwood. The wand is used to channel energy, to direct a cone of power, and to invoke God or Goddess.

Fire Meditation

Face South. Ground and center. Be conscious of the electric spark within each nerve as pulses jump from synapse to synapse. Be aware of the combustion within each cell, as food burns to release energy. Let your own fire become one with candle flame, bonfire, hearth fire, lightning, starlight, and sunlight, one with the bright spirit of the Goddess. Say, "Hail, Tana, Goddess of Fire!"

Wand Meditation

Ground and center. Hold your wand in your strongest hand. Breathe deeply, and feel the power of Fire, of energy. Be aware of yourself as a channel of energy. You can change spirit into matter, idea to reality, concept into form. Feel your own power to create, to do, to be an agent of change. Be in touch with your *will* — your power to do what you must, to set a goal and work toward it. Let your will flow into your wand.

The West

The West corresponds to the element Water, to emotions, to twilight, autumn, to blues, grays, deep purples, and sea greens, to sea serpents, dolphins, fish, to the power to *dare*. From the West comes the courage to face our deepest feelings. Its tool is the cup or chalice, which holds the salt water or ritual drink.

Water Meditation

Face West. Ground and center. Feel the blood flowing through the rivers of your veins, the liquid tides within each cell of your body. You are fluid, one drop congealed out of the primal ocean that is the womb of the Great Mother. Find the calm pools of tranquility within you, the rivers of feeling, the tides of power. Sink deep into the well of the inner mind, below consciousness. Say, "Hail, Tiamat, Serpent of the Watery Abyss!"

Cup Meditation

Ground and center. Hold your cup cradled in both hands. Breathe deep, and feel the power of Water, of feeling and emotion. Be in touch with the flow of your own emotions: love, anger, sorrow, joy. The cup is the symbol of nurturing, the overflowing breast of the Goddess that nourishes all life. Be aware of how you are nurtured, of how you nurture others. The power to feel is the power to be human, to be real, to be whole. Let the strength of your emotions flood the cup.

The North

The North is considered the most powerful direction. Because the sun never reaches the northern hemisphere, it is the direction of Mystery, of the unseen. The North Star is the center, around which the skies revolve. Altars face North in the Craft. North corresponds to Earth, to the body, to midnight, winter, brown, black and the green of vegetation. From the North comes the power to keep silent, to listen as well as speak, to keep secrets, to know what not to say. The Goddess as Dark Maiden, the new moon that is not yet visible, and the God as Sacred Bull are the totems of the North, and its tool is the pentacle, the prime symbol of the Craft. A five-pointed star with one point up, set within the circle of the full moon, the pentacle can be engraved on a plate, glazed on a ceramic platter, or molded out of "baker's clay" — bread dough and salt. It is used for grounding energy or as a platter for serving the sacred cakes.

Earth Meditation

Face North. Ground and center. Feel your bones, your skeleton, the solidity of your body. Be aware of your flesh, of all that can be touched and felt. Feel the pull of gravity, your own weight, your attraction to the earth that is the body of the Goddess. You are a natural feature, a moving mountain. Merge with all that comes from the earth: grass, trees, grains, fruits, flowers, beasts, metals, and precious stones. Return to dust, to compost, to mud. Say, "Hail, Belili, Mother of Mountains!"

Pentacle Meditation — The Five Stages of Life

Ground and center. Hold your pentacle in both hands. Breathe deep, and feel the power of earth, of the body. The pentacle is your own body, four limbs and head. It is the five senses, both inner and outer. Be in touch with your own power to see, to hear, to smell, to taste, to touch. The pentacle is the four elements plus the fifth — essence. And it is the five stages of life, each an aspect of the Goddess:

1. *Birth:* the beginning, the time of coming into being
2. *Initiation:* adolescence, the time of individuation

3. *Love:* the time of union with another, of full adulthood, sexuality, responsibility
4. *Repose:* the time of advancing age, of reflection, integration, wisdom
5. *Death:* the time of ending, of letting go, of moving on toward rebirth

Look at your pentacle, or draw one on a sheet of paper. Label the five stations, going clockwise around the points, and experience each stage in turn, as it occurs in a life span and within the span of each new activity or relationship. Trace the interlocking lines and reflect on their meanings. Love is linked to Birth and Death. Death is linked to Love and Initiation.

In the Goidelic tree alphabet, each of five stages was symbolized by a tree, whose name began with one of the five vowels:[5] (Goidelic refers to the Gaelic Celts [Irish, Scots, Manx] as opposed to the Brythonic Celts [Welsh, Cornish, and Bretons]).

A: Birth — *ailm,* silver fir
O: Initiation — *onn,* gorse or furze
U: Love — *ura,* heather
E: Repose — *eadha,* the aspen
I: Death — *idho,* the yew

Chant the sounds of the vowels and feel the power of each stage in turn. Touch your pentacle to your body, and let the life force of your own flesh flow into it.

The Iron Pentagram

(A pentagram is a drawn or written pentacle. This is a meditative tool of the Faery tradition and an important training exercise.)

Ground and center. In your Book of Shadows, draw a pentacle with interlocking lines and label the points, in order, clockwise: "Sex," "Self," "Passion," "Pride," and "Power."

Sex is the manifestation of the driving life force energy of the universe. It is polarity, the attraction of God and Goddess, the on-off pulse that sustains the universe, the orgasmic, ecstatic harmony that sings within each being.

Self is identity, individuality. Each of us is a unique manifestation of the Goddess, and that individuality is highly valued in the Craft. Self-love is the foundation of all love. "Celebrate yourself, and you will see that Self is everywhere."

Passion is the force of emotion that gives color and depth and vitality to life. Joy, sorrow, ecstasy, anger, fear, pain, love — the Goddess manifests in all human emotions. We cannot feel any of them in their full intensity unless we are willing to face them all.

Pride encourages us to create, to do, to share, to grow, and to enjoy the rightful fruits of our achievements. True pride is not based on comparisons or competition; it is an absolute sense of one's inner worth. Pride carries with it the responsibility of acting in accordance with one's self-respect and respect for Self in others.

Power is energy, inner power, not power over others. When the five points are in balance, the life force flows freely, filling us with vitality. Power is integrity, creativity, courage: the mark of a person who is whole.

Meditate on each of the points in turn, and then explore the links and connections: "Sex — Passion," "Self — Pride," "Passion — Power," and so on. Lie down with your arms and legs outstretched so that you form a star. Let your head and each of your limbs be a point on the pentacle. When you are "on the points," they will all be in balance. If some points feel weak, work on developing those qualities. Absorb the strength of the Iron Pentagram.

The Pentagram of Pearl

The Pentagram of Pearl is a meditative tool, like the Iron Pentagram. Its points are Love, Wisdom, Knowledge, Law, and Power.

Begin as for the Iron Pentagram.

Love is the moving energy of life. It is both blindly erotic and deeply personal, a passionate, prideful, powerful caring for oneself and others. It is the law of the Goddess and the essence of magic.

Wisdom and *Knowledge* can best be understood together. Knowledge is learning, the power of the mind to understand and describe the universe. Wisdom is knowing how to apply knowledge — and how not to apply it. Knowledge is knowing what to say; wisdom is knowing whether or not to say it. Knowledge gives answers; wisdom asks questions. Knowledge can be taught; wisdom grows out of experience, out of making mistakes.

Law is natural law, not human law. When we break natural laws, we suffer the consequences as a natural result of our actions, not as a punishment. If you break the law of gravity, you will fall. Magic functions within natural law, not outside of it. But natural law may be broader and more complex than we realize.

Power, again, is the power that comes from within, when love, knowledge, wisdom, and law are united. Power, rooted in love and tempered by knowledge, law, and wisdom, brings growth and healing.

Again, meditate on the points and the links between them. Lie in the pentacle position, feel the points as part of yourself, and become aware of your own imbalances. Absorb the beauty of the Pentagram of Pearl.

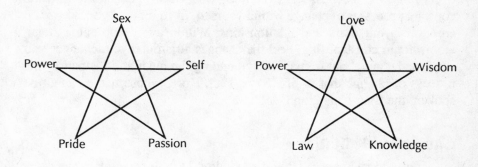

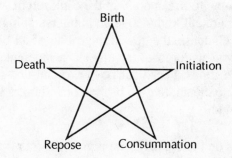

Center

The center of the circle is the point of transformation. It corresponds to pure essence, to timelessness, to transparent light, to the power to *go*, to move, change, transform. Its magical tool is the cauldron, which may be the traditional three-legged cast iron pot, or a clay or metal bowl. The cauldron holds fire: a candle, incense, smoldering herbs, or a bonfire. It may also be a cooking pot, in which fire transforms the food we will eat.

Transformation Meditation

Ground and center. Whisper softly over and over, "She changes everything She touches, and everything She touches, changes." Feel the constant processes of change within yourself, in your body, your ideas and emotions, your work and relationships. Within every unmoving stone, atoms are in constant flux. Feel the changes all around you, changes you have made, are about to make. Even ending the meditation is part of the process of change that is life. Say, "Hail, Kore, whose name cannot be spoken, the Ever-Changing One!"

Cauldron Meditation

Ground and center. Hold the cauldron in both hands. Breathe deep, and feel the power of transformation. You hold the Cauldron of Ceridwen, where the dead come to life. You hold the cauldron in which was brewed the broth that imparts all knowledge and understanding. The cauldron is the womb of the Goddess, the gestation ground of all birth. Think of the transformations you undergo every day. In a moment, you die and are reborn a thousand times. Feel your power to end and begin anew, your ability to gestate, to create, to give birth to new things, and let that power flow into your cauldron.

Meditations on the elements are part of the training of every Witch. After experiencing the energy of each magical element separately, the apprentice is taught to combine them, in preparation for learning to cast a circle.

The Circle Visualization Exercise

(You may lie down, sit comfortably, or get up and enact this exercise.

Face each direction either physically or mentally.)

Ground and center. Face East. Visualize your *athame* in your strongest hand, and draw an Invoking Pentacle. See it burning with a pale, blue flame. Say, "Hail, Guardians of the Watchtowers of the East, Powers of Air."

Walk through the pentacle, and see a great wind sweeping across a vast plain of waving grass. Breathe deeply, and feel the air on your face, in your lungs, through your hair. The sun is rising, and in its rays a golden eagle shines as it flies toward you. When you are filled with the power of air, say, "Hail and farewell, Shining Ones." Walk back through the pentacle.

Turn and face the South. Again, draw the Invoking Pentacle. Say, "Hail, Guardians of the Watchtowers of the South, Powers of Fire."

Walk through the pentacle. You are on a blazing veldt under the hot sun. It is high noon. Feel the sun's fire on your skin and absorb its power. In the distance, red-gold lions sun themselves. When you feel attuned to fire, say, "Hail and farewell, Radiant Ones." Walk back through the pentacle.

Turn and face the West, and again draw the pentacle. Say, "Hail, Guardians of the Watchtowers of the West, Powers of Water."

Walk through the pentacle. You are on a cliff above a pounding sea. Feel the spray and the force of the waves. It is twilight, and the blue-green waves are edged with violet as the sun disappears. Dolphins and sea serpents dive and play in the foam. When you feel attuned to the power of water, say, "Hail and farewell, Flowing Ones" and walk through the pentacle.

Turn and face North. Draw the pentacle, and say, "Hail, Guardians of the Watchtowers of the North, Powers of Earth."

Walk through the pentacle. You are in the midst of a lush, fertile landscape, on the slopes of a mountain. Around you are green, growing herbs nourished by fresh springs, and tall silent trees fed by the minerals and nutrients in the earth. In the distance, grain is waving in the fertile fields. Wild goats cling to the craggy heights above you, while below, herds of wild cattle thunder across the plain. It is midnight; the moon is hidden but the stars are bright. The Great Bear and Little Bear circle the North Star, the still center point of the whirling wheel of the sky. Say, "Hail and farewell, Silent Ones."

Visualize all four pentacles around you in a circle of blue flame. Above your head is an eight-rayed star. Breathe deep, and draw in power from the star. Let it fill you; feel it flood every cell of your body with light, a cone of light that extends deep into the earth around you. Thank the star, and let the light return to its source. Open the circle by visualizing the pentacles flying off into space.

Additional tools used in most covens include a cord, a necklace, a censer, and a Book of Shadows, which has been discussed in Chapter Three. The cord is the symbol of binding, of belonging to a particular coven. In some traditions, the color of the cord reflects the degree of advancement in the Craft of its bearer. The censer is used to hold the incense, and is identified with either the East or the South, Air or Fire. The necklace is the circle of rebirth, the sign of the Goddess. It can be of any design that is personally pleasing.

Of course, candles, herbs, oils, and incenses are also used in Witchcraft. Unfortunately, I don't have space to go into a detailed discussion of their uses and correspondences, especially as that information is given in the Tables of Correspondences and is available from other sources.[6] In general, a Witch depends less on traditional associations of herbs, odors, and colors than on her own intuition. If the "proper" materials aren't available, we improvise.

The tools are usually kept on an altar, which may be anything from a hand-carved antique chest to a box covered with a cloth. When used for regular meditation and magical practice, the altar becomes charged with energy, a vortex of power. Generally, a Witch's altar faces north, and the tools are placed in their corresponding directions. Images of the Goddess and God — statues, shells, seeds, flowers, or a mirror — take a central position.

Consecrating a Tool

(Tools can be charged — imbued with psychic energy — and consecrated within a group ritual, during an initiation, or individually. I will describe the rite for an *athame*. For other tools, simply make the necessary adjustments.)

Set up the altar as you want it, and light the candles and incense. Perform the Salt-Water Purification, and cast a circle by doing the Circle Visualization. Ask the Goddess to be with you.

Hold your *athame* in your strongest hand, saying, "Blessed be, thou creature of art. Do the *Athame* or Sword Meditation.

Touch it to the symbols of each of the four elements in turn: incense for Air, the wand for Fire, the cup for Water, and the pentacle for Earth. Meditate on the power of each element, and visualize that power flowing into the *athame*. Say, "May you be charged with the power of (Air, Fire, etc.) and serve me well in the (East, South, etc.), between the worlds, in all the worlds. So mote it be."

Pass your *athame* through the candle flame, and touch it to the central cauldron. Visualize white light filling and charging it. Say, "May you be charged from the center of all, above and below, throughout and about, within and without, to serve me well between the worlds, in all the worlds. So mote it be."

Draw or inscribe your own personal symbols on the blade or hilt. Trace over them with your own saliva, sweat, menstrual blood, or other secretions, to create the link with your tool. Breathe on it, and imagine your own personal power flowing into it.

Touch it to your heart, and your lips. Raise it to sky, and point it to earth. Wrap your cord around it (or imagine it, if you don't have a cord) and visualize a shield of light binding the power. Say, "Cord go round, power be bound, light revealed, now be sealed."

Earth the power, thank the Goddess, and open the circle by thanking each of the directions and visualizing the pentacles dissolving.

In casting a circle, the outer forms used are less important than the strength of the inner visualization. When the Priestess calls the Guardians of the East, for example, she feels the wind and sees the sun rising with her inner sight. She is also visualizing the flaming pentacles and the circle of light surrounding the coven. In a strong coven, one person may perform the outward actions, but all will be internally visualizing the circle and attuning themselves to the elements.

The outer forms can be very simple. Alone, it may be enough to simply visualize a ring of white light around the room, or turn to each direction in turn and tap the wall. A group may join hands and picture the circle, or one member may walk around the others. The circle may be marked out ahead of time with chalk, stones, string, flowers, leaves, or shells, or drawn invisibly with the *athame* as it is cast.

This chapter opens with a description of a formal circle casting. At first, trying to remember the words and actions, visualize the elements, and feel the power will be far more difficult than trying to pat your head and rub your stomach at the same time. But with practice your concentration will improve until the entire sequence flows easily and naturally. You may wish to create your own invocations, instead of using the ones given.

The energy field created by a circle can also be used for protection. This can be done very simply:

Protective Circle

Visualize a circle or bubble of white light around yourself, with the energy running clockwise. Tell yourself it is an impenetrable barrier no harmful forces can cross. If you have time, perform the Circle Visualization or quickly call each of the four elements in turn.

Permanent Protective Circle

(A permanent circle of protection can be established around your home or place of work. The following ritual can be done alone, or in a group with each person carrying one of the objects.)

Ground and center. Go around the house widdershins with a bell, a broom, and charged salt water. Ring the bell to scare away negative energies. Sweep away unwanted forces with the broom — or use a wand to wave them out. Sprinkle each entrance — each window, door, mirror, and major water outlets — with salt water. Also sprinkle the corners of every room. If necessary, perform a Banishing. Do the Salt-Water Purification.

Now go around the house clockwise, with salt water, athame, *and incense. Draw an invoking pentacle at each entrance with the* athame, *and then with salt water. Concentrate on forming a seal of protection that cannot be broken. Finally, with the incense, charge each entrance and corner, inviting good forces to enter. Say,*

Salt and sea,
Of ill stay free,
Fire and air,
Draw all that is fair.
Around and around,
The circle is bound.

Formally cast a circle in the room you will use for rituals. Chant and raise power to fill the house with protection. Then thank the Goddess, earth the power, and open the circle.

You can reinforce a protective circle by visualizing it. Do so before magical work or sleep.

The circle is cast; the ritual is begun. We have created the sacred space, a space fit for the Gods to enter. We have cleansed ourselves and centered ourselves; our mental bonds have dropped away. Free from fear, we can open to the starlight. In perfect love, and perfect trust, we are prepared to invoke the Goddess.

Notes

1.This set of invocations is written and paraphrased by me from traditional Faery invocations.

2. Mary Daly, *Beyond God the Father* (Boston: Beacon Press, 1973), p. 40.

3. Daly, p. 41.

4. Helen Diner, *Mothers and Amazons* (New York: Anchor Press, 1973), p. 169.

5. Robert Graves, *The White Goddess* (New York: Farrar, Straus & Giroux, 1966), Chaps. 10-11.

6. As a good reference on traditional materials, and an excellent source book for Dianic Witchcraft, see Z Budapest, *The Feminist Book of Lights and Shadows* (Venice, CA: Luna Publications, 1976) — reissued by Wingbow Press, Berkeley, CA.

Antiga

Antiga is a feminist and lesbian witch, educator, writer, artist, singer and workshop creator. She guides groups, facilitating change and growth through the workshop process, and develops her spirituality by creating celebrations and rituals based on female experience. Her fascination with language led her to an M.A. in linguistics. She then began to study how sexism is interwoven into our language.

Antiga's writing and art have appeared in many feminist publications. Her book, *What Can I Learn?* (by Mary Lee George) is an intriguing invitation to enjoy life as one learns. It is available from Sisters, PO Box

6513, Minneapolis, MN 55406 for $6.25. Her recent audio tape, *I Dance to Be the Woman I Can Be*, chants for use in rituals and other feminist songs, is available from Llewellyn Publications. Antiga is well known for her work at 'organizing for the Goddess' in Minneapolis/St. Paul and beyond. She is a graduate of Selena Fox's School for Priestesses held at Circle Sanctuary, and is becoming recognized for her work at archiving Women's Spirituality chants and music. Among her friends and coveners, Antiga is also known for her Hag Power sweatshirts and her immense courage in the face of disability and adversity.

In "Blood Mysteries," Antiga makes joyous rituals of women's menstruation, menarche, menopause and childbearing. She denies the male edict that women's blood is shameful, dirty, sinful or evil — and that women are also shameful, dirty, sinful or evil. She affirms the Goddess-within in all women and in women's blood. Following Antiga through her process of self-discovery and the making of blood prints, to her ritual of menarche and honoring rituals of women's blood, is a rite of passage women have long needed to experience. The joy in this article is profound.

Antiga can be reached at 2829 41st Avenue S., Minneapolis, MN 55406.

Blood Mysteries

Antiga

October 10, 9988 a.d.a.[1]

I t is new moon. If I were younger and still bleeding monthly, if I lived during times with no electric lights when people lived in small tribal groups and women bled with the moon and with each other, I'd be bleeding. Thirty years ago today one of my four children was born — I wonder if it was New Moon on that day 30 years ago when I was bleeding at birthing. That experience was not what I wanted it to be. It was medical instead of spiritual. The birthing was set up totally for the doctor's convenience without the slightest regard for what I might want or need. My frustration and anger at this set-up came out many years later in a poem I wrote about my third pregnancy.

Ames, Iowa 1960
Pregnant and
    no female friend to confide in
Scared and
    no woman to tell it to

A male doctor who patronizingly
    calls me by my first name
    while I'm supposed to
        respectfully
    call him Dr. So-an-so
A husband so afraid of
    his own fear that
    He's unwilling to know it's there
        not the person
        to listen to mine

Where are the witches, midwives
     and friends
  to belly dance and chant
     while I deliver
  to hold me and breathe with me
     as I push
  to touch me and comfort me
     as I cry?

Where are the womyn who know
    what it's like
    to give birth?

I now know that I wanted wemoon present: midwives to help the baby emerge, friends to celebrate, sing, dance and drum. The birth of all my children was taken from me by male medical doctors who had no respect for the sacredness of women's blood.

My woman's blood and the moon have been linked since the beginning of time. It was most likely the congruence of moon cycle and wimmin's bleeding cycle that birthed the idea of marking time.

Time (bleeding Time), moon and women have been connected since ancient days. Bleeding, whether monthly or at birthing, was a sacred time in womyn's lives. A time in which women attended and nurtured each other. A time for connection with the divine — with Earth who birthed us all and with each other. Such a sacred time was a holy day (holiday). Wemoon rested from everyday activity and gathered in the woods to give their blood back to the Mother Earth. If there were those for whom bleeding was uncomfortable, these women were tended to, comforted, and touched by others. It was a time for fun, for celebration, for silence, for being with oneself, for being with other wimmin whose bleeding was also sacred. This was a holy time in their lives.

It has been many many moons since women's blood was respected and honored. Yet somewhere in the genes of all of us is the memory of the sacredness of bleeding and moon and women.

Time is cycling around again to bring us to a conscious awareness of the sacred nature of our blood. Some of us have discovered that the beauty of our blood can create blood prints as we sit on paper to catch these images. Some of us are discovering the creativity that our bleeding time brings as we discard the patriarchal notion that our blood is dirty or evil. The patriarchal definition of menstruation has forced us to hate our female bodies and our female selves. It takes us away from listening to our bodies, from paying attention to what our bodies tell us we need. It tears our spirit away from our body, ripping our essence in two. It pits parts of us against other parts. When we are disgusted with our blood we are also disgusted with our spirit. Without the power of our spirit, we are unable to challenge a system that sets us against ourselves, against our sisters. As we discover the beauty and power in our blood, we honor our bodies, we honor the Goddess and are more easily able to love our female selves.

In modern society, there is shame surrounding the natural body function of bleeding every 28 days. It is seen in silences — not using the word menstruation or menopause in daily conversation. I recently was interviewed by a woman reporter from a large university newspaper. She had asked why the moon was so important in women's ritual. I explained the connection between the 28 day moon cycles and wemoon's 28 day menstrual cycle. I said, "Be sure to print the word 'menstruation' in your article." She was doubtful. "This is a university publication." Though not a four-letter word, she seemed to think that it might very well be an unacceptable word to print. The word 'menstruation' did not appear in her article.

Silence often indicates shame. I believe that in this case it does. So one of the ways we can cast off shame is to begin talking about menstruation and menopause in ordinary conversation in a matter of fact way. Though others might initially be shocked, hearing these words comfortably spoken again and again can strip our bleeding of the shame that patriarchal thinking has forced upon us. Louise Kessel, a North Carolina storyteller, has a wonderful tape[2] in which she talks comfortably about menstruation, "Menstruation Rap," and tells a tale of the beginning of menstruation "Menstrual Myth."

To unlearn what I'd been taught about womoon's blood and to learn to honor the beauty and power of my female essence through loving my menstrual blood took many many many moons. The shame around what was most female about me — my monthly bleeding — was forced on me at an early age before I had a chance to experience the creativity of my female blood that should have been my birthright. Shame stops me from glorying in my female self. Shame stayed with me through the birth of my four children. I did not have the nurturing of other women that should have been my birthright at those births. My birthing blood was not honored. It was ignored. Silence surrounded it. It was not until my children were teenagers that the possibility of viewing menstruation as anything other than shameful surfaced. The idea that menstruation might be respected, even enjoyed, came to me through a magazine of wimmin's spirituality. In *WomanSpirit* I read an article about a womon who made blood prints when she bled. She sat down on paper and bled onto the paper, creating art by using her body and her blood as the instruments for her creation.

I liked the idea and began doing it myself. I found what a wonderfully creative and renewing time my blood flow was if I respected my inner needs. I got terribly irritable if I had to do boring or other-directed tasks during my blood flow. Irritations which would not normally cause me much concern took on such proportion that I found myself in real trouble. In the feminist future that I'm creating, our lives will be arranged so that wimmin can have their bleeding time for themselves, for quiet, for spiritual development, for letting their creativity as well as their blood flow.

One thing I most enjoyed about doing blood prints was using my body as the instrument to work with and my blood as the medium. I developed different techniques as I gave myself more permission to experiment. At first, I would simply sit on the paper and make images. Then I learned to scoot backwards in two ways: one going straight back and the other moving from side to side. I sometimes sat on the same piece of paper several times. This gave me a repeat of a similar image. I caught my blood with a sponge or a menstrual cup and used the blood as ink. I wrote some of the work that I've written about blood right on the blood print. I also used the cup blood to drip on paper or I would fling lines onto the paper and finger paint with it. A friend who does blood prints folds the paper and presses it together to get her image. I did blood prints on cloth. The way cloth combines with blood is entirely different from the way blood and paper combine. It felt like a whole new art form to me.

And, through making blood prints, I came to understand the power of women's blood and the connection of blood to my spiritual essence, to my creativity. As I began to honor my bleeding in this way, I discovered that this time was the most creative of the whole month. I began to eagerly await my blood flow.

As I let others know what I was doing, their reactions were varied. Some thought it was disgusting, others were intrigued. My 17-year-old daughter thought it was strange but didn't mind as long as I didn't show my blood prints to her friends. She insisted that I put them out of sight when her friends came to visit.

I have shown my blood prints in two art shows. The first was at WARM, the women's art gallery in Minneapolis, with a group of other feminist artists. Later, I had a whole show of blood prints at the Women's Coffee House in Minneapolis. Reactions varied from admiration ("You've got a lot of guts to put that up in public"), to horror and/or refusal to look at the prints or read what's written on them once they know that it's really blood. Many strongly feminist wimmin have so internalized the belief that menstrual blood is dirty that they can't see the beauty in the prints.

Most important, doing blood prints helped me value my bleeding time as spiritually creative. Whenever possible, I took that time to be alone and to allow my sensitivity to guide me. I did other sorts of art work or writing during this time as well. I was giving myself the permission to do whatever felt good. To any wimmin who do not enjoy their bleeding, I suggest doing blood prints. I looked forward eagerly to each flow and missed it when it didn't appear.

When I had several of my blood prints copied I had the pleasure of watching the expression of disbelief on the face of the man photocopying them. He knew what they were.

Doing the blood prints led me into some thinking and research about how wemoon's blood was viewed in tribal societies. I was aware that the anthropologists, who were primarily male, studying so-called primitive societies, had concluded that womyn were segregated from the men during bleeding because they were unclean.

Looking to my experience rather than to research based on the assumption that women's blood was dirty, I realized that wimmin had created menstrual huts, rest from normal activities *for* themselves. The gift they gave themselves was time to rest, to slow down, to explore their spirituality.

To have taken this sacred time away from women the men would need heavy-handed propaganda, possibly with cruel enforcement. Looking at history (his story), we see that is exactly what happened.

When I realized this, I felt violent anger — scary to express, yet necessary for my emotional well being. Anger had been forbidden to me as shame had been forced on me. The prohibition and propaganda were beginning to make sense. Keeping women from knowing the power of their blood was one of the ways that women were kept in a subservient position.

After anger, what then? A decision to honor my menstrual blood, to love myself and my body by loving my blood. To create rituals and be a part in rituals honoring women's blood: rituals of passage for young women beginning to bleed, for old womyn ceasing to bleed, for all women who still bleed. To show my blood prints as art in wemoon's spaces. To let others know in whatever way possible that I love my female self, my female blood and my female spirit. To remember times of joy and creativity through my bleeding.

I remember a time I was camping alone at one of my favorite spots at Madeline Island on Lake Superior. My bleeding began as I was packing to return home. I wasn't prepared. Instead of rushing to the drugstore to buy pads, I decided to bleed onto my clothes, onto my legs, onto the car seat with reckless abandon. I allowed myself to enjoy the wet warm blood as it trickled down my leg and soaked my clothes. I allowed myself sensations that I had been prohibited from feeling. I felt female in every cell of my body and loved myself fiercely.

And I remember the time of my last bleeding. By this time, I was skipping many moons between each bleeding. So each time the blood came I rejoiced and felt the bittersweet knowing that it could be my last. The time that was my last, I began bleeding as we were riding the ferry across Lake Michigan to go to the Michigan Women's Music Festival. I had blank postcard size cardboard with me. I ran into the bathroom to make blood prints, then out on deck to show them to other women, then back to make some more, to show these. Will a time come when a woman could do this in public? The fun of being able to show the prints as soon as they were made was something I had not yet had. It felt like a fitting way to end 35 years of bleeding.

Though I no longer bleed monthly, I think of Starhawk's chant: "What is remembered, lives." So, I remember my bleeding with thanks that I came to love it before it ceased. I think also of the idea of wise blood: an ancient belief that old wimmin are the wisest of mortals because they retain their 'wise blood' in their veins.

In the years of my wise blood, an image important for my healing came to me. It relates to the blood in my veins.

I was in counseling for diabetes. The imbalance in my body frequently results in very high levels of sugar in my blood. I had a vision in which I saw black drops edged with fluorescent-yellow inside my body in my bloodstream. These black drops were woman hating that had been there since before I was born.

My counselor asked me, "How could those drops of women hating leave your body?" I immediately replied, "Through my fingertips." What

I need to do to monitor my blood sugar level is to prick my fingers several times a day to get drops of blood to put on a test strip. My counselor had me visualize the woman-hating drops gathering together and going out through the blood that I needed to test with. I did this and found that one time was not enough to release the woman hating that had been there all my life. So, I decided to continue doing this visualization as often as I could remember to do it.

At about the same time this vision came to me, I started drawing with the blood from my finger tips rather than wiping it off and throwing it away. Making art again with my blood helped make something bearable that is very hard to do: stick my finger so many times a day to draw blood.

One day I was attending a workshop on Shamanism led by Michael Harner, a well known scholar in this field, and found my blood sugar was very high. I did a shaman journey to search for healing for myself and got a vision of an image drawn with the blood from my fingers. I saw myself making a large manila envelope to put the drawing in. When I told my small group about these drawings, Michael happened to be sitting in on our group.

When he heard my story he said, "You have come very close to a method of praying from another culture. The Huichol Indians in North Central Mexico believed that spirits wanted blood because they had none. If a blood drawing were offered to the spirits, they would come and get it. So, they would do blood drawings and also put a prayer on the drawings. When the spirit took the blood drawing, s/he was then obliged to help the petitioner with the prayer on the drawing."

So I find my relationship with my blood different in my crone years and possibly even more powerful than it was when my wise blood poured out through my vulva monthly.

And as I talk more freely and openly about my experience, other women share theirs with me. My good friend Rachel Parker said: "I didn't stop having cramps until after I heard about menstrual huts. Cramps were my way of validating that I needed to be alone. When I learned to validate my need to withdraw in a straightforward way, I no longer needed cramps."

Jackie Rivers said: "I feel inwardly powerful when I'm bleeding. It's a good time for crying or meditation. I didn't know how powerful this time was for many years. Knowing the power of menstruation came at about the time I found witchcraft. I feel sad that I didn't have this awareness when my daughter began her bleeding."

Mary Rose Cassavant told me: "I never knew about the sacredness of

Invocation to North and Earth

The Menstrual Hut

Reeds and rushes
Rushes and reeds
Woven by women
Born of the Earth
A place to bleed with other women
A place to be with other women
A place to enjoy with other women
A place to return womyn's blood to the earth
A place for solitude
A place for sisterhood
A place for solidarity
A place for silence
A place for spiritual spontaneity
with other women

Maidens   Mothers   Matriarchs
Move
My
Imagination
Protecting women with Blood Taboos

Is it any wonder that patriarchy needed
to separate us from the Earth
to turn us against
our womanblood?

After saying "The circle is cast. The ritual has begun," the story telling begins. Louise Kessel's "Menstruation Myth" would be a good one to start with. Stories of personal experiences can be combined with talk of the times. "Some would say long, long ago. Some would say a mere blink of the eye in Earth's time" when womyn were honored and respected, when wimmin's blood was known to be sacred. After the prepared stories are told, then women divide into small groups — about three in a group — to tell their own stories. These stories might be painful, they might be joyful. After the storytelling, wemoon are invited to gather in a large circle and share with the others something from their stories: a word, a movement, a song, a drawing.

After the story sharing, there is a time to release the pain caused by patriarchal put downs of our bleeding time. This is a very good time to encourage screaming, foot stamping, whatever sorts of angry actions we are not allowed to take. Doing it in a group makes it possible for wimmin to participate who ordinarily would never do so. When asking women to join in, one can speak of returning this energy to the Earth for her to compost, to turn into rich soil in which wemoon loving will flourish. Take as long as this part of the ritual needs. There may be a lot that needs releasing.

The last part of the ritual is celebrating the power of our blood. A good chant for this is: "There is power in the blood of wimmin. There is power in the blood that transforms us." If space permits, dancing and drumming would be wonderful here. Any large pieces of red material that could be used for dancing would be fun. However it is done, raising energy for all wimmin to love their blood, their bodies, themselves, is a fitting end to the ritual.

It is New Moon. My coven is doing a ritual to honor our menstrual and birthing blood. We cast the circle by winding around us yarn in the colors of the Maiden, Mother and Crone (white, red, and black) while singing Goddess names. We anoint each other with Love oil "in perfect love and perfect trust." Once the ritual has begun, we talk about the importance of doing this ritual. We tell stories of joy about our bleeding time. We remember. One woman speaks of how difficult it is for her to speak easily about her bleeding time. We compare notes with other women, to see how their experience fits in with our own. Whether it's easy or hard, whether our stories are joyful or bittersweet, there is healing in speaking the truth of our experience, being listened to and believed.

The sacred circle is a place where each woman speaks her truth and all the others listen. We feel ourselves powerfully in that sacred place affirming the sacredness of our wemoon's blood. The connection made at the beginning of the ritual with the red, white, and black yarn becomes an emotional connection woven by the magic of our stories. The beauty and power of our womyn's blood is honored and celebrated. We do a guided meditation before raising energy asking for respect for and honor of women's blood.

The meditation takes us inside our body, asks us to explore our most female parts, to become our menstrual blood, feel the power in that blood as we flow to the world outside our body.

Here are the words I used in that meditation:

Breathe and center.

Go inside your body and visit the most female parts of you. Visit your breasts, your vulva, your womb, ovaries and fallopian tubes. Take time at each to explore. What does this part of you feel like? Is it moist? What color is it? What does it taste like? Smell like? Are there sounds associated with it? If there are parts of you that you are uncomfortable exploring, simply note which they are and move on.

Now go to (or return to) your ovary. Go inside and feel what it's like to be an egg ready to burst through the wall of the ovary and begin a journey with an unknown destination. You have pushed through and find yourself falling gently through a large tunnel. You continue falling, enjoying the gentle movement until you come into a large cave. The walls are blood red and inviting. Yet you continue to move until you find yourself in some light that seems quite foreign to you. You decide to rest and fall asleep.

Asleep, you find yourself back in the large cave. Now you are the inviting red blood on the wall of the cave. What does it feel like to be this blood? You have seen the egg move through the case and feel drawn to follow her. Part of you is dense, part liquid. You allow yourself to be pulled away from the wall of the cave, gradually, little by litle. At first just a bit of you lets go, then as more of you goes, the rest is drawn to follow. You flow into a smaller cave whose walls are deep flesh pink, incredibly sensual to touch as you flow by. As you come to the end of this cave, you see light ahead. Somehow your choices come to you and you consider how you want to enter this strange new world, and where you want to go.

Do you want to be washed away by and merge with water?

Do you want to join the soft moss of the Earth?

Do you want to find your place on paper or cloth and be dried by air?

Do you want to flow onto a woman's finger and be anointed onto a red candle celebrating this woman's blood flow? Do you want to enter the fire to be transformed as the candle burns?

You make your choice and, lo, it happens. Your choice of element takes you into an entirely different sort of existence.

After the meditation, we share anything we wish about what came to us. We end with the following chant as we ask ourselves to imagine what our lives would be like, what the world would be like if every womoon could bleed and birth inside a sacred circle.

Blessing to our menstrual blood!
Blessing for our birthing blood!
Blessing to our female body
Blessing to our spirit
Blessing for our connection with other women
Blessing for our self-love and love of each other
Blessing to the world that holds us sacred.

Notes

I want to thank Mary Rose Cassavant for typing this article for me when I was unable to see to do it myself.

Permission is given to copy all or part of this article for group or personal use.

1. 'a.d.a.': after the development of agriculture. See Merlin Stone's article, "9978: Repairing the Time Warp," in *Heresies,* Spring 1978, pp. 124-126.

2. "The Goddess Suite" by Cynthia R. Crossen and "Goddess Stories" told by Louise Kessel. Tapes and info. from Louise Kessel, PO Box 8, Bynum, NC 27228, (919) 542-5599.

3. As quoted in *WomanSpirit,* Spring Equinox, 1983.

4. Jean Mountaingrove, "An ancient message," in *WomanSpirit,* Winter Solstice, 1974, p. 13. Address: 2000 King Mountain Trail, Wolf Creek, OR 97497.

5. Bonne Holbrook, "Menstrual Ritual," in *WomanSpirit,* Spring Equinox, 1983, p. 36.

6. Alexandra Kollmeyer, *The Clear Red Stone,* 1982, In Sight Press, 535 Coedova Rd., Suite 228, Santa Fe, NM 87601.

Caridwyn Aleva

Caridwyn (Care'-id-wyn) Aleva and her partner Mari (Mah'-ree) are duly ordained ministers in the Church of Tzaddi, a non-denominational metaphysical church that acknowledges the spiritual validity of their pagan path. They are also spiritual healer-counselors and third degree Reiki practitioners. Co-founder of Coven Diana Parthenos, Caridwyn has facilitated personal growth and spiritual development workshops, study groups and circles for many years.

Caridwyn and Mari are co-directors of Moonwind, a center for those who seek and walk in truth. Mari is a conscious channel and a professional master hypnotist trained in Alchemical Hypnotherapy. The focus of her work is to assist people in moving forward on their life paths, contacting their inner wisdom and developing their unlimited potential. They both travel nationally to present seminars, workshops and rituals.

I met Caridwyn and Mari at a workshop at the Michigan Women's Music Festival, the same festival where their handfasting took place in 1987. Our meeting and the developing friendship between the three of us has changed my life. In 1989 I became an initiated member of the Coven Diana Parthenos. We have done much healing work together and these women have taught me a great deal. Finding Caridwyn and Mari and the Diana Parthenos women, I found the family I had sought for many years. *The Goddess Celebrates* was envisioned as a book of friends, a circle of women writing about ritual in the spirit of sharing and exchange. It is with great joy that I present "Handfasting Ritual for Mari and Caridwyn" in this anthology.

For more information about workshops, channeling, Reiki, or healing, contact Caridwyn and Mari Aleva at Moonwind, PO Box 85986, Westland, MI 48185, (313) 326-7561.

Handfasting Ritual for Mari and Caridwyn

Caridwyn Aleva

In Wicce we have a ritual to celebrate a relationship which already exists. This ritual is called Handfast(en)ing or Trysting, a word meaning 'meeting' and also 'trust.' We are here today to join Mari and Caridwyn in bonds of commitment according to ancient rites.

With these words began the most meaningful ritual of my life. Here we were standing up in front of a crowd of friends, family and acquaintances and making a commitment to love and care for each other in this lifetime and beyond, even if we love others as well.

Traditional patriarchal "marriage" ceremonies include a commitment "Till death do us part." In Wicce we believe that life is a cycle of birth, death and rebirth. Thus, handfasting does not recognize death as ending a relationship. Handfasting, trysting, establishes a bond of trust and loving care for each other no matter what our future relationship may be in this life or any other and no matter who else we may bond with or "marry."

Mari and I had been lovers for almost five years. We were both in our forties when we met. Our relationship developed quickly and with great intensity. For both of us this union provided more emotional support, more loving and caring, than either of us had ever experienced in a relationship before. We swiftly moved to an exclusive commitment and exchanged rings and other symbols of our growing love. We shared in birthing the Coven Diana Parthenos. We thrived in our developing spirituality. In addition, Mari began to take part in many of my lesbian feminist political activities. We attended NOW conferences and demonstrations together, and we marched side by side in Lesbian and Gay Pride Day Parades.

In our process of growth our path led us to a number of difficulties, and for a period of several months we stopped seeing each other. My enabling behaviors, those survival techniques that I learned as the brutally abused child of an alcoholic father who died when I was seven years old, began to get in the way of my communicating with Mari. My underlying fear of abandonment began emerging and I started trying to "fix" things before they went wrong. Then I would get angry because the "fixing" behaviors that I thought would keep her from leaving me were contrary to what I believed was appropriate.

Mari, on the other hand, had grown up in an atmosphere that did not allow emotional displays, especially anger. While she had taught herself to be openly loving, anger was an emotion she did not understand. When I got angry, she would retreat, hoping she could ignore the problem until it went away. Her withdrawal only confirmed my fears of abandonment. My angry attempts to get through her wall of withdrawal were seen as attacks. In January of 1986 we reluctantly agreed to part.

I sought help and support in Al Anon and Adult Children of Alcoholics groups as well as individual therapy. Four months later we started seeing each other just as "dates." Mari started therapy also at that point. She had quipped to friends that if she ever got involved with me again, she'd need a shrink! It was too soon. My needs and Mari's were in conflict in too many areas as we both were working on old unfinished business.

Several months later in the fall of that year we began tentatively to reach out to each other again. Our efforts to restore the best of our prior relationship and to improve the problem areas led us to a long period of couples counseling that continued for more than a year past our Handfasting. We were starting a totally new relationship that we found exciting and challenging. We were also being very cautious as both of us had experienced feelings of betrayal and pain.

At our Winter Solstice Celebration (Yule) that December Mari took me by surprise by asking me in front of all our circle sisters to join her in trust (tryst). Our months apart had given us each the space to make a number of changes in our behaviors and expectations. We had both missed very much the special energies that assisted us to enhance each other's growth. Our renewed relationship was filled with romance and excitement coupled with the practical experience of learning and using better ways to communicate our needs to each other, and more productive ways to work together.

Now we were taking a new step forward. We were starting to build a home together. By making a public statement of our bond of trust, respect and love, we felt we would invite the assistance of all our friends and family in building a solid and lasting relationship. Many of our friends were incredulous that we had been able to rebuild our relationship when it had seemed completely shattered the year before. It was a long and arduous task, and many acquaintances were inspired by our example.

We decided to have our Handfasting at the Michigan Women's Music Festival, held each year in August. A lot of our dearest friends were regulars with us at "Michigan," and many more agreed to be there at our celebration even though they didn't relish the thought of primitive camping. Friends from all over the country would be able to share our joy and add their own unique energies to the celebration.

Our dear mutual friend Marlene, who first introduced us in 1982 and was instrumental in helping us to re-connect, agreed to stand up for Mari. Mari and Marlene have been friends since 1972. My younger daughter agreed to attend and stand up for me. I felt this was an incredible gesture of love on her part since she had just been married the month before and was a bit uneasy about the conditions we chose for our trysting. It meant a lot to me to have her support.

Mari and I had led Handfastings for friends in the past. This time it was to be our own, and we wanted to include everyone possible in the proceedings. We knew one of our coven sisters (Bonnie Rita, my soul sister and co-founder of Coven Diana Parthenos) would be unable to attend because she was going to graduate school in Europe. The other two initiated members of Diana Parthenos were Anna Divine and Amethyst Crystal Rainbow. We asked them to serve as High Priestesses.

Anna Divine, Bonnie Rita, Mari and I were the driving force behind the formation of Diana Parthenos. Bonnie and I started working on forming a coven during the summer of 1982. Many women visited our rituals and study groups. There were others who shared in our birthing ritual for the coven at Winter Solstice (Yule) that year. The four of us, however, formed the continuing base of women who worked together over the months and years to forge the coven into a living entity. Together we struggled with the issues of how to assemble a ritual format and make it work. We learned how to handle and direct energy by trial and error. The four of us together always made magick. As others joined us in circles, we often found their energies compatible and dynamic. When the magick was not as strong, we experimented until it began to happen. When results were evident, we examined the mixture of people and energies and began to understand why some people and some modalities blend well.

For over a year every ritual was preceded by a full evening of planning together. We also always spent a few minutes before any ritual to let the guests know what we had planned. We would include any ideas, suggestions and ritual items as well as giving guests the opportunity to participate if they wished. Eventually we were working together so smoothly that we often assisted each other without even being consciously aware of how we did it. Needless to say, our bond transcends time and space. When Bonnie Rita moved away, we continued to keep in touch through writing, visits and phone calls.

When Anna's first grandchild was born in another state, we drove together for a "visit," picking up Bonnie Rita on the way, and held an intensely moving welcoming/naming ceremony for the baby. While the baby's father was present during the whole ritual, he never guessed what we were doing. Anna's daughter knew because of her own circle work, and she never questioned our intent or gave a hint of it to her husband. Magick happens when we make it happen. Our protection techniques, "cloaking devices" if you will, have always worked. We often hold rituals in public places (the Michigan Renaissance Festival is one of our favorites — such a convenient cover) and have never had a problem.

Amethyst Crystal Rainbow began circling with us in 1986 and attended a study group that I facilitated for women on the Goddess and Ritual. The hour drive from her home made working with us a major commitment. She continued studying and preparing for her initiation into the coven. Mari and I and Rainbow and her lover were going through many changes, and we grew closer through shared experiences of both trauma and growth.

In the spring of 1987, Rainbow accepted a promotion to a position in another state. She asked if we would consider moving her initiation date from Candlemas to sometime before her early summer move. In this way she could keep a "family" tie with us and leave Michigan as a coven sister. She wanted to keep our connection strong so she would continue developing in the Craft. Her growth was moving swiftly and she was becoming a gifted healer. Diana Parthenos was beginning to weave a net across the country.

Mari and I put together our own ceremony using much of the material that we had used in other handfastings and adding the special touches that held deep meaning for us, including some information channeled from Mari's spirit guide Helm. It is our belief that a public celebration of bonding is an important part of making a relationship work. While marriage is not succeeding very well in the statistics, we have found that handfasting, by its very nature of being non-legal, non-binding and totally voluntary, is a way for couples to build a ceremony that expresses exactly what that couple needs in order to maintain a loving and lasting bond. Every couple we have handfasted is still together.

Since Handfasting is a celebration of a relationship that already exists, it is particularly meaningful to celebrate a Handfasting at an anniversary or a special time of change. Mari and I had just joined households in May. This ritual marked a new period in our life together. It was also the fourth Michigan Festival we were attending together.

At ELF Fest in Lothlorian in May, we both purchased silver crescent moon necklaces with suspended crystals hanging within the moon circle. We agreed that we would wear these till our handfasting and exchange them then so that we would carry the other's energies at all times. Our "Handfastening" would be done by linking our identical silver bracelets. These had been created for us by M'Lou, a gifted artist in the women's community. Each bracelet featured a double women's symbol.

Friends from all over the country, from Oregon and New Mexico to Minnesota and Massachusetts, took part in the ritual. Many special friends had attended our rituals both at the Festival and in our homes for many years. Our audience included all ages from a nursing infant to our beautiful crone circle sister Benita who celebrated her seventieth birthday soon after. Altogether over seventy-five people took part. The variety and uniqueness of each woman's clothing or lack thereof was a special touch to be remembered and treasured.

I have used circle names, first names or nicknames to be able to honor each woman who contributed to our Trysting while retaining a sense of anonymity. In addition to those helping with the ceremony, PJ took photographs and Shirley provided video coverage complete with interviews of participants and those attending. We had handfasted PJ and her lover Jan two years before and we were pleased that we would now be sharing our anniversary with these special friends.

Shirley, an intimate friend since 1983, had often joined us in Goddess study groups and circles. She was actively searching for her own expression of spirituality. As her ultimate cosmic joke, she claimed to be a true believer in the Goddess Atha, protector and Matron of all atheists.

As with any outdoor ritual, the weather was crucial, and this Festival was marked by much rain. We had arranged to hold the ritual at the Meditation Circle, a quiet grove with an altar of a huge piece of old wood with many branching levels for offerings to the Goddess. It had been raining off and on all day, so at the last minute we arranged to use a workshop area that included a tent in case we needed to take cover. Friends ran back and forth to gather items we forgot to bring and leave notes about the change of location. The confusion was a true test of our ability to maintain a loving demeanor under pressure. The biting flies didn't help either.

Shopping carts full of food, clothing and ritual equipment were stored in the tent where Mari and I donned our ritual garb and checked on our bridesmaids while we had the jitters together.

Mari wore multi-colored tie dyed spaghetti strap tee shirt and harem pants with a multi-colored jacket and many necklaces and crystals. She also wore a blue sapphire and pearl circle pin crafted by her jeweler great grandfather. It had been worn at every wedding in her immediate family since 1960. Even my daughter wore it at her wedding the month before.

I was clothed in a loose light blue sun dress with a full-feathered earcuff blending downward from my red hair, tinged with silver by the Goddess (not my hairdresser). My red medicine bag hung around my neck. My older daughter Stardrop had made it for me seven years earlier as a charm to bring love into my life. I also wore a four-inch oval pottery neck-lace of a nude Goddess surrounded by pentacles and a gold pendant of a crescent moon Goddess, a birthday gift from Mari.

Our priestesses were dressed in white wearing the multiple crystal necklaces we had gifted them for leading our ceremony. Anna Devine was dressed in a short chemise, and Amethyst Crystal Rainbow wore a long white gown with the red cord we made for her initiation a couple of months earlier.

Our altar was a bale of hay covered with a white cloth and a silk scarf depicting mythical griffins. A pair of pewter chalices, a handfasting gift from Rainbow, stood ready to use for sharing the cup of wine or sparkling cider near the end of the ritual. My athame and Mari's rose-colored ritual shaker lay in the east, a blue Amazon Earthworks bowl for the cleansing salt water in the west. The salt itself was in a green ginger jar my friend Jeanne had brought from Arizona. A plate of various foods symbolizing roots, stems, leaves, flowers and fruits was ready for another part of the ritual. In the south a fire glowed in the votive candle holder our coven sister Bonnie Rita had given us. We had to include her presence in some way. In the north a candle the color of red earth burned in an old glass and pewter candle holder given to me by our friend Judith, who was not at the festival this year. A lavender lace, dyke-crafted teddy bear named Lucy-Bear from Mari's legendary collection sat in the northeast awaiting this new begin-ning. The center was graced by an ivory candle symbolic of the triple

Goddess with three angels singing and playing instruments to shower our union with music and joy.

The following ritual can be used with slight changes for any couple, lesbian, gay or heterosexual. Some of the format and words are borrowed or adapted from the Handfasting Ceremony in Z. Budapest's *The Holy Book of Women's Mysteries, Part II*. Wherever possible I have given credit to the author of any song or reading when I know who it is. Some of the ritual words and poems were written by me for other rituals. The unique readings, chants and words used can be changed to suit the individual needs of any couple. Following is the way we chose to celebrate our Love in Trust.

Handfasting (Commitment) Ceremony
August 15, 1987
Mari and Caridwyn

Arriving guests are anointed on their third eye with China Musk Oil by Bonnie Benita the Crone and Lamia. China Musk is a favorite scent Mari and I often use for rituals or meditation. We first found it at the Michigan Renaissance Festival. It quickly assists us to enter altered states and is often used by us for self purification.

Guests are seated and given programs by JB, Jan, Corky and others. The program includes a invitation to all guests to remove their shoes if they wish, to form a circle around the markers and to join in the songs and chants where indicated.

The guests were already in various states of comfortable undress typical of the Women's Festival. Some wore only tops, while others wore only skirts or shorts. The invitation to remove shoes is an additional way to move into sacred space by getting in direct touch with the Earth. This was, after all, the weekend of the Harmonic Convergence.

Shishi:
In Wicce we have a ritual to celebrate a relationship which already exists. This ritual is called Handfasting (Handfastening) or Trysting, a word meaning 'meeting,' and also 'trust.' We are here today to join Mari and Caridwyn in bonds of commitment according to ancient rites.

With her long wavy hair flowing over her black gown, Shishi was a friend with whom we had shared many rituals and times of discovery and growth. Three months earlier Mari and Shishi designed, promoted and presented a wonderful weekend workshop of psychic awareness and spiritual growth exercises for women. I shared a bit in the planning though I was in the middle of the hard work of moving into Mari's small two-bedroom apartment from a home I had lived and raised four children in for 18 years. For me this had been a wonderful confirmation of the fact that our lives were not totally dependent on each other. We could work and grow with others and not cling too tightly to each other. No one can fill another person's every need. Our love had space to include others.

Kybele:
Here before the earth and sky, know that this ritual is blessed
by the Goddess of Life and Death and Beauty. This is not a
ritual that binds lovers as in patriarchal marriage, because to
own another person, or to be unequal in a relationship outrages
the Goddess of Love. She flees when reins are put upon her. As
long as love stays, blessings on this relationship stay as well.

Kybele, dressed in camping shorts with many pockets, was a shining example of womanly strength and gentleness combined. A recent friend, she had met our circle sister Shirley the year before at the festival. A few months before our ceremony, Shirley had packed up and moved to New Mexico to join her. Kybele's life was filled with crystal work and herb lore. Her western accent and loving care added another element to our mystic circle.

Margareth reads from The Prophet *by Kahlil Gibran:*
You were born together, and together you shall be forever-
more.
You shall be together when the white wings of death scatter
your days.
Ay, you shall be together even in the silent memory of God-
dess.
But let there be spaces in your togetherness,
And let the winds of the heavens dance between you.

Love one another, but make not a bond of love:

Let it rather be a moving sea between the shores of your souls.
Love gives naught but itself and takes naught but from itself.
Love possesses not nor would it be possessed;
For love is sufficient unto love.
Sing and dance together and be joyous, but let each one of you
     be alone,
Even as the strings of a lute are alone though they quiver with
     the same music.
Give your hearts, but not into each other's keeping.
For only the hand of Life can contain your hearts.
And stand together . . . yet not too near together:
For the pillars of the temple stand apart,
And the oak tree and the cypress grow not in each other's
     shadow.

Margareth, a friend we had not seen for a couple of years, brought her lilting British accent to the circle. When Mari and I began dating, a trip to visit Margareth and her lover was one of the first plans Mari suggested. She was so sure Margareth and I would enjoy knowing each other and becoming friends. It was not easy, however, as we were both strongly opinionated feminist activists. Luckily we also knew how to agree to disagree. Margareth had fought a heartbreaking battle to gain custody of her children in a landmark lesbian custody case, winning only half the battle in court. She rendered lovingly the wise and moving words from *The Prophet*.

Drawing the Circle: *Bonnie Benita the Crone takes the broom and sweeps behind all guests from East to South, West, North and ending in East again, repeating:*

Here I mark our sacred place,
Safe beyond all time and space.

All others whisper "Mark . . . mark . . . mark . . . mark."

With her striking silver-white hair like a crown, Bonnie Benita the Crone was lively in a full skirt and a Goddess pottery necklace as she swept the earth with a decorative broom. Benita is another circle sister with a long history of political activism stretching back to my earliest baby years. Besides being proudly pagan and an outspoken feminist, Benita has spent time in jail to back up her political and environmental concerns. She also has long-standing experience in hammering out consensus in groups striving for equality in action. Once when Mari playfully asked me what I wanted to be when I grew up, I said, "Benita."

Cleansing circle and guests: *Lamia, in her beautiful hand-painted tee shirt and shorts, takes bowl of salt water from altar and starts in East to sprinkle each guest with it, saying:*

From heart and mind remove all fault,
I purify with water and salt.

Others whisper "Purify . . . purify . . . purify . . . purify."

Lamia is a circle sister and another political activist who supports many wholistic health alternatives. She was very encouraging in my efforts to address my co-dependency and addiction issues. Our circle work has always stressed the cooperative nature of ritual and the importance of choices. We always include a non-alcoholic alternative to wine when wine is included in our ceremonies. Lamia went beyond this in supporting my need to be in totally safe, substance-free space while I was working on my issues.

Charging circle and guests: *Shishi uses a feather to gently send patchouli incense at each woman present, saying:*

With fire and air beyond all time,
I charge with energy divine.

Others whisper "Charge . . . charge . . . charge . . . charge."

With the sweet hint of patchouli still mixing with the warm, damp woods scent, the two priestesses began calling the elements by drawing invoking pentacles in each direction.

Invocations of Elemental Powers
East:
Spirit of the whirlwind, living in the whirlwind,
Come down from the whirlwind, join our circle now.

Spirit of whirlwind, join our circle now.

Anna Divine gives Indian wedding cup to Mari and Caridwyn who have been standing in the East, saying:

Share the breath of life.

Mari and I bought the Indian wedding cup in Las Vegas when we were there for the wedding of Mari's daughter in 1983. The pottery wedding cup was white with black designs and symbols. It looks like a vase with two necks and a handle between. It is possible for two people to drink from it at the same time if they are standing closely side by side. To honor the element air, symbol of the east, we chose to change the use of the cup by each gently blowing into one side while the other inhaled from the other side.

South:
Spirit of the fire, living in the fire,
Come out of the fire, join our circle now.
Spirit of fire, join our circle now.

Amethyst Crystal Rainbow says:
Share the warmth of an embrace.

The fire element, identified with the south, represents strong will, determination, passion. A hug seemed very appropriate.

West:
Spirit of the river, living in the river,
Come up from the river, join our circle now.
Spirit of river, join our circle now.

Offering the ritual bowl of salt water, Anna Divine says:
Anoint each other with the water of life.
(Each anoints the other's forehead.)

North:
Spirit of the mountain, living in the mountain,
Come down from the mountain, join our circle now.

Spirit of mountain, join our circle now.

Amethyst Crystal Rainbow gives Mari and Caridwyn the pot of clay, saying:
May you always have the strength of Mother Earth and hold
Her power in respect.
(Each marks the other's forehead with clay.)

To invoke the center the two priestesses stood on opposite sides of the altar to draw the invoking pentacles.

Center:
Spirit of the center, living in the ether,
Ground us on the earth plane, complete our circle now.
Spirit of center, complete our circle now.

We chose to invoke the Goddess energy at the same time the center was addressed. We feel the center, or spirit, is the activating energy which combines the other four elements into the pattern of life.

Anna Divine raises her arms, saying:
Hail Artemis, Diana Parthenos, Moon Goddess, ever changing, ever the same, remind us to honor all women, whether Maiden, Matriarch or Crone. Center and balance our lives, complete our circle now.

Mari and Caridwyn are joined by their witnesses in the East.

Amethyst Crystal Rainbow anoints Mari and Caridwyn saying:
I purify you from all anxiety, I purify your mind from fear (anointing forehead), I bless your hands to do holy work (anointing hands).

Anna Divine smudges Mari and Caridwyn, saying to each:
I charge your eyes to see holy ways, your lips to speak divine words, your breasts formed in strength and beauty, your genitals I bless for strength and pleasure, and your feet to walk a worthy path.

A.C. Rainbow challenges:

Who enters here?

Mari and Caridwyn say together:
I, Mari (I, Caridwyn), enter this circle in perfect love and perfect trust.

All respond:
Welcome to the presence of the Goddess.

A.C. Rainbow: Who is witness for Mari?

Marlene: I, Marlene, am witness for Mari.

A.C. Rainbow: Who is witness for Caridwyn?

Daughter: I am witness for Caridwyn.

All respond:
Welcome to the presence of the Goddess.

Next came a solo by Mary singing "Testimony" (By My Heart) written by Ferron. (Everyone is invited to join in the chorus.*)

There's godlike, and warlike, and strong like only some show
And there's sadlike and madlike and had like we know
* But by my life be I spirit, and by my heart be I woman,
And by my eyes be I open, and by my hands be I whole.

They say slowly brings the least shock, but no matter how slow
    I walk
There are traces, empty spaces and doors and doors of locks
* But by my life be I spirit and by my heart be I woman,
And by my eyes be I open, and by my hands be I whole.

You young ones, you're the next ones, and I hope you choose
    it well
Though you try hard, you may fall prey, to the jaded jewel
* But by your lives be you spirits and by your hearts be you
    women,

And by your eyes be you open, and by your hands be you
   whole.

Listen, there are waters hidden from us, in the maze we find
     them still
We'll take you to them, you take your young ones, may they
     take their own in turn
* And by our lives be we spirit and by our hearts be we women,
And by our eyes be we open, and by our hands be we whole.

Mary's voice rang clear and sweet on the afternoon air. Mary's
reputation as a hostess is legendary. We have spent many happy times with
her and often camped together up north and at Saugatuck. It was at Mary's
Halloween party in 1982 that Mari and I had first expressed our romantic
interest in each other. She had offered her home for us to hold our reception
later that month.

Caridwyn's daughter and Marlene link Mari and Caridwyn's bracelets.

Lamia:
Trysting, or handfasting, or promising ritual is an ancient way
of bonding which we need to reestablish. When precious
metals were too expensive or unavailable, lovers' hands were
bound together and then ritually separated to symbolize one
bonding of two separate individuals.

We approach trysting from a universal point of view. The
bonds called down on the couple are loyalty forever. The
words exchanged are promises to take care of each other in this
life and in the life beyond.

A.C. Rainbow: What bonds do you, Mari, affirm?

Mari: Love and eternal friendship, peace, growth, sorrow and joy.

A.C. Rainbow: What bonds do you, Caridwyn, affirm?

Caridwyn:

184

Love and eternal friendship, the chance to see the dawn together, marvel at a leaf and bless the snow.

Anna Divine, unfastening bracelets:
By this symbolic breaking of the bond your bracelets have formed, may you break away from all fear, and rejoin your lives, united but separate, in beauty, community and peace. Carry this symbol of your love for each other and the Earth, your love for yourselves and the Goddess in us all.

Mari and Caridwyn face altar.
Anna Divine holds plate of foods while A.C. Rainbow says:
I invoke you, Goddess of all life, to witness the joining of these two spirits. I invoke You by the foods here present,

by the roots for a strong foundation for this relationship,
by the stems for standing firm and proud,
by the leaves to grow and prosper together,
by the flowers for joy and laughter,
by the fruits for a long and enduring relationship,

Descend into this circle of Life and bless this tryst.

Mari and Caridwyn feed each other, saying:
May you never hunger.

Mari and Caridwyn offer each other the cup, saying:
May you never thirst.

Anna Divine:
Do you, Caridwyn (Mari), promise to take Mari (Caridwyn) as your friend and lover for this lifetime and beyond, to care and to be loyal to, to love even if you love others as well?

Caridwyn (Mari): I do.
(Repeat for the other.)

Marlene and Caridwyn's daughter unfasten necklaces and trade from one to the other.

Anna Divine:
By the exchanging of these crystal necklaces, charged by your energy, your bond of love and friendship is sealed.

Marlene's lavender, pink and blue East Indian gown set off her petite elfin presence. My daughter, also a tiny woman, wore jeans and a light blue cut-off top. What a change from her wedding the month before where she wore my poi de sois wedding gown from thirty years ago. It had been quite a task to alter my size 12 to her size 3.

Caridwyn's daughter and Marlene hand Caridwyn and Mari each other's crown. Each crowns the other saying "Thou art Goddess."

Mari's crown was a golden chain-linked medieval creation that, like a loose net, covered her golden curls, allowing a stray wisp to sneak out here and there. My crown was a brass circlet with a pentacle rising above my third eye like a tiara. We both acquired them at ELF, the "Elf Lore Family's" nature sanctuary in Indiana.

Jumping the Broom. *Mary and Sue carry broom forward.*

A.C. Rainbow:
Jumping the broom is a symbol of setting up housekeeping together. *Mari and Caridwyn hold hands and jump.*

A.C. Rainbow: I now pronounce you lovers in trust.

All: Blessed be.

We ignored the request to "Do it again for the camera." Everyone was cheering. The intensity was incredible. It had reached a peak. We both felt how special our bond had become.

Pamela:
At this time Mari and Caridwyn would like to share the cup of sparkling juice (passed by JB) or wine (passed by Margareth) with you, their friends. Please wait till the fourth round to join in the chant.

Claudia L'Amoreaux

How many women remember their first menstruations with joy? For most adults the experience was far from positive, and women today want better for their daughters. As we reclaim women's bodies and wombs, menstruation becomes not a curse but a joy. In this light is Claudia L'Amoreaux's article "Welcome to the Circle of Women." She has created a menarche ritual for women looking back at their own first bleeding experiences, and wishing to regain what they lost, and a ritual as well for the new generations of young women coming of age.

Claudia's work grows out of her belief in the healing power of nature and community. She has been active in the Women's Spirituality movement, facilitating groups on dreams, myth and ritual, and rites of passage. Knowing that for women, healing begins with reclaiming the natural rhythms of our bodies, she has created a contemporary menstrual hut that she maintains and makes available to her Santa Cruz women's community. She teaches fertility awareness, believing that knowledge of our own cycles leads to empowerment. She has studied traditional healing practices of many cultures, especially the use of medicinal plants and trance states, as well as the contemporary healing arts of archetypal psychology, Jungian Sandplay, and hypnosis.

She has also been very involved in alternative education, teaching all ages of children in all kinds of settings. Inspired by the educator John Holt's vision of learning, Claudia joined the Growing Without Schooling movement in its earliest days, creating support groups and cooperatives for families wanting to educate their own children. She currently directs The Whole Earth Learning Center, a resource center for children, parents and educators, offering new approaches to holistic education.

Claudia is also an editor and writer. She co-edited *Celebrating Women's Spirituality*, an engagement calendar for 1991 from The Crossing Press, and wrote the rituals for the cross quarters that are included in it. She has been instrumental in the editing and production of *The Goddess Celebrates*. Claudia is writing her own book on empowering children and is producing a video on women and ecology. She writes:

> I relearned ritual sleeping under the moon and stars, hearing the wild boars foraging at night in the oaks, plunging naked into the cold waters of the rock-walled grotto, greeting the dawn, eating grapes ripe on the vine, and living, loving, fighting, dancing with a band of gypsies on the collarbone of Duncan Peak, in northern California.

Claudia was born in the southwest desert, came of age in the Ohio River Valley, and now makes her home in Santa Cruz, California, close to the sea. Contact Claudia at 2-1645 E. Cliff Dr., Santa Cruz, CA 95062.

Welcome to the Circle of Women

Claudia L'Amoreaux

My 11-year-old daughter, Zoe, is making the metamorphosis from girl to woman. I can't look at her body enough, it amazes me so, the long pubic hairs where a few months ago there was golden fuzz, the vital little breasts getting fuller and fuller every day. She is very aware of herself becoming a woman in a way that borders on exaltation at times. The extraordinary changes in the body and mind of this being I know so intimately are opening me to a dimension of myself that I didn't know existed.

Her self-awareness has brought into focus my complete lack of memories of the changes in my own body prior to menarche. And I am awed that this could be — how could I possibly not remember the first strange new hairs sprouting forth? How could I not notice and even measure the magical growth of my breasts? When I first discovered the absence of such memories, I experienced a profound sense of loss of some crucial part of myself. I felt an urgency to restore this part, and not just vicariously through my daughter.

This has led me into what I often refer to as an archeological dig — into my own past and into the puberty rituals of other cultures that might offer valuable insights. I realized that substantial elements of my self identity as a woman were created during this important phase of my life which happened to be in the repressive '50s and early '60s when the Breck girl reigned supreme as a model of the feminine. And I have begun to recognize the wounds to that emerging young woman that still exist and effect me now.

Memories of my first menstruation center on an image of discovering pasty brown stuff in my underwear. Feelings are all negative — revulsion, disgust, embarrassment. These feelings were amplified by the unpleasant location of my discovery in the stuffy, chlorinated air of the basement of my junior high school. It was swim class, the pool was in the basement and I hated swimming. There seemed to be one giant conspiracy to make me feel ugly. We had to wear stretched-out cotton tank suits that looked like hand-me-downs from 1920. Never given time to dry our hair afterwards, we very-self-conscious 12-year-old girls had to pass to our next class looking like what we called "drowned rats." The *one* and only good thing about getting my period was that it was the only valid reason besides illness for being "excused" from swimming. I have no memory of telling my mother or father or even friends about this event. There was no joy and certainly, no experience of joining the circle of women.

Soon after breaking ground on my archeological dig, I was having a bodywork session with a friend who practices Rosenwork massage. Through deep relaxation and following the natural movement of the breath, this form of bodywork facilitates very profound states of consciousness. In the session I had a vision — an extremely vivid vision: *It is night. I am in a circle of women all sitting on the ground. We are lit by shimmering firelight from the fire in the center of our circle. Our bodies are naked and we are all covered with an orange-red paint.*

An Australian aboriginal legend tells how, at the time of creation, the Unthippa women caused blood to flow from their vulvas in such large quantities that it ran into the ground and formed the world's deposits of red ochre.[1] I recognized the orange-red body paint of my vision as ochre — revered by people all over the world for thousands of years as the sacred blood of the Mother Earth. This vision touched me in the center of my being. I felt the lack of such a naturalness of body, and connectedness to the elements at a time in my life when I so much needed it. I knew that I sought a rite of passage that would welcome me into that circle and through the vision I realized I could create that for myself now.

I started to get an idea of the kind of rite of passage I wanted. It was a ceremony that connected me with all my sisters through time and culture, and that honored my female body and the link of this body to the earth. I wanted it to emphasize the interconnectedness of all life forms and I wanted it to help me feel welcome and positive as I crossed over into my new status as adult, and hopeful and empowered to contribute to the well-being of the planet, in cooperation with other women and men in my community. I needed that, I wanted that, and the young woman still alive in me who's uncertain of herself, disconnected from her body, doubtful of her abilities to cooperate and effect change, that young woman especially needed this rite of passage.

As I thought about the ritual, I felt my mother and my grandmothers very much with me, participating in this ceremony that none of us had, through me. I collected pictures of myself and of them at puberty which took me back in time over a span of more than 80 years. We all shared, in varying degrees, this alienation from our bodies and nature.

My mother and I live in different cities. I called her to tune her in to the magic that was brewing, and to invite her to participate by sharing with me the story of her first menstruation which I would speak in our ritual circle. This was a beautiful moment of intimacy between us—I had never heard her story. I know she felt honored to be included in this way, and she said she would join us that evening in spirit.

I shared my "ochre" vision with my women friends. I told them of my desire for a ritual and asked for their help. They answered my request with an abundance of beautiful ideas. At this point the ritual began to take on a life of its own. We decided to sit up together all night under the stars and see the dawn in together. We drew our inspiration for this partly from the Navajo Blessingway ceremonial.

The Blessingway is the central ceremonial of the Navajo. It is performed to bring blessings in all phases of life from birth to old age. A major portion of the ceremonial recounts the adolescence rites performed for Changing Woman, one of the most important Navajo deities. The conclusion of the ceremony for the adolescent girl is called the no-sleep. On the last night of the rite she must remain awake all night and not sleep until the following sunset. She is told, "If you absolutely go without sleep until sunset it will be very well, you will then have gained everything without exception."[2]

We came together on an October night near Halloween. I had found some full-face plastic masks that were half black and half white. To begin, we sat together on the grass under some tall eucalyptus trees and painted our masks, each of us admiring the others.' Dissatisfaction with our own emerged as the common theme. Later in the night the masks would come to life in the glow of the firelight as we traded them around the circle, discovering the power of our own masks on another's face. Our original dissatisfactions and judgments slowly melted into appreciation of our unique styles.

After the mask making we began preparations for a ceremonial meal. Looking back on it, I think this was the heart of our ritual. What happened there was unanticipated, magical and healing. With an ease that startled us, the table was set with flowers and symbols and a feast was prepared in what seemed like no time. As we sat down together we reflected on the power of our cooperation and felt great appreciation for our mothers who labored day after day for years preparing meals for their families, taking care of the household chores, most working outside jobs as well. As we tapped into our mothers and grandmothers, we tapped into womankind. Our meal became an affirmation of the largely unacknowledged work of food preparation and homemaking that still falls for the most part to women all over the world and an honoring of the importance of these elemental acts.

After the meal we made an altar outside on the ground with universal symbols of the feminine and our photographs spread out in a large mandala. We sat around it in a circle. We lit a small fire for warmth in the windy autumn night.

We shared the stories of our coming of age, bringing painful memories out into the open air to breathe beside us and be honored. We shared our mothers' stories and our grandmothers'. We took our shirts off, painted our breasts and faces with red clay gathered by one of the women in the southwest, and danced in the firelight. It is not often today that we as women dance together naked. That alone is a very healing act.

At times during the night we wished that we had inherited a ritual for such an occasion for it is not always so easy to find the words and songs that express our feelings. But we discovered that when we set out with trust and humility, we receive assistance. There is great wisdom inside each of us, and the same first creator of ritual that spoke the words to the chants and gave the instructions for the ceremonies in dreams and visions to the ancient ones is there in *our* dreams and visions guiding us to create the ceremonies and rites of passage that will assist us in our lives today and empower us to create a world of blessings for all beings.

We saw in the dawn together. And we felt ourselves new, and renewed. This experience was tremendously empowering. In my enthusiasm, I recounted this night to other women I knew. They were always very stirred by it and wanted to create similar healing ceremonies for themselves. I was facilitating dream groups at the time and I decided to offer a group called "Rites of Passage — Healing the Feminine." Five of us came together and a depth of healing energy was tapped. I would like to share the form of our circle as an inspiration to other women to come together to create your own rites of passage. May my sharing be a spark to light your fire.

The form of this group is designed to nurture a natural intimacy and appreciation for the uniqueness of each woman and the bond of commonality that unites us. As you meet and share, create a space to speak honestly and openly, revealing yourselves — do not critique each other. Bear witness, hear each other deeply in the telling of your stories. While one is sharing her story, this is the challenge to the others — to be fully present to hear the story, seeing it come to life in your mind's eye. Allow each other to be lost, frightened, weak, courageous, strengthened, self-assured — trusting that the speaking is the healing. The root of the word healing is wholeness. Wholeness embraces the entire range of experience.

I have found the following story of Nelle Morton's from her book, *The Journey Is Home* (Beacon Press, 1985), a powerful source of guidance in group work:

> It was in 1971 that I received a totally new understanding of hearing. It came from the lips of a most ordinary woman in a workshop I was conducting in Illinois . . . . The last day of the workshop, the woman, whose name I do not know, wandered off alone. As we gathered sometime later in small groups she started to talk in a hesitant, almost awkward manner. "I hurt," she began. "I hurt all over." She touched herself in various places before she added, "But I don't know where to begin to cry, I don't know how to cry." Hesitatingly she began to talk. Then she talked more and more. Her story took on fantastic coherence. When she reached a point of the most excruciating pain, no one moved. No one interrupted her. No one rushed to comfort her. No one cut her experience short. We simply sat. We sat in a powerful silence. The women clustered about the weeping one went with her to the deepest part of her life as if something so sacred was taking place they did not withdraw their presence or mar its visibility. Finally the woman, whose name I do not know, finished speaking. Tears flowed from her eyes in all directions. She spoke again: "You heard me. You heard me all the way." Her eyes narrowed then moved around the group again slowly as she said: "I have a strange feeling you heard me before I started. You heard me to my own story. You heard me to my own speech."
>
> I filed this story away as a unique experience. But it happened again and again in other such small groups when we allowed the pain to reach its own depth, or as another woman told me later: "You went down all the way with me. Then you didn't smother me. You gave it space to shape itself. You gave it time to come full circle." It happened to me. Then I knew I had been experiencing something I have never experienced before. A complete reversal of the going logic. The woman was saying, and I had experienced, a depth hearing that takes place before speaking — a hearing that is more than acute listening. A hearing that is a direct transitive verb that evokes speech — new speech that has never been spoken before. The woman who gave me those words had indeed been heard to her own speech.

Choose a symbol — it could be a crystal, a branch from a tree, or a red rock — something meaningful to the group to serve the function of "talking stick." Pass this around the circle and while a woman holds it, she and she alone speaks until she feels complete. Each woman must hold in her awareness a sense of the time she is taking — that it be in balance with the others, neither taking too much time, nor too little. Let the talking stick go all around the circle, one woman at a time sharing her story. Then open the circle for responses to each other's stories. Take care not to give advice, correct or argue but come from your own experience of what the stories made you feel and remember.

In our first gathering we shared the place of our origins with intimate detail, describing the terrain of the land where we were born, feeling what this landscape has contributed to the essence of who we are. We took our time, showing pictures of ourselves as babies, our mothers, our fathers, sisters and brothers, embracing the tender memories and the painful.

The second week we explored who we were as young girls. What were our dreams, our joys, our fears, our pains? What were our most glorious moments? What were the most embarrassing incidents? In reaching back through time and telling the stories, we establish a pathway to that young girl, opening an energy flow that, for many women, has been blocked for years. We regain the original dreams and vital energy. We reclaim our unique strengths and beauty. We restore wholeness.

The third week we revealed our experiences of puberty, each one of us telling the fears, despairs, aloneness, disgust, embarrassment that were common to most of us and seeking out what sustained us, what gave us courage and joy in dark times. We shared pictures of ourselves at puberty (and our mothers and grandmothers if we could find them). Few women knew their mothers' stories prior to the group. Asking our mothers about this central experience of their womanhood became for many of us an opportunity to establish a much deeper, honest flow of communication and opened new levels of understanding between us. I have found it much easier now to talk about sexuality with my mother, especially about her experience of menopause. She has become a valuable resource for me on this other central rite of passage that I am approaching.

We told of our first sexual experiences, including the big taboo of masturbation, and reflected on how these experiences have affected us throughout our lives. This third gathering was the midpoint of our five-week journey together. Our friendship and ease and intuitive knowledge of each other had grown deep since our first circle together.

The fourth week we stated what we desire most for ourselves today, what we want to affirm, celebrate, heal. We clarified what we each wanted in a rite of passage. The ritual began to form. Ceremonial food was a key element. One of us told of a Japanese tradition, "red rice," that is served when a girl has her first period. It is sticky glutenous rice cooked with red aduki beans. Another woman had a red blanket she would bring that we could each wear around us at some point. I told of a part of the Navajo girls' rite of passage called the kinaaldá ceremony. In the ancient myth the young woman runs with Salt Woman. I felt a strong affinity to this part of the Navajo ritual and knew I wanted to run in my rite of passage to feel my body, my strength, my vitality. One woman said she would bring red crepe paper to make belts that would link us. We decided we would each bring a few symbols that were especially significant to us, and music.

We talked briefly about the general structure of the rite and we trusted that we could go with the flow of energy on the night of our ritual, the summer solstice. We left each other with a vow to pay special attention to our dreams during the week between meetings.

The fifth week our ritual poured out of us with a deep intuitive wisdom. We began by linking hands and creating our circle. We passed around a feather and burning cedar to "smudge" ourselves as a cleansing and purification. Each woman shared the symbols she had brought, telling why they were meaningful to her.

Then each of us took our turn as young woman crossing over. For my turn, I lay down on my back on some pillows. A woman was at my head, one at my feet, and one on each side. I remember vividly their nurturing touches, gently massaging me. They verbally praised my beautiful body, telling what they especially loved about me. They placed gifts in my hands and on my heart, forehead, throat, belly — a seashell, a crystal, flowers, a cherry on my pubic bone.

When they sensed I was ready, they helped me up, each woman supporting my weight, and wrapped me in the red blanket. They were praising my beauty, inward and outward, and all said to me, "Welcome to the circle of women." I had tears of joy. I was amazed by the power of this experience. There was something very magical about being wrapped in that red blanket, and being verbally praised and welcomed into the circle of women. The passage was intensely real for each of us, transcending time. We *were* truly our maiden selves crossing over. We discovered the truth of our womanhood in a new way.

Afterwards, we had an extraordinary feast of red foods — a wild mix of watermelon, raspberries, cherries, pomegranate, strawberries and aduki rice. Then we gathered up some blankets and firewood and ran together two blocks to the beach at the end of my street. We made a blazing fire and each of us danced alone for the others our womandance. We wove the red crepe paper around us, binding us as one circle, and then each of us tied off the paper encircling our waists into our own belt to celebrate the sacred bleeding we share. We honored the fullness of summer solstice and the ripening of ourselves. I could feel a deep peace radiating from the young woman in me that affirmed and renewed me to the very core of my being.

My daughter has been the initiator on this journey, raising the challenge. Living with her through this mysterious time has given me the great gift of reclaiming and healing the lost and wounded parts of my young feminine self. It has broadened my journey in search of meaningful ritual. Now, when she is ready to be welcomed into the circle of women and the community of adults, I can appreciate and celebrate her passage to womanhood and my passage to a new phase of mothering from a place of strength in myself, having created and experienced my own unique rite of passage. I have eased the hold of the '50s on me and I feel a new freedom to actively engage the challenge of the '90s. I give thanks.

> Earth's feet, by means of them I shall go through life!
> Its legs, by means of them I shall go through life!
> Its body, by means of it I shall go through life!
> Its mind, by means of it I shall go through life!
> Its voice, by means of it I shall go through life!
> Strands from the top of its head, by means of them I shall go
>   through life!
> Blessing extending from mountains that encircle its
>   surroundings, by means of it I shall go through life!   .
> I shall be long life-happiness, before me it will be blessed,
>   behind me it will be blessed, it has become blessed
>   again, it has become blessed again! . . .[3]
> —From the Prayer of the Eight Words, *Blessingway*

Notes

1. Lyall Watson, *Lighting Bird* (New York: Simon & Schuster, Inc., 1982), p. 202.

2. Leland C. Wyman, *Blessingway* (Tucson, AZ: The University if Arizona Press, 1970), p. 167.

3. Ibid., p. 299.

Jeannine Parvati Baker

Jeannine Parvati Baker is the author of *Prenatal Yoga and Natural Birth* (1974, 1986), *Hygieia: A Woman's Herbal* (1978), and *Conscious Conception: Elemental Journey Through the Labyrinth of Sexuality* (with Frederick Baker, 1986). She is mother to six children, all born naturally — Loi (21), Oceana (16), Cheyenne (16), Gannon (11), Quinn (6), and Halley Sophia (4), and is a speaker, astrologer, midwife, herbalist, and aspiring crone.

With her husband, Jeannine created the Six Directions Foundation, a non-profit educational and charitable corporation for healing sexuality, fertility, birth, family and our earth. They conduct Freestone Innerprizes which includes Hygieia College (a mystery school in womancraft and lay midwifery), Hermetic Astrology Services, JP's Book of the Moon Club, Optimal Family Health Catalog and Joseph General Store, as well as Family Vision Quest Journeys into southern Utah. They seasonally tour as the Alchemical Bakery Word Medicine Show and homeschool their children.

Most women know Jeannine first as a midwife and healer. She combines the ancient priestess skills of midwifery and women's herbalism with modern holistic knowledge and uses ritual with psychology in her work. In everything she does her respect for women, women's bodies, children, babies, and the birthing process shows through strongly and clearly in a society where patriarchy has taken these things away from their guardians, women. She combines the ancient and the new to aid, comfort and heal women and their babies for today's wholeness in a fragmented world.

Says Jeannine Parvati Baker about women's birth rituals and the Navajo Blessingway:

Ritual has the ability to tap into the roots of one's soul and access the multiple levels of reality involved in pregnancy and birth. The Blessingway Ceremony has stood the test of time in helping actualize the visions and dreams of the family and community for the upcoming birth.

In "Rituals for Birth" she describes the dream council and Blessingway traditions, ancient tools for women in modern childbearing. In "Healing Cesarean Section Trauma: A Transformational Ritual," she offers healing for the too many women who have experienced birth through the traumas of the medical system, their womanright of natural childbirth taken from them necessarily or not.

Contact Jeannine Parvati Baker at: Hygieia College, PO Box 398, Dept. GC, Monroe, UT 84754.

Rituals for Birth

Jeannine Parvati Baker

From the heart of Earth, by means of yellow pollen
blessing is extended.
blessing is extended.
On top of a pollen floor may I there in blessing give birth! . . .

With long life-happiness surrounding me
may I in blessing give birth!
May I quickly give birth!
In blessing may I arise again, in blessing may I recover,
as one who is long life-happiness may I live on!
        —Navajo chant from the Blessingway Ceremony

The Blessingway Ceremony held before childbirth is as old as the Navajo people. In its myths and chants it chronicles the birth and puberty of Changing Woman and the birth of her twin sons. As one of the only rituals centered on the *feminine* rights of passage, this ceremony has been a major source of inspiration to midwives and birthing mothers in creating new birthing rituals. Giving credit to their source of inspiration, these contemporary rituals have come to be called blessingways by the women creating them. I first became acquainted with blessingways while practicing midwifery in Santa Cruz, California, through Raven Lang.[1] Immediately I began to hold these ceremonies in my own practice and found it to be a remarkable "prenatal ritual." This was 11 years ago. The Blessingway Ceremony radically changed my way of assisting the full empowerment of the woman-with-child and how I helped parents give spontaneous birth. It provided me with the first public demonstration of shamanic midwifery. It clarified my role in birth as ally, rather than savior, priestess, or doctor. Through birth rituals, I became more aware of how to empower a woman to birth her own baby. Ritual has the ability to tap into the roots of one's soul and access the multiple levels of reality involved in pregnancy and birth. The Blessingway Ceremony has stood the test of time in helping actualize the visions and dreams of the family and community for the upcoming birth.

The Blessingway is a very positive ritual, affirming that the woman will have a natural and beautiful birth experience. The experience of pregnancy and anticipation of childbirth often constellates very primal fears. In my years as midwife, I have found it important to address these fears — the shadow side with its frightening monsters. With my background in archetypal psychology, I've found dreamwork to be one of the best prenatal rituals possible. I assist mothers-to-be through prenatal dream council to clear the road for birth by acknowledging the monsters within and without who might impede a spontaneous birth. Similar to Tibetan Buddhism, where the hungry ghosts are embraced, rather than ignored or forced away, the dream council incorporates the negative psychological forces and spirits into the process of birth preparation. Rather than repression, which doesn't work in birth, in dream council, I encourage acceptance of the dark side. With the earth being round, whatever we try to push away comes back round (through the back door) in the process of giving birth. It is optimal to look at our fears, accept them and transform them into power (the shamanic way). It is so very easy to observe in birth that what one resists, one co-creates. Dream council can help change resistance into acceptance, even of one's most catastrophic fantasy and fear.

Death is perhaps the greatest fear. Any childbirth education which avoids the possibility of death is incomplete and impedes the full shamanic power inherent in giving birth. Birth and death are the flip sides of the same coin. Both rites of passage, birth and death, are affected by culture and its mythology. When we accept the possibility of death-in-birth, we may open up to the mythic dimension of our culture which gives us the bigger picture. This mythic perspective allows for self-transcendence and a spiritual experience in childbirth.

Listening to the dreamworld puts us in touch with more subtle experiences, imaginal realms, and the soul-making power of birth. If we are only focused on birth being an athletic event, a mere (though all consuming) physical process, we miss the opportunity to unify our mind/body/spirit and therefore we unconsciously scatter our energies. The dream council gives us practice in focusing our feelings, images, and responses to intensity in a unified consciousness. Within the dream, fears might surface about giving birth and through being attuned to this, much healing encouragement is revealed. I've found pregnant women to experience tremendous trust (prerequisite for surrender) as the dreams drew out a natural knowing of birth, once the road had been cleared of the inner monsters.

Having met the demons, a woman is ready to affirm her inherent ability to birth her child. The Blessingway Ceremony initiates one into the Feminine Mysteries, through which we begin our identification with the Goddesses. We are touched by Changing Woman, who midwifes our passage from maiden to mother. In Blessingways, we learn to give birth to ourselves — that is, we deliver ourselves from the patriarchal notion of women being helpless victims of our biology into being fully expressive of our unique forms of sexuality, such as giving spontaneous birth. Childbirth can become an act of worship, of sacred sexual expression, given not only to the family and community but to our Goddess as well.

The Blessingway ritualizes the community's support of the pregnant family. It gives the mother practice in accepting the focus of the tribe and the intensity of that. The mother learns to graciously accept gifts for her baby, as she will accept the birthforce (as labor pains — each one bringing her the gift of her baby earthside). She is honored for being the one to bring forth new life to the tribe. By being in the sacred circle of Blessingway, the mother realizes she is *one* with the great round of being. According to where one sits on the medicine wheel, the circle of life, a specific role is to be played. For the mother, her role is that of co-creatrix. The dream council has prepared her with the imaginal tools, the inward skills, to play this role magnificently. The Blessingway Ceremony seals upon her the supportive trust of her people in the task ahead. She is empowered to do what is best-for-life.

To perform a Blessingway Ceremony; first decide if it is to be with women only (and girls — infants of either gender are fine) or for families, including the fathers, brothers, etc. We hold Blessingways of both kinds and find a special healing in each.

For families, we deepen the bonding of the men to babies, and to their lovers as mothers, thereby securing more equal parenting of the baby. To bring about a healing on this earth, the masculine energies must be gentled. Birth does that to men. Therefore preparing the father to receive his child makes him a more conscious birth partner and more likely to be softened, more in awe of life. So Blessingway helps to bring about a more balanced world and a true partnership society, by bringing men into the ecstasies of birth and fulfillment of infant and child care.

The description of Blessingway Ceremony will be for women only. If you are planning a Blessingway for families, just include the father alongside the mother with his father (or the husband of the midwife) grooming and washing the father of the new one. Side by side, in the north, mother and father.

To begin; call a meeting and instruct your guests to prepare themselves ceremoniously. As in preparing for sexual encounters, the more foreplay, the better! (Thanks to Nan Koehler[2] for this simile.) Ask your guests to bathe and wear ceremonial clothing, also to bring a gift for the mother/baby. This gift can be a song, a dance, a poem — as well as the more standard baby shower items. If desired, ask for a pot-luck dish for the feast following the Blessingway.

The ceremonial site can be wherever the mother feels fullness of joy and empowered. Often it is held on the site where birth is planned to occur. Equally as often, the ceremony is conducted in a favorite wilderness place (or at least outside). Wherever, great care is shown when preparing the site.

A circle is defined (with cornmeal, or stones, etc.). An altar is created with the special articles from the mother's medicine bottle. The mother ideally sets up her own altar (mesa, shrine, puja table). Sometimes the midwife will do this for her. Statues or drawings of the Goddesses who claim her are placed on the mesa. A symbol for each element to be included is placed in the four directions with the fifth for ether in the middle. For example, for the earth element, a crystal — for water, a bowl of water or seashell — for fire, a candle — for air, incense or feather — for ether, a conch shell or mandala.

The altar can be open for others to place their power objects upon too. Medicine bags, rings, eyeglasses, watches, etc. (everyone has something) can be added to the altar. In my own practice, toddlers participate, and so the altar would need to be sturdy or elevated.

One gift I always bring and place on the altar is my birthing beads. This idea came from an African tribe. The midwife would carry the birthing beads to each delivery for the mother to hold. After the mother gave birth, she would add another bead to it. I began this ritual in 1978 and the beads tell the story of many women I've attended bedside as midwife. I give the beads to the mother-to-be at the Blessingway and she holds them during childbirth, adds a bead, and eventually returns it to my medicine basket. It is one of my most powerful allies in midwifery as it carries the courage and testimony of women who have beautifully made the passage. In a long labor, I've been known to tell some birth stories as the mother fingered the beads, like a rosary or mala, with sacred respect. Six of the beads represent my own birthings. In other words, I walk my talk and have birthed naturally six babies, the last three with my husband and I being midwife, and two of those underwater. The beads are from the ecstatic births of Loi Caitlin, Oceana Violet, Cheyenne Coral, Gannon Hamilton, Quinn Ambriel and Halley Sophia Baker.

Within reach of where the mother sits, place a ball of natural fiber yarn, a special comb or brush, a towel, a bowl of very warm water (covered) and cornmeal. Herbs and flowers which have fallen to the ground naturally can be placed in the bowl of water. Do not pluck the plants, as the energy in the Blessingway must be consistent with the image of pure, spontaneous birth (e.g., without forceps or being "plucked"). With the same attention to symbolic detail, soil from a riverbed where the stream runs smooth and uncrooked, is raked in the direction of the waterflow and brought to the Blessingway, to be placed next to the cornmeal. The cornmeal may be ground ceremonially beforehand (or sometimes during the singing).

Each guest is smudged (i.e., incense burning in an abalone shell is brushed around the body with a feather — cedar branches and/or lavender make ideal incense) before sitting around the medicine wheel. The mother is also smudged entering, sitting upon the honored "throne" of pillows, usually in the direction of the north. The place where the mother sits traditionally is a pile of corn seeds so that she is slightly higher than the rest of the circle, exalted if you will. Her midwife sits next to her, or in the direction of the west.

If the mother is to be her own midwife, she begins the ceremony by explaining the program. Otherwise, the midwife begins by speaking. "The ceremony goes as follows; first prayer, then song, next ritual grooming and washing, then gift-giving and lastly more song and prayer." An optional feast may follow. The Blessingway is set as close to the expected due date as possible (and full moons are classically the time). If the mother feels like labor has begun or is imminent, she may want to forgo the feasting.

The prayer is offered as an expression of gratitude. The whole group merges their mindful attention on the word medicine of prayer. Special thanks is given to Changing Woman (Creatix, Heavenly Mother, or Whomever is on call that night, etc.) for the blessing of being a woman, a mother. The ancient ones, the Grandmothers are invited to share a moment in time with their daughters in sacred circle so that all which passes is done in love. Let the will of our Divine Mother be manifest in Blessingway.

Favorite circle songs are then shared, gently building up in strength, like early labor so often does. The entire Blessingway Ceremony is a template for childbirth. The beginning rituals are like nesting and early labor. The grooming and washing like active labor. The gift giving like giving birth and the closing songs/prayer, delivery of the placenta and post-partum. A shamanic midwife learns how to read a Blessingway diagnostically and mythically, sharing what she saw with the pregnant woman in order to clear the road better for birth.

Possible suggestions for songs are —

We are opening up in sweet surrender
to the luminous love light of love (repeat)
We are opening, we are opening (repeat)[3]

(Or substitute the word "love" with "Source" or "Goddess," or replace "love" with "my birth" or "childbirth.")

Sing —

I am an open bamboo
open up and let the light shine through (repeat)[4]
(Or substitute the words "Babe" for light and "come" for shine.)

And sing some more;

From a woman we are born into this circle
From a woman we are born into this world (repeat)[5]

After singing, the ball of yarn is brought out. A few words about Spider Woman weaving the world can be shared as each woman present in the circle takes the ball of yarn, in turn, and wraps a bit of it around her wrist. When all the women are bound together by the circle of yarn, a few words about being *one*, sisters and united through the *One Mother* can be told. Then each breaks off the yarn and wraps the dangling pieces around her wristband. Though it appears *as if* each are now separate, we still are all cut from the same ball of yarn. Each woman wears the yarn bracelet as a reminder of the Blessingway until the mother gives birth. Then, tradition has it, the yarn is burned.

Ritual grooming precedes the washing. The hairstyle of the mother to give birth is changed. Navajo women wear their hair in butterfly whorls, or down. When a woman is to become a mother, she ties her hair up in a chignon. Anglos just change their hairstyle. If she is wearing her hair tied up, down it comes to symbolize the change of mind needed to be with the young, more free flowing. If she has her hair down, it is brushed and tied up on her head to symbolize the change in her mind from carefree maiden to responsible mother. Traditionally, it is the mother of the pregnant woman who combs her hair but the closest sister will do.

Then comes ritual washing of the feet by the midwife. If the woman is her own midwife, the woman who will act as her doula (i.e. helper for post-partum care) does the washing. The midwife is humble and awake to her proper position at birth: at the feet of the numinous mother.

Cornmeal is rubbed onto her feet to dry them. Then a towel is used to brush off the caked cornmeal and shine up her feet. This is a purifying practice which, through reflexology, clears the road for birth. The most precious substance of the culture is used, the body-offering of the Corn Mother herself. This demonstrates what a privilege it is to give birth for the people.

After the grooming and washing, gifts are given. Like birthforce waves, they usually come slowly at first and build up momentum gradually. Then the rush of gifts at the end (when folks realize they might be the last to present their gift if they don't hurry up). How attentive and gracious a mother while receiving these gifts is indicative of how open she will be to the movements of labor and delivery. A shamanic midwife keeps breathing in an open manner and observes how the mother breathes throughout the ceremony. Adjustments/suggestions on how to greet "gifts" can be shared after the ceremony (or during, through body-language and mental affirmations). When I present my gift, the birthing beads and whatever else, I follow closely, paying particular attention to how my body feels, where my breath is, as I give my gift. This I will also share with the mother later.

After the gifts, more song. Great closure comes from singing —

Humble yourself inside of your Mother
You've got to know what she knows so (repeat)
And we will lift each other up,
higher and higher
And we will lift each other up.[6]

And sing —

The earth the water the fire the air
returns, returns returns, returns (repeat)
Ay yay ay yay ay yay ay yay ay
yo ay yo ay yo ay yo (repeat)[7]

Lastly sing —

I am a circle, you are healing me
Unite us, be as one,
Unite us, be as one.[8]

Finally, the closing prayer. Again, first and foremost is gratitude for
the Blessingway Ceremony itself and all the participants, seen and unseen,
who have graced the circle with their presence. Gratitude for the Creatrix
who has entrusted this tribe with a new one. Thanks is given for whatever
may come in birth and beyond and affirmations of trust and surrender are
given unto the Mystery. The circle is now complete, and open to celebrate
LIFE.

Before the guests begin to feast or celebrate and leave, pass around a
sign-up list for after birthing care. Everyone present at the ceremony can
help out post-partum by doing housework, cooking, laundry, errands and
baby-sitting older siblings if needed. To magnify the joy of Blessingway or
any ritual, the give-away follows. For the mother, her give-away is childbirth and sharing the vision which might come at birth. For her community,
it is serving the mother and baby when most needed, early postpartum.

Birth is a woman's spiritual vision quest. When this idea is ritualized
beforehand, the deeper meanings of childbirth can more readily be ac-
cessed. Birth is also beyond any one woman's personal desires and will,
binding her in the community of all women. Like the birthing beads, her
experience is one more bead on a very long strand connecting all mothers.
Rituals for birth hone these birthing beads, bringing the light to each facet
of the journey of birth. Let us share these rituals so that the necklace of our
births will be added upon and our gift of life will shine about the breasts of
Changing Woman. May they adorn Her in beauty all ways. Blessed be.

Before me may it be blessed,
Behind me may it be blessed,

Below me may it be blessed.
Above me may it be blessed,
In all my surroundings may it be blessed,
May my speech be blessed!
It has become blessed again,
It has become blessed again,
It has become blessed again,
It has become blessed again!
   —from the Navajo Blessingway Ceremony

Notes

1. Personal communication with Raven at the Lama Foundation wherein we were both speakers at "Birth & Rebirth: A Spiritual Childbirth Conference" for midwives and others who care about birth, Taos, New Mexico, 1979.

2. From Nan's "Blessingway Ceremony" article, unpublished, 1987.

3. Opening song for Blessingway, "We are opening up in sweet surrender," *Songs of the Earth,* Anna Kealoha, p. 133.

4. Opening song for Blessingway, "I am an open bamboo — open up and let the light come through." Ibid., p. 133.

5. Opening song for Blessingway, "From a woman we are born into this circle — from a woman we are born into this world." Neoteric.

6. Closing song for Blessingway, "Humble yourself inside of your mother — You've got to know what she knows." Ibid., p. 128.

7. Closing song for Blessingway, "The earth, the water, the fire, the air — returns, returns, returns, returns." Ibid., p. 118.

8. Closing song for Blessingway, "I am a circle, you are healing me — Unite us, be as one." Ibid., p. 129.

Healing Cesarean Section Trauma: A Transformational Ritual

Jeannine Parvati Baker

Birth is life's oldest ritual. Our society has lost much of the prenatal and post-partum supportive, preparatory and completion rituals for natural birth. Instead we've replaced them with medico-rituals which make natural birth much harder to experience. And so it is to ritual that we turn to heal the trauma of surgical childbirth.

Delivery of babies by Cesarean section surgery needs healing of the whole being, both mother and baby, sometime in the post-partum period. Ideally, the sooner a mother is willing to feel the pain of her loss and insult upon her body, mind and soul, the better. However, we can't push the river. When a mother is able to, she will experience her grief. Then it is appropriate to offer her the following ritual to assist in deeper healing and forgiving. C-sec can be revisioned to be an initiation into soul-making but first, the release of the pain, the healing — and then empowerment.

Cesarean section is a major psychological event of our times for mothers and one which will continue to affect those involved for a long time. Better to integrate the experience and find the personal meaning, the purpose if you will, for the surgery. The assumption is that all things serve on this earth from the psycho-spiritual perspective. There is tremendous potential for deepening one's understanding of the meaning of life when the road of denial and pain has been cleared. As the Chinese say, "The bigger the front, the bigger the back." The more trauma involved, the greater opportunity for transformational healing.

Preparing the ceremonial space: How the mother and baby enter the ritual space is extremely important. This is the central metaphor to be healed — leaving a space and entering new ground. The new ground is where the ritual takes place. It is prepared by cleaning and smudging the room — or circle of ground outside — where the healing ceremony will be held. Flowers, plants, crystals, rocks, cornmeal, etc. may be used to define a womb-like space just big enough for mother and newborn to sit in. Also include something to symbolize the placenta (a large, pancake-shaped rock or a lumpy pillow, etc.) and two cords (or three if you had twins!! Woven belts make good cords.) Choose something to symbolize your mate (marriage bundle, wedding memento, or something from the person of whomever you will share the birth). Also in this circle she places her own personal medicine bundle, power objects, etc., and one offering which she will either bury or burn. Possible suggestions for an offering are: a crystal (if she's chosen to bury it) or a poem or statement of what she's willing to let go of now if she's chosen to burn her offering. Finally a jar of earth (if the ceremony is to be held indoors) can be set in the sacred circle. First create this space before the actual entrance into the circle for ritual.

The mother next prepares herself by bathing and anointing her belly with special oil. She wears her ceremonial dress from pregnancy (or at least her favorite pregnancy dress). She puts her hair up. (If she has too short hair to put up, then wear a barrette or comb or ribbon.) The baby is prepared in the same way, except if it is warm enough, have the baby be naked.

Now she is ready to begin. Mother and baby stand outside the circle and pray. First by citing all the things she is grateful for, then praying for guidance — that this ritual will be for healing and all that passes will be pleasing unto her God-Us (Spirit). Then she carries the baby and steps into the circle, witness to her movement, thoughts and feelings. This is a particularly portentous moment. *How* she enters her sacred circle will reveal how to heal the trauma of Cesarean.

Begin with centering and grounding rituals and any opening prayers, mudras, poses or practices which are already familiar. If the mother hasn't experienced ritual before, here is a suggested format:

Sing —
She been waiting, waiting
she's been waiting so long
she's been waiting, waiting
for Her children to remember
to return. . . .[1]

Sing —
Where we sit is holy
holy is the ground
forest mountain river
listen to this sound
Great Spirit circling

all around us. . . .[2]

And Sing Some More —
Holy Spirit you are welcomed
in this place, Holy Spirit
you are welcomed in this place
Come upon us every one
Thy perfect will be done
Holy Spirit you are welcomed
in this place. . . .[3]

After singing, the mother prays for what she wants, clearly, humbly and with affirmations of surrender to those forces much bigger than the desires of this person. Express gratitude again for being a mother, trusted to care for Goddess' baby(s) and pray to be worthy of this trust. Express love for the child in words and action. The baby may be still on her lap or may have crawled away by now so that there is a semi-permeable membrane around the sacred circle which lets babies in and out without altering the focus of the ceremony. It is fine for little ones to move about while the mother remains planted on her new ground.

Next, give an offering to the four directions and mother earth. If the ceremony is outside, this is more powerful. Take some soil in hand during this offering to the mother earth and rub it on the mother's belly and the baby's belly (if accessible). Indoors, the small jar of earth is now used. While offering to the earth, focus on the scar from surgery. Visualize both the scar on mother's belly and the mother earth as healed — no personal wound, no collective pollution. Lastly, give an offering to the Great Spirit, the Goddess, Heavenly Parents (or whomever or whatever the mother calls the Mystery). Light some incense, a candle (something of the fire element) to represent spirit. Let the flame and smoke carry the prayers heavenward.

The mother takes the placenta and ties the cord between it and her belly. If the baby is lying still, or within range of the circle, another cord is tied between the baby and the placenta.

She next listens to the mother's heart. A drumbeat helps, but, without the sound of the drum, focusing on one's own heartbeat as a pulse, a rhythm, is sufficient.

Deeper into the inner sounds and rhythms the mother goes as she meditates on her experience of giving birth. The mother visualizes the labor and those choices which lead her to being sectioned. Not only her choices, but all her attendants' influences. One by one, she visualizes these decisions and forgives herself and any others involved in them. The mother focuses on the image of each birth attendant with compassion and under-standing. To complete this part, the mother visualizes herself being cut open, delivered and sewn back up. She expresses any feelings she has, and forgives all, including herself. Now she takes her hair down. (Or takes out the ribbon, or barrette.) Then the mother takes her offering to be buried and does so, or, if it is to be burned, throws it into the fire (woodstove, abalone shell, or ash tray, etc.).

Place the placenta symbol on the mother's belly. Breathe deeply down to the rock or pillow. Visualize the intactness, integrity and strength of the womb and abdomen. Image a gold glow all around the incision scar. The wound reveals the cure. Invite a message from the old scar and listen for the word medicine which comes. Ponder these things in the mother's heart.

Now the mother takes her baby in her arms and begins the closure. She may sing her own heart song or any other which truly moves her toward love. Possible suggestions here are:

Listen listen listen to my heart song
listen listen listen to my heart song
I will never forget you
I will never forsake you
I will never forget you
I will never forsake you.[4]

And Sing —
Help us on our way, God-Us
help us on our way
help us on our way, God-Us
help us on our way
we're healing, we're healing
we're healing.[5]

And Sing Some More —
We are sisters on a journey
shining in the sun
remembering the ancient ones
the women and the children

the women and the children.[6]

Then comes the closing prayer. Include acknowledgement to one's personal expression of Spirit and speak gratefully to that force bigger than each of us for the healing ceremony. Gratitude for the mother's own birthmother is appropriate here — and all the foremothers which made her possible. Connecting imaginally with one's heritage of birthmothers is empowering.

Hopes for future purebirths may be shared aloud. And that which was learned in this Cesarean will benefit subsequent deliveries. Stating precisely just what was gained from surgical childbirth continues the healing process. Remember, all things on earth serve.

Lastly, close the prayer by asking for the healing of our mother earth, that she will no longer be cut, poisoned, raped and her children torn from her body. (Cut — agribusiness, mining and deforestation; poisoned — chemicals, nuclear radiation and drug abuse; raped — treated like an inert, unfeeling being by men; tearing children from her body — extinction of animal and plant life and the senseless violence humans perpetuate upon one another. These are symbolized in C-sec; the scalpel, the anesthesia, the abduction of the baby, and the severance of natural birth bonding.) The mother commits herself and her children to being change agents for evolution and vows to align her personal desires with the collective will of nature. She knows better than anyone else, how our mother earth must feel and dedicates her family to making their earthwalk a gentle one.

Blessed Be, Amen and Ho!! It is done.

Mother and baby then leave the sacred circle, again watching closely for how one experiences leaving the holy place. Outside of the circle, the mother unties the cords between herself, baby(s), and placenta. The placenta is then buried (if a rock). If it is a pillow, this is now used for ceremonies only from that time on.

Ceremonial feasting may follow, or at least, a warm drink to represent the first feeding. Focus on the nourishment which comes so gracefully from the mother with joy and thanksgiving.

Birth is life's central mystery. No one can predict how a birth may manifest. Birth belongs to a people, not an individual person and reflects the morphogenetic field (the invisible connections each human has with others of our species). Our dominant culture is anything but "natural" so it is no surprise that childbirth, even with the most natural lifestyle lived by an individual family, sometimes needs intervention and medical assistance. This is not to say that any one mother's efforts to have a natural childbirth are futile. Just that birth is bigger than one's personal desires.

Healing the trauma of Cesarean will facilitate deeper bonding to the baby, cleanse the old wounds, and provide the new ground from which to transform a horrific experience into one of great power. Wherever there is fear, there is power. On a tissue level, old unexpressed pain constricts physiologic processes, such as childbirth. It is very natural to fear giving birth again after a Cesarean. This inhibits the fullness of joy in sex, especially seminal intercourse. If one is afraid of the trauma of childbirth, there is an avoidance of the act which brings about pregnancy. So this ritual has the excellent side-effect of also bringing more ecstasy into sexuality.

This ceremony is also invaluable preparation for a V-BAC (vaginal birth after Cesarean) for it "feeds the hungry ghosts" which clamor for attention in subsequent births. It is will known amongst midwives that the birth(s) after a Cesarean constellate the surgery — and the laboring mother must psychologically give vaginal birth to the surgically removed baby before she can deliver her present baby spontaneously. This ceremony clears the road for purebirth (natural birth without assistance). Whatever dynamic which was involved in impeding the previous birth is still present until it is understood — and forgiven. The most effective tool to use during this healing process is prayer. For example, if a mother was sectioned at seven centimeters of cervical dilation because she was "stuck" or the baby was distressed or whatever, during her next labor, when she is seven centimeters, a prayer circle would be indicated if needed.

Share this ritual with all of our sisters who have been abused and/or rescued from the surgical knife. This ritual can be done privately — or for the community with extended family and friends sitting around the sacred circle to pray and sing along with the mother. However, if there are others present, it is extremely important that the mother perform all the actions of the ritual and is not a passive recipient of the healing process. She will be strengthened by the knowledge that she is the prime mover in healing herself — and that nobody else can do it for her. Having been sectioned, a woman retains an imprint of being rescued. As birth is an expression of all our lives, each moment a mother can be aware of being co-creatrix rather than victim of her experiences, is "preparation" for V-BAC. This ritual therefore is most healing when initiated, practiced, and completed by the mother herself, rather than it being done for or to her. This doesn't negate the need for community but refocuses responsibility where it can best bring about purebirth.

We can change the morphogenetic field and transform our culture into one which reverences the original ground of our being, mother's womb and then, by extension, we can heal our earth by healing birth. And where do we begin? Right where we are. Healing one mother is healing our earth.

1/1990 Utah

Notes

1. Anna Kealoha, *Songs of the Earth,* p. 160.
2. Ibid., p. 179.
3. Traditional Christian Church Hymn
4. Parmahansa Yogananda
5. Neoteric
6. Anna Kealoha, *Songs of the Earth,* p. 172.

Every effort was made to acknowledge the songwriters. If we have overlooked any credit, please inform us so that we can rectify the omission.

Uzuri Amini

I met Uzuri Amini at A Woman's Place Bookstore in Oakland, California. Before five minutes had passed, she had done an impromptu psychic reading for me, and I a small healing for her. There was an instant recognition between us of sisters, healers and women traveling a like-minded path. She is a deeply gentle and deeply powerful woman.

Uzuri Amini is a writer, spiritual counselor, artist, and performer. She was a facilitator at Her Voice, Our Voices: A Women's Summer Solstice Camp in 1985 and 1986. Her Flowers of the Goddess, clay originals, are featured in her article, "Eye of the Vulture" (with Luisah Teish) in Issue 8 of *Woman of Power* magazine (Winter, 1988). They are vulva images, helping Uzuri to "fulfill my role as Oshun's daughter by combining a project of art and sexuality."[1]

Committed to healing childhood sexual abuse in herself and other women, Uzuri is the developer and facilitator of "Healing From the Root," workshops for women survivors. She travels and presents the "Moon-daughters Healing Hut" workshop with Luisah Teish. Uzuri regularly speaks at conferences about her healing experiences as a survivor of childhood sexual abuse and presents workshops for women-of-color survivors. She is the mother of a son and daughter, and has three grandsons. Uzuri is currently working on a manuscript about her spiritual journey three years ago to Southeast Asia and New Zealand.

In "A Path of Change: Healing from Childhood Sexual Abuse," Uzuri Amini describes how "psychodrama and metaphysics" helped her to overcome the impact of childhood sexual abuse on her life. She describes in meditations and ritual, ways to heal the child within, to release memories that hold back growth and wholeness from women who were traumatized as children. Childhood sexual abuse recovery is a major concern of the women's and Women's Spirituality movements today, as women come to grips with early devastating pain, learn to overcome it and move forward, and learn to affirm and validate their lives.

Uzuri Amini is a priestess of Ochun, the Yoruba Goddess of love, healing and art. She was initiated by the Ochun Society in Oshogbo, Nigeria, at the directive of the King Ataoja in the Spring of 1989. She is nurtured and advised by Luisah Teish, author of *Jambalaya*. Together they have taught workshops and conducted rituals across the United States. Says Uzuri:

> You will find a short prayer to Elleggua at the beginning and end of the chapter. Within our tradition all things begin and end with Elleggua. In writing the chapter I attempted to give information about the tradition, but also to keep it as loose as possible for women to adapt it to their own needs.

I am very pleased to present in this book rituals derived from this tradition, and rituals healing women from childhood sexual abuse.

A Path of Change:
Healing from Childhood Sexual Abuse

Uzuri Amini

Elleggua, Destiny Messenger, Crossroad Guardian, Opener of all Doors, open the door to manifest the cleansing change, righteous release and personal peace for each spirit seeker who reads this work. Aché.

I am a survivor of childhood sexual abuse. With many women I share indelible memories that were kept secret as I persevered through years filled with guilt, shame and remorse about the sexual abuse I experienced. The continual mental, emotional and psychic pain I endured diminished my self-esteem as I fought my way through early motherhood, marriage, divorce and single parenthood.

As I lived my life I found my childhood experiences impacting my personal relationships, the parenting of my children, my work and my intimate love life. At some time in my life almost daily an encounter or interaction would trigger a memory or feeling tied to my childhood sexual abuse experiences. Those experiences created a personal hell I lived in my waking and sleeping hours.

I sought remedies in transactional analysis groups, one-to-one counseling and self therapy. Each process proved to be only a piece of my healing puzzle, leaving me a constant seeker of the magic formula that would lessen the depth of my inner pain.

My search continued until I found both psychodrama and metaphysics. I was lucky enough to learn and utilize both healing systems to effect changes in my life and ignite my personal healing process. As I worked on healing myself, metaphysics and ritual took on important roles in cleansing myself of old hurts, negative inner programming and self-alienation.

As I grew stronger I opened more to my spiritual self. My healing progressed further and further along until I felt ready to share and work with other women survivors.

Over the past three years my spiritual self has Divinely been led into the Yoruba tradition. This tradition is an earth-centered religious system from Africa with its roots in universal forces. It teaches a discipline of ancestor reverence and kinship between humans, plants, earth and animals as a central part of everyday life. Here I have found ancient healing knowledge that I integrate with the spiritual systems of the women I counsel to effect healing.

Childhood sexual abuse is a worldwide problem of great magnitude, with spiritual implications for the survivor and society, which is worthy of our diligent attention. The information I share with you is gleaned from my own healing experiences and the experiences of various survivors with whom I've worked. In future writing, I will explore the spiritual aspects of this societal malady. Within this chapter I offer a sampling of metaphysical methods in hope of helping you with your healing process. For more background information check the reading list at the end of this chapter.

As you begin your healing process, it is important that you don't isolate yourself. This doesn't mean that you have to go into the world and declare yourself a survivor. But it is important to have at least one friend or confidant you trust to be there for you. This provides you with a caring supporter who can help you with the meditations (presented within this chapter), and help you in your healing process.

Throughout this chapter you will see names with an asterisk beside them. This symbolizes the pseudonym used for that person.

Reclaiming the Inner Child

As a survivor beginning this process, you confront the self alienation of your little girl. This part of yourself has worked hard for you from the beginning of the abuse. She carries the secret, devises defense mechanisms, shares your nightmarish fears, memorizes the memories, cries with you when the pressure of your secret threatens your life and over and over relives your abuse. Our little girls are vigilant in their efforts to protect us, and determined to be heard. Yet, it is easy for us to forget this important part of ourselves because of how hard she works and the pain she can elicit when she visits us.

I first encountered my inner little girl in a psychodrama group. She surfaced in one of our opening exercises. I remember how numb I was to her existence and hastily removed her from my presence by placing her essence in the closet where we kept the varied props we used to carry out our dramas. I left her there for over two years. It was only after I began my metaphysical studies that I was able to make peace with her and re-integrate her into my life.

My inner little girl's name is Sara. I met and began talking to her in an active meditation. I found her an energetic companion, open to adventures in the world, immensely wise and full of healing advice for me.

Prepare now to rescue this part of yourself, shunned and forgotten under the weight of your childhood sexual abuse. She is a powerful ally, waiting to be activated to help you remember those forgotten pieces of your life you seek, to be the catalyst for releasing your stored rage or that inner comforter you need in the middle of the night. Your little girl waits to be recognized and acknowledged.

Here I offer a meditation to start you on your way to that little girl within.

Set aside some time for yourself when you will not be disturbed. Relax. Take a deep breath from the bottom of your belly and let it out slow. Take another deep breath and let it out s-l-o-o-o-w. Take another deep breath and as you let it out s-l-o-w see yourself moving back in time. Let the years drift away. Further and further you move through your past. High school . . . junior high school . . . elementary school . . . kindergarten. Think about yourself when you were a little girl. See yourself going places, in your neighborhood, with your friends. (If you have difficulty visualizing the young child you, then imagine scenes that relate to the youngest age you can remember.)

Enjoy the feeling of sliding down a slide, climbing a tree, visiting your special place, or playing with some important toy that was yours. Now visualize everyone else fading away except the little girl that is you. Look at this child. Observe what she looks like, how she's dressed, and what toy she may hold.

Move closer to her and ask her name. Listen. Ask her what gift she brings to you. Listen. Ask her what she wants from you in return. Listen. Now ask her if there is anything special she would like for you to do to honor her. Listen. Next, ask her how you can get in touch with her again. Listen. Thank her for coming and speaking to you. Tell her goodbye and if it seems right and okay, hug her.

Take a deep breath and let it out slow. Take another deep breath and let it out slow. Another breath and when you feel comfortable return to the room and open your eyes.

Take a little time and think about who and what you just experienced. You may want to write about your experience and act on the information you've obtained.

Among my clients their little girls have requested everything from stuffed toys to rides in the amusement park. Others have asked to be remembered every day and have taken on roles as spiritual companions.

One of my clients, Karen,* found after doing this meditation, that her inner little girl was actually two little girls: Pat* was between three to five years old and Rena* was about ten. Karen found Pat very talkative, full of energy and ready to tackle the world. But the greater challenge was Rena who stayed mute until she felt comfortable with Karen, realizing that Karen wouldn't abandon her now that she was found.

Karen continues to relate with her little girls regularly. They in turn have become an integral part of her healing process and her life.

One way to integrate your little girl into your everyday life is to create an altar just for her. Begin by finding a piece of cloth with a design that appeals to your little girl. Maybe it has candy canes on it or figures you remember from childhood. Perhaps the cloth is baby soft and pliable. Let the cloth be the beginning foundation for the altar. Now find that special spot to put your little girl's altar.

If you already have an altar, you may want to clear part of the space for your little girl's altar. If you don't have any altar space set aside, consider space on your dresser, chest of drawers, on your mantel, or a bookshelf. One woman I know created an entire playroom for herself, filling it with toys, dolls, kites and other items that pleased her little girl.

Once the place is established, you can begin to put items on the altar for your little girl's pleasure. Put any games you may have played as a child on the altar, like jacks, pick-up-sticks or a jump rope. Maybe you had a little yellow rubber duckie in your tub as a child. Go out and purchase one now and put it on your altar. Next put items or toys you wanted but didn't get as a child. And don't forget to consult your little girl to see if there is anything she wants on the altar that you may have forgotten. Occasionally light a candle and put flowers on the altar.

Don't forget to follow through and do what your little girl asks you to do to honor her. Sara asked me to buy her balloons. So I regularly purchase a helium-filled balloon for her or I buy a package of balloons, blow them up and spread them around my apartment. As I walk from room to room Sara delights in the joy of these colorful, light balls. One day I hope to fulfill her request for a thousand balloons on our birthday.

Now you can move to the really fun part . . . play with one or two toys at least once a week. Put your rubber duckie in the tub with you when you take your bath. Invite a couple of friends over and play jacks. Go to the park and enjoy the swings, slides, sandbox, and other fun things. Have a slumber party. Take your little girl on adventures.

Continue communicating with your little girl. Visit her again and again. Speak to her about problems or issues you're attempting to solve. You will find her wisdom enlightening and loving. So relish being yourself as you nurture this important part of you.

Nommo

As the bond to your little girl grows, you can begin to re-shape your life by using the power of the word. Within the traditions of Westland Central Africa this is called *nommo*. Everyone has this ability, yet we tend to overlook its usage in our everyday lives to solve problems and create peace. For you, *nommo* can be a useful tool in alleviating your inner guilt and shame.

Begin speaking your truth, as you know it. Escape the silent prison, the secret sexual abuse placed upon you. Use *nommo* to share your experience with someone you trust; to remove that inner rage that doesn't let you sleep; to speak to the pain you see in another survivor; and to re-create the emotional, mental and spiritual environment that you live in.

Create affirmations that assert positive healing in your life. For example, you can state, "I am healed of the shame I experienced because of my childhood sexual abuse. I am. I am. I am." Repeat this affirmation or your personal self affirmations over and over with feeling and meaning. Let *nommo* work as your personal word warrior. And each time you speak your truth, be healed by *nommo*.

Useful Suggestions for Healing

Many survivors experience recurring dreams, nightmares or even images involving their childhood sexual abuse while interacting or making love with their current mate, spouse or lover.

It is helpful to do work in your third chakra. This energy center is your power and survival chakra. Images and experiences that diminish your self-esteem and inner power are retained here. Unresolved issues in this chakra lead to physical ailments, like ulcers.

A useful technique for releasing these images is to sit quietly after doing some deep breathing and project a stored picture from out of your third chakra three feet before you. Examine the image. Next destroy the image in any fashion that suits you. You can burn the image in flame or zap it away with your finger or visualize a laser that cuts the picture into tiny pieces that blow away.

Repeat this process over and over on a single image until it no longer appears. Do not be discouraged if the image doesn't stop appearing for some time. The image has been within you for a long time and will take some time to remove.

I found this process to be a very moving one that pushed my emotional button, causing me to cry a lot. Looking at the pictures that were a part of my abuse experience brought up the powerlessness I felt at that time in my life. But I had discovered a tool of empowerment, as each image contained less and less energy with subsequent use of this technique. So remember, don't be afraid to cry when you feel the need, because you are involved in an empowering process.

Psychic Confrontation with the Abuser and/or Family Members

As your healing process continues, you may find yourself needing confrontation with your abuser or family members who may have played an active/inactive role in the abuse situation. Sometimes this is possible, but other times physical confrontation can't happen because of death or lost communication; or you may not be in a place to handle a one-on-one confrontation. Your healing process does not need to stall at this point. An active meditation is an effective tool to accomplish your confrontation goal.

Before you begin your meditation, select a clean, quiet space. Put any power objects you feel important to your healing near you. This will help you to have a clear, focused meditation, so there are no discordant vibrations to interfere with your healing work.

In doing your meditation, it is important that you have a protective psychic barrier around you. A clear bubble, approximately 15 feet from all points on your body is a good beginning. This barrier protects you from psychic attack by anyone you may interact with during an active meditation. So let's begin!

Sit down and take several deep breaths to put you in a meditative inner space. Now erect your bubble 15 feet above your head, 15 feet below your feet, 15 feet from your right shoulder, 15 feet from your left shoulder, 15 feet in front of your chest and 15 feet behind your back.

Feel what it feels like to be in your own safe protective space. No entities are allowed within your safe, protected space except various aspects of yourself (like your little girl, the mermaid you, the gypsy you, etc.), your spirit guides, and your deity.

Now call forth an image of the abuser three feet in front of your bubble. Speak to the abuser and say whatever you need to say to them. Talk from your heart. Verbally release any stored anger or feelings you haven't expressed. Ask questions. If the entity does not want to listen to you, remember you are in control. You can put a big ear in their heart, glue them to their chair or stick them in the middle of a giant spider web.

After you have said all you have to say, go into yourself and find the burdens you've carried all these years and give them back. If you are working with the abuser, give back the shame, the guilt, the grief, the powerlessness you have experienced. Let your inner little girl speak her truth and give back anything she needs to return. Visualize the person receiving those items back. Now see them walking way from you on their path of light.

Take a deep breath, let it out slow. Take two more deep breaths, return to the room, and open your eyes.

Barbara,* a former client, found this technique a good one in confronting her mother. She used this method to release a portion of the pent-up anger she felt toward her mother for not protecting her from a series of childhood sexual assaults. After utilizing this active meditation several times, she was able to meet with her mother and talk about her issues and concerns about her childhood.

Later Barbara told me how important it was to her that she not "lose it" in front of her mother and that she credited her confrontation success with using the active meditation beforehand. Rosa,* another client, found the meditation useful after she confronted her parents about the sexual abuse she experienced.

"After confronting my parents about the abuse from my grandfather I still used active meditations to deal with patterns that are being repeated now that the secret is out. I talk to my dad (in active meditation) when he creates a crisis so the focus is on him and he wants me to take care of him."

If you are ready, this meditation can also be used to forgive the abuser or others involved in your abuse experience. Deciding to forgive your abuser or others is a personal decision you have to make. If you do not choose to use this tool, don't make unnecessary judgments against yourself. Do what feels the most comfortable to you.

The Ritual

You may reach a point in your healing process where you want to activate healing energy around you through the use of ritual. Inspired by the Yoruba tradition, I originally conceived the following ritual to help Rosa resolve some stagnating issues in her healing process. This ritual is offered to you as a guide and you can modify it to suit your specific needs.

This ritual invokes the energies of three Yoruba deities: Yemaya, Ochun, and Oya.

The first deity, Yemaya, the goddess of the ocean, is the giver of all life and the mother of us all as the oceans are the source of all living things. She provides the womb to which we can return and be reborn. Her number is seven and her colors are blue and white. Offerings to her are cornmeal, molasses, watermelons, seashells, and other things you find in the sea.

Oya, Goddess of the winds of change, blows into our lives and strikes her lightning to change our lives. Few lives are the same after being touched by her. Her number is nine. Burnt orange, red, and purple are among her colors. Offerings to her include red wine, eggplant, and grapes.

The sweetness of living comes with Ochun. She is the river that flows around obstacles in our path as she handles our sexual needs. Five is her number and yellow, gold, and coral are some of her colors. To her bring French pastries, oranges, cinnamon, pumpkins, and especially honey.

For clarity in the following ritual, the woman being helped will be called Enduring Woman. She will need three women to help her. Each woman should be chosen carefully for her energy and compassion.

The first woman will take the role of Transformation Woman. It is her responsibility to organize and lead the ritual. To her falls the task of making sure everyone knows her part and follows through.

Able Woman assists the first woman in planning and executing the ritual. She also helps in the preparation of the woman experiencing the ritual.

Backbone Woman is very important because she is the one that will stand at Enduring Woman's back and provide the mental, emotional, and spiritual support she will need throughout the process.

Next choose a date and time for the ritual when everyone won't be rushed. Also consider a place of privacy where there's access to water, a stream, a river or a secluded bathtub.

Two weeks prior to the ritual, Enduring Woman thinks of all the experiences she wants to release and lists them on paper. Muslin cloth and red paint need to be purchased. The cloth should be torn into strips wide enough on which to write words. Next, Enduring Woman selects words she associates with her abuse experience, and paints them on the cloth strips. The strips are then placed within her home in an area where she can regularly see them. She will also need new clothes to put on during the ritual. She might choose a red dress for courage or a white dress to symbolize the cleansing energy she has released in her life following the ritual.

Rosa shared her pre-ritual preparation experience:

> "The process of preparing the words for the ritual was very healing. I didn't realize the power these words had over me. When I first made my list, there were some words I did not want to write (penis, intercourse, love, etc.). Terror rose inside of me.
>
> "When I got to the stage of painting the words on the cloth, I went into a trance state and didn't have any emotions. I was numb. But having the words hanging in my closet helped me to gain control and power over the experiences they represented.
>
> "During the work with the words in the ritual I was able to release a great deal of emotion and bound up energy. The healing circle was complete when I reclaimed words I wanted (vagina, trust, sex, etc.), to feed me in healthy and positive ways in my life."

Ritual Day

Transformation Woman, have Enduring Woman wear clothes that symbolize what she experienced as a child. She removes all her jewelry. Smudge the area(s) to be used and construct an altar with something on it for each of the aforementiond deities. Include any power objects you feel are appropriate. (Example: crystals, stones, a special piece of jewelry, a doll, etc.). Also have items to represent the four elements. You could use a candle for fire, a bowl of water, a rock for the earth and the air is all around.

Come together and salute the four directions. Invoke the energy and power of each woman's matriarchal line by calling the names of each woman's female ancestors and the names of any other woman who is known to be an abuse survivor.

Next invoke Yemaya, Ochun and Oya with the following invocation:

Yemaya, Dream Creator, Full Moon Mama, Isis of the Veil, we come asking you to open the path to your knowledgeable watery depths to help *Enduring woman's full name* find within herself the knowledge and peace she needs to complete this work today. Take her into your nurturing arms and wash her clean of the disrespect borne by her body as you soothe the little girl within.

Empress of the Storm, Lightning Mother, Divine Warrioress, Oya, send your cleansing wind to change this life of pain to one of known courage. Help Enduring Woman to blow away the shadowy abusive remembrances of childhood that plague her mind and keep her from living a fulfilling life. Bring your transmuting power as a gentle breeze that cools and calms while relieving her inner torment.

Ochun, Keeper of the Sweet Rivers of Life, Sensuality Queen, Passionate Love Weaver, Beauty's Light in the World, let your spicy nectar flow through Enduring Woman and cleanse her female organs of any violence or trauma they have suffered. Bathe her in your abundant golden sweetness and light to bring new feelings of joy to replace her tears of woe.

We thank you gracious divinities for these blessings which you bestow upon Enduring Woman today. Aché.

Each woman now lights a candle on the altar, beginning with Transformation Woman and ending with Enduring Woman as she states her affirmation for the day. During Rosa's ritual, as Transformation Woman, I affirmed that all of the stagnating issues she experienced daily would be washed away and not haunt her anymore.

After this is done, Backbone Woman takes Enduring Woman to some private place with the word cloths. Enduring Woman sits with her word cloths, thinking and reviewing her words; the feelings they evoke; the experiences and people she associates with them. As she goes through this process, Backbone Woman helps Enduring Woman talk about her sexual abuse experiences. She also encourages her to let out her feelings by crying, screaming, hitting the words or stomping on them — any and everything short of tearing the words up. Remember, this is a time of intense release and should not be hurried.

While Enduring Woman and Backbone Woman work together, Transformation Woman and Able Woman are preparing the next part of the ritual . . . a cleansing bath.

In a large bowl, mix together one can of evaporated milk, a quarter cup of salt and two quarts of water. Holding the bowl and using one hand to stir the mixture, first Transformation Woman, followed by Able Woman and later Backbone Woman each expresses their affirmations for Enduring Woman's future. These affirmations should include thoughts about her releasing old negative patterns and self-destructive attitudes, receiving the healing Enduring Woman seeks and other positive things she will need for a good life after the ritual.

Your affirmations could be a chant, like — "Good life, good health, lasting love, pleasurable sex, and financial abundance is *Enduring Woman's Name* now and always." Don't be afraid to affirm all of the good your imagination can muster for Enduring Woman's future.

Next, give Enduring Woman a bowl and some soap to wash her words. Let her continue with her process until all her words have been washed and rinsed. When she has finished this part of the ritual, Enduring Woman gives the bowl with the word cloths to Able Woman.

If you are doing the ritual by a river or the ocean, fine; otherwise run water in the bathtub. Have Backbone Woman accompany Enduring Woman to where the bath will take place. At this point Enduring Woman needs to close her eyes and take a few moments to think about the change she is bringing into her life. Her eyes need to remain closed until Transformation Woman tells her to open them again.

Next, Enduring Woman steps into the water. Transformation Woman turns her very quickly counterclockwise several times to signal the beginning of change within Enduring Woman. Now the clothes Enduring Woman is wearing to symbolize all the trauma she has suffered are quickly ripped off. Ripping away clothes is a widely practiced way to rid a person of trauma. The strips of cloth are associated with the Dead and thus the trauma is *made dead* by this ritual.

Transformation Woman slowly pours the cleansing mixture over Enduring Woman's head. Then backbone Woman helps Enduring Woman out of the water, dries her off and dresses her.

As this is happening, Transformation Woman and Able Woman lay a path with the word cloths from where Enduring Woman received her bath to the altar. When Enduring Woman is dressed, she is led to the first word, and steps upon it. Next she reaches down, picks up the word, holds it to her heart, says the word aloud and a positive affirmation about the word. Step by step, this process is repeated until she reaches the altar.

(Special Note: All of the words do not have to be used, but the ones deemed most important by Enduring Woman should be included.)

At the altar Enduring Woman lays the collected word cloths upon the altar and steps back. Each woman in turn bestows her gift to Enduring Woman for the future. This is the place where continuing support can be pledged to Enduring Woman, or the promise of helping at some other point in her healing process or even the gift of sharing fun between the inner little girls of the women can happen.

Thank your ancestors, each of the deities you have invoked, and release each of the four directions.

After the Ritual

It is important that Enduring Woman has some space to relax after the ritual. She may find herself famished and in need of food as this work takes a lot of energy. Days after the ritual she may need to talk about the ritual, how she feels, what she's accomplished and how she wants to proceed with her healing. It is important that the women who participate in the ritual make some time for this part of process in their lives, providing Enduring Woman with a bonded support network to help effect the changes she sought in her life.

Rosa found herself doubting the work she did months after the ritual. She had found the clouds of depression and self-hatred threatening on her horizon again. Once again she was feeling engulfed within her old stuff and very needy.

We made time and talked about the ritual. Together we examined her gains, how her daily living process had changed since the ritual, and how her levels of trust and trust issues were changed or resolved. This enabled Rosa to work through her resultant past issues about her childhood sexual abuse in a new way.

The most important thing is that someone is there for Enduring Woman throughout her healing process. When everything else is not working, caring and giving friends are invaluable.

Before I Forget

There are a lot of other things that can be done metaphysically to help a survivor's healing process. Many of you know or will discover those things as you work on your own healing process. Remember that there are as many methods or techniques as your imagination can conjure.

As you go forward with your healing, here is a short list of books you can read to learn more about the Yoruba tradition, and other healing traditions and options you can use in your healing process.

Bass, Ellen and Laura Davis. *Courage to Heal*. Harper & Row, 1988.
Gil, Eliana. *Outgrowing the Pain*. Launch Press, 1984.
Wippler, Migene Gonzalez. *Tales of the Orishas*. Original Publications, 1985.
Teish, Luisah. *Jambalaya*. Harper & Row, 1985.

Elleggua, thank you for opening the doors to healing for each woman who reads this work. Aché.

Notes

1. Uzuri Amini and Luisah Teish, "Eye of the Vulture," in *Woman of Power* (PO Box 827, Cambridge, MA 02238), Issue 8, Winter, 1988, p. 56.

Penina Adelman

Penina V. Adelman is the author of *Miriam's Well: Rituals for Jewish Women Around the Year* (Biblio Press, 1987). She has an MA in folklore from the University of Pennsylvania, has attended the Pardes Institute in Jerusalem, and is a recent MSW from the Boston University School of Social Work. With a special interest and expertise in Jewish women's rituals, Adelman leads performance workshops on them at Harvard and Brandeis Universities and at Omega Institute. Her articles on ritual have appeared in *Reconstructionist Magazine* and *Genesis 2*. She is also co-author, with Selma Williams, of *Riding the Nightmare: Women and Witchcraft* (Atheneum Press, 1978).

Miriam's Well is a Wheel of the Year ritual book for Jewish women and others that explores women's connection with the cycles of life and the turning seasons. This beautiful book contains a ritual for each of the thirteen lunar months, the thirteen New Moon celebrations of Rosh Hodesh. The monthly holiday of the New Moon has been identified traditionally with women in Jewish teachings, folklore and practice. It is used by modern women as a vehicle for returning Judaism to meaning for active female participants in today's world. Many women celebrate Rosh Hodesh with monthly ritual or study groups. *Miriam's Well* is a contribution to Jewish women's revisioning of religious Judaism, a movement begun in the 1960s.

Says Penina Adelman about Rosh Hodesh and women:

Rosh Hodesh . . . was a natural vehicle by which these groups could wrestle with the issues they needed to resolve in order to remain active participants in their own heritage. Some groups used a lecture/study format with invited speakers and a designated text; other groups combined improvisational dance, meditation, chanting and creative visualization in their hunger to learn about their female ancestors and role models of the present. What most groups do have in common is a wish to return to traditional sources as a way of reinforcing Jewish identity instead of breaking from it completely. The members of a Rosh Hodesh group gain strength from the tradition in grappling with it or integrating it with their new beliefs and practices.

In the process of reclaiming and celebrating Rosh Hodesh, the women of the groups reclaim women's lives, herstory, traditions and rites of passage, as well.

I am delighted to present two rituals from *Miriam's Well* — Penina Adelman's rituals from Jewish women's heritage and tradition — in this anthology of women and ritual. They are important and meaningful rituals for all women, and an honored addition to this book.

Iyyar: A Menopause Ritual

Penina Adelman

Iyyar
April/May
A Time to Keep
And A Time To Cast Away

This month's ritual has been designed[1] with an awareness of our mothers, grandmothers, and great-grandmothers who were earlier inhibited — even in the community of Jewish women — from marking the cessation of menstruation, of *derech nashim* (the way of younger women as in Genesis 31:35) and the release from the physical tasks of childbearing and childrearing. Now wholly freed, our female ancestors would have been ready "to give birth" to their personal creativity, to dip into Miriam's Well without the distractions and responsibilities of family.

We hope to convey a positive tenor to this life cycle event which has been feared and misunderstood by so many men and women in the past.[2] Once a woman has reached the age beyond which pregnancy ceases, her gender identity is often blurred by society. She is in a transitional state, experienced by those interacting with her as being full of power and danger.[3] During the tumultuous fourteenth century when the Black Death struck in Europe, those women who managed to survive the disease and live to old age were thought to be witches.

In interviewing post-menopausal women to arrive at an appropriate ritual marking their "change of life," I found unanimous reactions. All indicated they would forgo any ritual ceremony that emphasized menopause, fearing a societal backlash which might discriminate against them as they advanced in age. Most said they did not feel very different physically after menopause. The aging process itself was their emphasis; the gradual body changes. These were linked not only to menopause, but to the entire process of aging. Whether these same feelings and attitudes will persist when contemporary young women reach *their* menopause is now being speculated.[4]

Some women may choose to mark the end of menopause with a "mature age bat mitzvah" if they have never had one as an adolescent. Setting a goal such as learning to read and speak Hebrew, to read Torah, to lead a prayer service, teaching a Jewish text within the forum of a bat mitzvah, at an age well beyond 12 or 13, is the way many older women are choosing to reenter the tradition after years of alienation from, or passive appreciation of, Jewish ritual.

Others may wish to invite friends who experienced menopause already or are presently undergoing it. My own mother has said that she could not imagine participating in a menopause ritual, but would have liked to get together with her friends to share experiences of those important years of change.

Hithbagrut[†]

Bring: The Book of Ruth (several copies); a group gift for the *mithbogeret*. (As preparation, read the Book of Ruth.)[5]

Setting: Home of the *mithbogeret,* the menopausal or post-menopausal woman, here named Tamar. We are in a sitting room. Have pictures of the woman as a baby, young girl, young woman, bride, mother, grandmother. Flowers and greens of the season decorate the room. Attending are all the female relatives of the *mithbogeret* who can be present — sisters, daughters, mother, aunts — as well as her good friends, including members of the *Rosh Hodesh* group.

Themes of Iyyar

Keeper: *Iyyar* is a transitional month which falls between two major holidays — Pesach, in the month of *Nisan,* and Shavuot, in *Sivan.*

From the second night of Pesach, we count forty-nine days (seven weeks) until Shavuot, the Feast of Weeks. This period is called the *Omer.* When the Temple still stood in Jerusalem, each family would count a sheaf offering of grain to bring to the Temple on the pilgrimage festival of

---

†Like *bagrut,* the term for the young girl's Coming of Age, *hithbagrut* means "maturity, coming of age." However, *hithbagrut* is a reflexive noun, implying a process which reflects a previous maturing process that has been ongoing, a second "coming of age."

Shavuot. The purpose of this may have been partly a way of blessing the Spring harvest which would also be celebrated on Shavuot.[6]

In the act of counting, the Rabbis saw an opportunity to keep track of an inner harvest of spiritual qualities. Every week of the *Omer* was to emphasize a particular attribute of God. Each day of the week then represented a different permutation of the divine attributes.[7]

In the context of this *Rosh Hodesh Iyyar* marking Tamar's *hithbagrut,* one may think of the counting of years and deeds and events which make up a woman's life. Given are seven distinct stages of life corresponding to the seven weeks of *Omer:* conception, pregnancy, birth, childhood, womanhood, motherhood, and maturity.

In the seven-week counting of the *Omer,* we find the suggestion of seven ritual activities which may be performed during the *Rosh Hodesh* celebration for any given month. We take as our impetus the Rabbis' notion of seven divine attributes to be explored and emulated for the purpose of healing the ills of the universe. We have designated these activities: meditation, ritual immersion (*mikveh*), singing, prayer, storytelling (*midrash*), text study (*talmud torah*), eating and drinking.[8]

Omer as a Period of Mourning

Keeper of *Iyyar:* The period of the *Omer* which includes the entire month of *Iyyar* is considered by observant Jews to be a time of mourning. Wedding ceremonies, hair cutting, and playing music are prohibited. The reasons for this are unclear, ranging from a plague said to have killed the disciples of Rabbi Akiba in the early centuries of the Common Era, to the influence of a Roman superstition which held that during this time of year, the souls of the dead wander into the land of the living.[9]

We do not view menopause as a time to mourn the "end of fertility," as have many in the past. Our purpose in coming together today is, rather, to understand and recognize the meaning of menopause for women who have experienced it or will soon enter its phases. Today we have an opportunity to think of new ways for women to mark this time in future years.

Sign of Iyyar

Keeper of *Iyyar:* The astrological sign of the month is the Bull, *Shor. Nisan* is the month during which seeds are planted. The bull ploughs the earth, bending its broad neck to the ground, dragging a heavy load. The bull tends the change from the new Spring growth of *Nisan* to the first Spring harvest of *Sivan*. The rhythms of the earth reverberate throughout the strong body of the bull.

Kavannah

Keeper of *Iyyar:* In some cultures, once a woman has passed the age of childbearing, she is known as the "Wise Woman" of the community. In her reside the knowledge and values of her people which she transmits to the young. Hers is the status of a venerated elder.

This contrasts sharply with the devalued status of the aging female in our own culture.[10] Today we intend to question this and to learn about the experiences all have had during menopause in order to instill new and positive expectations in our children and grandchildren.

One of the major misconceptions we need to address has to do with sex and the older woman. In Judaism, sex has never been linked only to procreation. On the contrary, in addition to procreation, sex exists for the sake of pleasure, wellbeing, and harmony in a marriage. Therefore, when a woman has passed the age of childbearing and even earlier, she is encouraged by Jewish law to enjoy sex with her partner.[11]

Are there any other *kavannot*?

Each woman voices her own intention for the ritual.

Woman: To mark the passing of physical fertility and to rededicate ourselves to a greater focus on spiritual, intellectual, and artistic creativity and fertility.

Woman: To say good-bye to the womb, *rechem,* the center of childbearing.

Woman: To praise and give thanks for the cycles of life which pulsate through our bodies.

Woman: To say good-bye and good riddance to tampons and sanitary napkins and pads and foams and jellies and diaphragms and pills and anything else I've left out — forever!

Tamar, the *Mithbogeret:* I would like this to be a ritual of transmitting wisdom, *hokhmah.*

In Greek, the word for "wisdom," *sophia,* was identified with a female figure. In Hebrew *hokhmah* is a word of the feminine gender. The connection between wisdom and women is clear in Hebrew literature. In the Bible, the wise women of Tekoa and Abel in 11 Samuel 14 and 11 Samuel 20, respectively, are examples of what seemed to be a convention in Israel at that time — a woman of the community who knew how to choose her words wisely and communicate the desired message. She was perhaps a female counterpart to the Hebrew prophet, God's instrument of communication with the people of Israel. More examples are found in Proverbs 14:1 and in the poem recited to the woman of the household on Sabbath evening, "A Woman of Valor." One of the last lines speaks of her mouth, which "opens with wisdom."[12]

In fairy tales, the woman with special powers, with the knowledge of creation and destruction, is either an evil witch or a good fairy godmother. Both are frequently characterized as older women.[13]

In this *hithbagrut* ritual, we teach and lead a discussion based on two stories of mother and daughter figures where the mother passes on her life's wisdom to her daughter. They are the stories of Naomi and Ruth in the Bible, and Demeter and Persephone from Greek mythology.[†]

([†]We suggest that each *mithbogeret* design her own ritual just as in the *bagrut* ritual [*Sivan*]. One woman may write a song or a poem, another may wish to teach a text, another may express the meaning of menopause by talking directly about it, sharing her personal experience, her "wisdom" with the group.)

Storytelling

All should have a copy of the story of Ruth and Naomi, or should have read the story in preparation. Tamar, the *mithbogeret,* then tells the Greek myth in her own words.

Demeter and Persephone

Once there lived a goddess who ruled over the earth. She had power over agriculture, causing abundant growth of cereals and grains. In this way she echoed Naomi and Ruth, women of the land. Demeter had one lovely daughter, Persephone, as fair as the first flower of Spring.

One day Persephone wandered far from her mother to pick flowers which beckoned. Steeped in the fragrance of those blooms, she was startled by Hades, the dark god of the Underworld. He seized her and pulled her down to his cold, damp kingdom beneath the earth.

Demeter sank into despair when her beloved daughter did not return. She entered into mourning, forgetting to bring new buds into being. She grieved for her daughter, even refusing to eat or sleep. Thus, the earth was allowed to wither.

When at last she sought aid from the gods to find her daughter, she was told that if Persephone had not eaten food in the Underworld, she could return unharmed to this world. Though Persephone had not been tempted by food, Hades was able to break her resolve with a single ruby seed of a pomegranate. Knowing that if he could induce her to nourish herself in his domain, he could have her as his wife, he strove to make her taste food. Because of that one seed, she would now have to divide her time equally between Hades and Demeter, between the land of darkness and death and the land of light and life.

That is why the Greeks say that the earth blooms half the year and withers during the other half. When Persephone descends to her husband, Hades, Demeter forgets to bring the buds into being.

Tamar describes the link between these stories in which an older woman passes down special knowledge to a younger woman, and the onset of menopause in which the transmission of wisdom among the members of a women's community is crucial. She tells of her own experience of menopause and asks the other women to share theirs. The younger women who are present share their fears and fantasies of menopause and ask questions of the older women.

Meditation and Movement

Woman: Since menopause involves a new relationship with one's body, we now meditate on ending that segment of our life characterized by an active womb.

This meditation begins with a movement exercise called "Aura-Brushing." The "aura" is the psychic field around an individual. This aura may be affected by fatigue, illness, depression, isolation. The purpose of "brushing the aura" is to symbolize making a fresh start by discarding the cobwebs which drain one of energy.

We start by forming groups of threes, one woman standing in the middle, one on each side of her.

Now the woman in the middle should close her eyes. The other two will begin to whisk the air upward from her feet as they whisper her name repeatedly. They whisk from her feet, her legs, her trunk, up to her neck and head, whispering all the while.

Each woman in the group takes turns standing in the middle while the others two brush her "aura."

Woman: I composed this meditation especially with you in mind. Tamar, as you and I have been working together, I know the kind of imagery you might use for yourself.[14]

It is important to note here that the process just mentioned is a crucial one for the *Rosh Hodesh* ritual. As pioneers in new ritual, we continue to scrutinize our conceptions to create meaningful ceremonies. In this case, Tamar asked for help in saying good-bye to her once-active womb. Another woman might require a different image journey.

Woman: While we composed the following for Tamar, all may participate, even those not yet at menopause. But do not feel you must participate. You may wish to close your eyes, sending healing energy to Tamar. Or, you may wish to start with this visualization and then let your own imagination take over. Some of you may want to leave the room. How you decide to participate is your own choice.

Now, begin by finding a comfortable position. Close your eyes and focus on your breathing deeply in and out. . . .

See yourself carrying your womb in a crystal jar. Look at it carefully. Take the jar with you to Jerusalem. Carry it carefully up to the Mount of Olives. Find a spot on the Mount of Olives and begin digging a hole with your hands.

Dig deeply, and when the hole is deep enough, place the jar containing your womb deep into the Jerusalem earth. Cover the jar carefully. Know that your womb is buried safely, forever. Before leaving the spot where your womb is buried, thank your womb for all that it has given you. Thank the earth for protecting and housing your womb.

Cover the spot with a smooth, white Jerusalem stone. Walk to a nearby waterfall. Stand beneath it and feel yourself cleansed from within and without. Return home knowing that you will continue to be creative and productive. Feel yourself strong and in perfect health.

When you are ready, open your eyes.

When the meditation is over, some of the women share what they felt. Others remain silent, choosing to listen. Tamar is very peaceful, talking about what this ritual evening has meant to her.

Gift

The women present Tamar, the *mithbogeret,* with a gift, one they have made or bought.

The Keeper of *Iyyar* invites all to partake of the food and drink on the table.

Notes

1. This ritual for a woman who has reached menopause has not yet been performed. It is hoped that those women who have marked *Rosh Hodesh* each month for several years will be inclined to view this month's ritual content as one Jewish woman's personal expression in coming to terms with menopause. Each woman will find her own way. A ritual which has been performed and recorded is Irene Fine, *Midlife* (San Diego: Women's Institute for Continuing Jewish Education, 1983). It also makes suggestions for creating a ritual. However, the book steers clear of an adequate recognition of the physiological implications of menopause for women's self-concept. The ritual was not created specifically for women.

2. Williams and Williams (aka P.V. Adelman), pp. 60–61. See also Myerhoff.

3. See Douglas.

4. Doress *et al.,* "Women Growing Older," *Our Bodies, Ourselves,* 1985 ed., pp. 435–472.

5. Book of Ruth, *The Writings.*

6. Kitov, Vol. 2: 356–374.

7. Kitov, Vol. 2: 363–366.

8. See "How to Start a Group."

9. *Encyclopedia Judaica,* Vol. 12: 1382–1389.

10. Paula Gantz, "Our Golden Years—You Should Live So Long!" in *Lilith,* Number 10, Winter, 1982–1983, pp. 6–9; Louis Lowy, *Social Policies and Programs on Aging* (Lexington, Mass.: Lexington Books, D.C. Heath and Company, 1980), pp. 16–17, 176–177.

11. David Feldman, "The *Mitzvah* of Marital Sex," pp. 60–80 and "The Legitimacy of Sexual Pleasure," pp. 81–105 in Feldman, *Marital Relations, Birth Control and Abortion in Jewish Law* (New York: Schocken, 1968).

12. Claudia Camp, "The Wise Women of II Samuel: A Role Model for Women in Early Israel?" in *The Catholic Biblical Quarterly*, Vol. 43, No. 1, January, 1981, pp. 14–29.

13. The witch in "Hansel and Gretel," the evil queen in "Snow White," the fairy godmother in "Cinderella" are various examples of "wise women." See Brothers Grimm, *The Complete Grimm's Fairy Tales* (New York: Pantheon Books, 1944). See Tales 15, 53, and 21 esp.

14. This meditation created by Carol Rose, August, 1984.

Tevet: A Ritual for Mourning a Loved One

Penina Adelman

Tevet
December/January
A Time to Weep

Bring: Bibles, large decorative box or jar, *Yahrzeit* candles, photos, cakes and wine.

Setting: A living room, at the home of the Keeper of the month. It is in the depth of winter. We sit on pillows and on comfortable chairs. The walls of the room are hung with views of ancient and modern Jerusalem. The room is brightly lit with candles and shaded lamps. Since the theme of *Tevet* evokes sadness and mourning, light is essential for balance. (Dark feelings in a dark room will drain the participants of energy, whereas abundant light will function in dynamic tension with the darkness, enabling energy to flow freely.)

Themes for Tevet

Keeper: *Tevet* is a transitional time in the middle of winter when there are no major holidays. The month's principal event is the Fast of the Tenth of *Tevet*.

On that day, Nebuchadnezzar, the evil King of Babylon, laid siege to Jerusalem, the Holy City. Three years later, after continuous siege, the Temple was destroyed. The tenth of *Tevet* marks the beginning of the Destruction for which we fast on *Tisha B'Av*, the Ninth of *Av*.[1]

During this month we re-experience the destruction of Jerusalem, spiritual center of the Jewish people. Fasting symbolizes our mourning state because the central emblem of our faith, the Holy Temple, has been violated.

It is appropriate at this time to remember the deaths of loved ones, by a *yahrzeit,* the one-year anniversary. I would like to invite all those here who have lost someone within the past year to join with me in marking the transition from formal mourning to gathering our memories of their lives into our own.

Each woman marking a death is given a *yahrzeit* candle.

This is the *yahrzeit* of my grandmother's death, so I shall light a candle for her.[2] (The others light candles.)

Some study Torah together at the *yahrzeit* in honor of the deceased person.[3]

Among the Hasidim the *yahrzeit* is considered to be a time of both sadness and joy. The Hasidim drink and eat, dance and sing, in honor of the dead. I would like to mark the *yahrzeits* of those who have died in this way. This will enable us to experience a ceremony both ancient and modern, like the *Rosh Hodesh* ritual itself. There is a tradition among Jews, one which is prominent throughout the Middle East and other parts of the world, the tradition of women mourners.[4] As the prophet Jeremish has said:

> Thus says the Lord of hosts. Consider, and call for the mourning women, that they may come and send for the wise women, that they may come; and let them make haste, and take up a wailing for us, that our eyes may run down with tears, and our eyelids gush out with waters.[5]

Sign of Tevet

The goat, *G' di,* is the astrological sign of this month. The goat works its way slowly, laboriously up the mountain of winter. Though the path is treacherous, the goat never slips or falls. Sure-footed, firmly centered in the earth, the creature eventually reaches the summit. During *Tevet,* as we focus on the cycle of death and life, we are like that goat, slowly climbing up from the depths of sadness and grief into the light of faith and renewal.[6]

The women share memories about their loved ones who have died, and bring them to life in speech for those present.

Woman: Tell us about your grandmother. What was her name? What memories do you have of her?

Keeper of *Tevet:* My grandmother's name was Sophie which comes from the Greek "Sophia," wisdom. Her Hebrew name was Sarah.

The Keeper shows photos of Sophie, explaining the origin of her grandmother's name. She shows an old jar which once stood on the counter of her grandmother's kitchen.

Keeper: This is a "Memory Jar" in which I keep trinkets, objects and whatever reminds me of my grandmother.[7]

Storytelling:

The Keeper of *Tevet* tells stories and anecdotes about her grandmother. The memories traverse the range of emotions from wistfulness to sadness to happiness to grief and back again.[8] An example follows:

> I remember "Granma's" hands. They were always busy doing something, making something. She was stirring the rich brown batter for the honey cake or kneading the soft puffy dough for the Sabbath *challot*. She was polishing the stove till it shone like new, or scrubbing dirty footprints off the kitchen floor. Then there were her geraniums which she trimmed, pruned, watered and admired as if they were her children.
>
> In the last years of her life, "Granma" was not able to continue her activities. She had an operation on her hand. The doctor crossed the nerves by mistake, and the loss of use in her right hand left her bereft and helpless. Still, I try to remember all that she used to do.[9]

The Keeper begins to weep and the other women form a circle around her, arms around each other's waists, shoulders.

Group Wailing

Group wailing is inspired by the accounts of the wailing women in Jeremiah and other writings from the ancient Near East.

One woman begins to wail and moan softly in a manner that sounds like a form of blues singing.

"Sometimes I Feel Like A Motherless Child" (spiritual), sung with or without words, is very likely to inspire sadness and grief which is waiting beneath the surface to emerge.

Some follow the voice of the singer, others harmonize. Then, in the magical way in which song is able to open the heart, some begin to weep.

This is a very powerful and moving exercise. However, it is not for everyone. One must not feel obligated to weep. In fact, those who do not feel like weeping can give support and comfort through their physical presence and through the sounds of their voices. The purpose of group wailing is to lend strength in numbers towards the act of unburdening oneself of personal grief. The group provides a safe haven for the individual to weep and mourn, not in isolation as she is accustomed to do in this society, but in a supportive, understanding environment.

In reciprocal fashion, the individual's loss provides the group members with the opportunity to experience grief as well, both for their own personal losses and for that of the Keeper.[10]

Singing

As the wailing ends, the voices of the women revert to song. One woman sings a tune based on the words of the hasid, Rabbi Nachman of Bratzlav, an Eastern European sage and storyteller of the late eighteenth and early nineteenth centuries.

> *Kol ha-Olam kulo gesher tsar me'od* . . . (All the world is a narrow bridge)[11] . . . She sings another tune by a modern Hasidic rabbi, "Return again." [12]

Healing Circle

Woman: As we stand here in the circle, let's focus on the name of the person whose *yahrzeit* is this evening, as well as others we have lost whose names come to mind. As Absalom, the ill-fated son of David knew, it is a sad thing to have no one "to keep my name in remembrance." [13]

We could say these names aloud, inviting the spirits behind the names to come into the circle with us. In this way, we recognize the continuity between life and death, the circle of existence which permeates all being. We agree with Rabbi Simeon who noted in *Pirkei Avot, Sayings of the Fathers,*

There are three crowns: the crown of learning, the crown of

246

priesthood, and the crown of royalty; but the crown of a good name excels them all.[14]

As names come to mind, the women mention them, pausing between each name to let that name have its place within the circle.

Woman: My great aunt Mira, who died this year.

Woman: My friend Nurit who died of cancer this year.

Woman: My father who died ten years ago this month.

Keeper of *Tevet:* I had a dream this month. I know it was about my grandmother even though in the dream her name was Luthi. The story is a message from my grandmother, I think. Until this dream I had not been able to accept her death. I'd like to tell you about it.

My grandmother used to tell this story about a mysterious figure named Luthi, who had migrated to Israel after the Holocaust. She would only say that Luthi was the one who taught people how to grieve after the Holocaust when everyone felt too dead inside to shed another tear.

Storytelling:

Luthi's Story[15]

My grandmother, Sophie, often spoke of the market in Vilna where she had grown up. On Friday mornings just before the Sabbath, one Jew was not afraid to help another. Here in America, she used to say, "Every Shopper for Her/Himself and May the Fastest Hands Win!" She told me this story once about how, as a young woman, she met Luthi.

It was shortly after World War II in Cleveland on the day before Pesach. Sophie had gone to the grocery store for some last minute shopping. Aronin's Market was stuffed like a cabbage with people frantically buying for the Holiday of Matzos. In the mélée somebody tugged at her elbow.

"Can you tell me where is the *kosher l'Pesach* cooking oil?" asked a tiny woman with an ancient face, soft and shriveled like a peach which has lain in the sun too long.

"Nobody helps an old woman," she complained, in the same way my grandmother complained when she could no longer read the recipes she had written down on crackled pieces of paper.

Sophie left her cart and guided the elderly woman by the arm to a bin with only a few bottles of the pristine oil left.

"Thank you," smiled the weathered peach. "This I will remember. You're a good girl."

As my grandmother pushed her cart to the next aisle to find spices, she saw, to her surprise, a small self-contained woman standing in the center of a crowd of curious listeners. People were whispering, as they do when a celebrity is in their midst, "Come, hear Luthi tell stories. That's Luthi. You *must* hear her."

Luthi's face bloomed as she told her stories. Her earrings sparkled, her eyes beckoned, her mouth luxuriated in each well-chosen word. Was this the same woman who, a few minutes earlier, had been too helpless to find oil?

With the whole store listening, she invited every one of those frantic shoppers down, down, down to the hidden world beneath Aronin's Market where the Pesach hubbub did not yet exist, where there were no stores, no shopping lists, no demands on anyone's time.

As she spoke, all found their way down to the basement of the grocery store. At the bottom of the stairs, instead of the expected piles of discarded flour sacks and canned goods, there were more steps. They were covered with grass and were actually part of a graduated playing field. The green color faded by degrees as it sloped downward over the steps. Suddenly, the crowd was outdoors. Spring seemed far behind. Now winter approached slowly, heavy-footed, a dark bear on the prowl.

Luthi stood at the bottom of this green stairway, beckoning. One by one, she called out the names of those present. Where had she learned them? Those who had not yet been called watched the others go down to her silently. Then Sophie was called. She stood face to face with Luthi, her heart drumming inside her chest. In every direction were small holes, no bigger than hands. Each one contained a single flower which stood straight up.

Sophie asked Luthi if she had a sister and Luthi said yes. She asked if Luthi's sister were winter and she were summer, and again Luthi said yes.

Sophie crouched before an unopened flower and tried to pry it open. "You mustn't open it," Luthi warned. "It's not ready."

My grandmother examined the flowers more carefully. She knew each one by name. Then she realized that the names that had been called out were the same as the names of the flowers.

Luthi explained, "There is a cycle of people and flowers, their names and growing seasons interchangeable. This garden could have been called Auschwitz or Dachau or Treblinka.

Each person has a story. That story is the seed from which the flower grows. Tell the story. Bury your pain in the earth like a seed. Your flower will grow."

My grandmother would later say, "No one ever explained death that way before. We lost so many of my family back in Vilna, we thought it was bad luck to talk about it; that more death would come of talking about death. But Luthi showed us that from telling the pain, by giving it a name, we could grow new life from our seeds of grief." Sophie was never afraid to talk about death or other subjects most people avoided. Her openness was a gift.

When I awoke from my dream, in that instant I beheld my grandmother's face, and at least I knew with my heart that she had died.

Meditation:[16] Precious Pain

Woman: Now I'd like to meditate. This has helped me in the past in grieving for those people I have lost. As in the story, this meditation will focus on the cycles of life and death. If you want to join me, close your eyes and find a comfortable position. Pay attention to your breathing, in and out, in and out, in and out. . . .

As thoughts come in, just watch them and let them go. All the while keep remembering your breathing, in and out . . . in and out . . . in and out. . . .

Now let your mind come to rest on a person who is no longer in your life, someone whom you loved very much at one time, someone you may still love to this day.

Who was this person? How did you come to know him or her?

What brought you together? What caused your lives to inter-mingle?

Remember how it felt to be with this person. . . .

Now it is time for this person to leave. . . . Allow yourself to experience the pain of that separation. . . . Imagine that your pain is a precious stone which you wrap carefully in material you choose. Take care of your pain. Protect it. Cherish it. Keep it.

This pain is also your memory of the person who you have lost. Find a safe place for this pain and keep it there so you can return to it when you need to.

This pain can also be your teacher. What has your pain taught — about loss, about your relationship with this person, about yourself? Consider what you have learned and hold it inside for a while. . . .

When you're ready, open your eyes.

Keeper of *Tevet:* Let's say Kaddish now. My grandmother used to tell us how much she had wanted to say Kaddish for her father and, of course, she was not allowed to do so. Kaddish is one of my favorite prayers. The words sound like rocking, like a mother rocking a baby — *Yitgadal v'yitkadash shmei rabbo. . . .*[17]

The women recite the prayer affirming the wonder and awe of this universe. All join in the call and respond. Then the Keeper invites the women to read original poetry and prose in the Kaddish mode.

Keeper of *Tevet:* We've come full circle, from grief and mourning to joy and praise, the way our ancestors have always managed to do before us. Let's eat cakes and drink sweet wine now in the Hasidic tradition of *yahrzeit.*

All eat and drink. The *yahrzeit* candles flicker in the darkness in memory of those who have passed away.

Notes

1. Kitov, Vol. 1: 325–327; II Kings 25 and Jeremiah 52.

2. Lamm, pp. 202–203.

3. Schauss, p. 299. Suggested for study are these Torah portions about death: Moses' death in Deuteronomy 31: 14–34 and Sarah's death in Genesis 23: 1–20.

4. *Encyclopedia Judaica* 8: 1461; Waldemar Janzen, *Mourning Cry and Woe Oracle* (NY: 1972), p. 16; Rosenblatt, Walsh and Jackson, *Grief and Mourning in Cross-Cultural Perspective* (New Haven: 1976); Y. Sabar, "Lel-Huza: Story and History in a Cycle of Lamentations," *Journal of Semitic Studies*, Vol. 21: 1 and 2, 1976.

5. Book of Jeremiah, 9: 16–17.

6. For a tale of a goat appropriate this month, see "Rabbi Menachem Mendl of Kotsk and the Goat," in Wiesel, pp. 251–252.

7. The idea for a "memory jar" is from Erlbaum ms., p. 6.

Take a box or jar, one that belonged to or was given to you by the person whom you wish to remember. Fill it with your written thoughts and memories of the person. Write down anecdotal experiences or favorite expressions and place them in the container. Decorate it. Put pictures and special objects inside it.

If you fill the container with tangible things, you can always open it and experience these things again and again.

What requires more dedicated energy is to fill the box or jar with meditations—ideas you have written down—and then to tie a ribbon around it or seal it and hold onto it. You need never open the container again. The simple act of holding it, looking at it, and meditating with it transforms the container into an ark for your memories of the person.

8. If it is difficult to remember specific stories about the deceased person, see Zeitlin, et al.

9. P.V. Adelman's memory of her paternal grandmother, Bella Jenkins Williams who passed away before Pesach, 1981.

10. For Group Wailing in another context, see chapter on Tammuz.

11. Hasidic melody from Zeller cassette tape.

12. Tune by Rabbi Shlomo Carlebach; words by Rafi Katz.

13. II Samuel 18: 18.

14. Tractate *Pirkei Avot* 4: 17

15. Personal tale of P.V. Adelman.

16. This meditation is based on ideas from Matia Angelou and Lili Goodman.

17. For other interpretations/explanations of Kaddish, see Schauss, pp. 294–295 and Lamm, pp. 147–187. See Weidman-Schneider, pp. 143–148, for controversy over Jewish women saying Kaddish. An excellent description of one woman's attempt to say Kaddish for her mother is by Sara Reguer, "Kaddish from the Wrong Side of the Mehitzah," in Heschel, pp. 177–181. The basis for women's exemption from saying Kaddish is discussed by Biale, pp. 10–43. For the prayer itself, see Birnbaum, pp. 49–52.

Carol Christ

Carol Christ has helped to shape Women's Spirituality from the very earliest days. Her 1979 book *Womanspirit Rising: A Feminist Reader in Religion* (Harper & Row) was co-edited with Judith Plaskow and is one of the germinal works of the beginning Goddess movement. It presented such writers as Mary Daly, Merlin Stone and Z Budapest, writing about religion, the Goddess and ritual. Her own article in it, "Why Women Need the Goddess," introduced many women to spirituality and is a women's classic. Her 1986 *Diving Deep and Surfacing* (Beacon Press) explores the stages of women's spiritual journey and presents women's writing as sacred texts. Her most recent book, *Laughter of Aphrodite: Reflections on a Journey to the Goddess*, (Harper & Row, 1987) tells her own journey from theology to *thealogy*, her own way into Women's Spirituality and religion.

She is co-chair of the women and religion section of the American Academy of Religion. A native of California, she discovered her spiritual home in Lesbos, the island sacred to Aphrodite and a spiritual mecca for many women. She currently spends much of her time there writing, creating rituals and teaching about the Goddess at the Aegean Women's Studies Institute. Carol Christ is a dedicated feminist, thealogian, educator and peace activist.

In "Eleusinian Mysteries," Carol brings the flavor of the ancient world to women of today, and brings a sense of timelessness and current magick to women's basic ancient mystery, that of mothers and daughters.

She writes about the Goddess in *Laughter of Aphrodite*:

> The symbol of Goddess has much to offer women who are struggling to be rid of the "powerful, pervasive, and long-lasting moods and motivations" of devaluation of female power, denigration of the female body, distrust of female will, and denial of the women's bonds and heritage that have been engendered by patriarchal religion. As women struggle to create a new culture in which women's power, bodies, will, and bonds are celebrated, it seems natural that the Goddess would reemerge as symbol of the newfound beauty, strength, and power of women.

Eleusinian Mysteries

Carol Christ

I n the Aegean Women's Studies Institute our learning begins with trips to the Parthenon and the National Museum, but our spiritual beginning comes at Eleusis, a site sacred to Demeter, the Grain Mother, and Persephone, her Daughter, Queen of the Underworld.

The rituals of Demeter and Persephone at Eleusis were practiced for some 2000 years, from the fifteenth century B.C.E. to the end of the fourth century C.E. Demeter and Persephone are Goddesses of the agricultural cycle, Goddesses of the death and rebirth of the seed crops, Goddesses whose rites were later spiritualized to symbolize the death and rebirth of the soul.[1] The rites of Demeter and Persephone are said to derive from agricultural rituals for women only known as the Thesmophoria. In classical times the rituals of Demeter and Persephone at Eleusis were among the most important in all Greece.[2]

We go to Eleusis because we too want to celebrate the mysteries of mother and daughter. For those of us who are reared on myths and stories of fathers and sons, it is healing to know that once the deepest mysteries of the universe were symbolized in a story about the relationship of mother and daughter. The story of Demeter and Persephone resonates with echoes of the powerful but little-celebrated relationship we have had with our mothers and our daughters.

Our rituals at Eleusis in the summers of 1981 to 1986, are among the first to have been celebrated there in conscious recognition of the Goddesses since the forced closing of the ancient temples about 400 C.E. These rituals have been among the most powerful experiences of my life. It seems as if there is an enormous energy dammed up on the site waiting to be released. Whether that power is the natural energy of the place (all the Greek temple sites are at naturally powerful spots, as Vincent Scully has shown[3]), or the cumulative energy of worshippers, or the power of the Goddess, I do not know.

We travel to Eleusis by bus along a highway built in part over the sacred road that celebrants once walked. The ruins of the ancient temple (which is little visited by tourists) lie at the apex of the heart-shaped Bay of Eleusis. To the side of the sacred way is a shallow cave, undoubtedly once known as the womb of the earth, but later said to be the opening through which Persephone descended to the underworld. The site appears desolate. The temple can barely be distinguished from the other ruins. Only those who know can imagine that this was once one of the most important ritual centers in all of Greece. A single phrase runs through my mind, "So much has been lost, so much has been destroyed." I find myself thinking how different our world might have been if we had known a religion that celebrated womanhood and our bonds with our mothers, our daughters. We come to Eleusis to remember that once there was a time when we were not despised, when we did not learn to despise ourselves. The desecration of the site makes us feel in our bodies the desecration of ourselves. A solemnity overtakes us as we try to imagine how much has been lost, how much we have lost.

Joining hands in a women's circle we meditate on our coming together as women, something that is not so easy to do in our culture. "We have come together as women to learn about our history and to create a community. And so it is appropriate that we come to this place, where the bonds of women with women, mother with daughter, daughter with mother, were celebrated. We come with a sense of new beginning, and we call on ancient Goddesses to give us strength."

We make an altar on the base of what was once one of the columns within the temple. We bring grain, seeds, fruits, and flowers. A beautiful pattern emerges as each woman places her offering on the altar. Someone brings honey and then everything is wet and glistening. We join hands again, this time around the altar we have created. We breathe deeply and draw the beauty, the nourishing power the earth has given and we have brought to the site, into ourselves. Then we reenact the story. Our telling, inspired by Charlene Spretnak,[4] rejects the rape of Persephone as a patriarchal addition. We speak of season and cycle, mother and daughter. As one of us tells the story, two move to the center of the circle and enact the drama.

"In the beginning Demeter gave birth to a daughter and named her Persephone. For a time, mother and daughter were as one. The mother stroked her daughter's hair and told her many things. As they danced together plants and flowers sprang up. The cycle of the seasons is the dance of mother and daughter. For aeons the cycles continued in the same way.

Then one day Persephone realized she was a woman and knew that she must find her own way. Day by day she wandered farther and farther from her mother, until one day she could not find her way back. She was frightened, but she knew she must continue. In her wanderings Persephone learned many things. She knew joy. She knew pain. One day she came to a chasm and heard the cries of the dead. Taking a torch she climbed slowly down. The moans of the dead ceased when they saw the light she had brought them. When Persephone did not return, Demeter was desolate. She mourned and she raged. She draped herself in a dark cape and she cried until she could cry no more. 'No life will come forth from me until my daughter returns,' she said. All the growing things on the face of the earth began to wither and die. 'No life will come forth from me,' she said."

Here at the place of the separation of mother and daughter, we begin to tell our own stories. Our stories of separation between mother and daughter. We speak of daughters taken away from their mothers by angry husbands. We speak of times when our mothers did not understand our lives. We speak of times when we did not understand our mothers. We speak of alcoholic mothers. We speak of daughters who made their mothers fear. We speak of loss. We speak of separation. We speak of anger. We cry. We cry together. We embrace one another. We embrace each other as mother and as daughter. The healing begins. Demeter and Persephone run to embrace each other. We speak of reunions. We speak of daughters who learned to appreciate their mothers. We speak of mothers who can name their daughter's strengths and celebrate. We speak of moments when we saw how alike we are. And of how we learned to appreciate our differences. We embrace each other again. We anoint each other with water. We offer fruit to each other. We join hands again and thank the powers of the place. We close the circle. Each woman takes one flower from the altar and leaves it in a special place on the site. We say that in so doing, "we consecrate the site for women's mysteries once again."

Persephone Visits Alum Rock Park

It is important that we celebrate the land in which we live, forging connections to her. Several years ago I came to know well a particular group of trails in Alum Rock Park in San Jose by walking them several times a week. I saw the grasses dry out, watched the ground rejoice with the rains as the creeks filled with rushing water, and celebrated first green shoots emerging. It seemed natural to have a spring ritual in this place where I had followed the daily changes of the seasons. Because it was spring, I also wanted to celebrate Persephone's return and honor the ancient bonds of mother and daughter.

We meet in the parking lot. When we have all arrived we put on our flower crowns and walk to the alum (sulphur) springs. In a bowl filled with healing water, we dip our fingers and repeat the self-blessing ritual. "Bless my eyes to see your ways. Bless my ears to hear your sweet sounds. Bless my nose to smell your essence. Bless my lips to speak of you. Bless my breasts formed in strength and beauty. Bless my sex without which we would not be. Bless my feet to walk in your paths. Bless me, Mama, for I am your child."[5]

Then we walk up the steep hillside in silence, meditating on the journey of Persephone up from the underworld and on the recent journey of the green plants up from under the soil. After about half an hour, we arrive at a resting point.

Each woman is guided, one at a time, to the center of an enormous California bay laurel. There she is asked to fold herself into a fetal position, to feel herself in the womb of the mother, to know herself nurtured and protected in the womb of the earth. Each woman stays here as long as she wants. When she is ready to be born, we help her out of the tree, shouting, "It's a girl! It's a girl! Oh good, it's another girl!" Our faces are radiant as we emerge.

After we have all been born, we proceed up to the meadow at the top of the hill. Each woman picks one green sprig or flower, which for her symbolizes the rebirth of spring. Each finds a stone in the meadow and places it under the oak tree next to the stones we had left the year before. (When I had looked a few days earlier to see if the stones were still there, a green-and-yellow-striped snake had slithered out between the rocks.) We put our flowers and green shoots on the stones, and offer the food and juice we have brought.

We make a circle, part a few lingering clouds, raise the power, and reenact the myth. We speak of the union of mother and daughter. Of their dance of creation. Of Persephone's need to find her own way. Of Demeter's loss and how she sat on a stone and wept. And of their joyous reunion.

Then each of us takes her stone and holds it in her hands. We name the loss, the bitterness, the grief that has turned to stone within us. We speak of mothers, fathers, grandmothers who have died, lovers who left us, separations too painful to bear. We cry and share our sorrow.

We return our stones to the altar, pour water over them, saying that just as water wears away stone, so the stones within us can be worn away.

Each of us gives the flower or green shoot she has brought to one of the others, making a wish. "I give you my strength." "I give you my laughter." "I give you my ability to clean up messes." And so on, until we have each received a piece of new growth and a wish. And then we feast.

Later we close the circle and make our way down the hill.

Return to Eleusis

My initiation deepens each time I visit the sacred places. During one of the rituals at Eleusis, I express my desire to give birth to a daughter, and am profoundly challenged. Unexpectedly, Caroll, a Jungian analyst who has been deeply influenced by my work but whom I have just met, steps into the center of the circle, looks me in the eyes, and says, "I don't know whether or not you will ever have a physical daughter, but you have many spiritual daughters, and I don't think you're taking responsibility for them." I feel as if I have been addressed by Demeter. Over the next days, weeks, and months, I think about what she has said.

During the previous years I had been deeply depressed about my work. The community of feminist scholars in religion had fragmented after the initial bonding created by our critique of patriarchal religion. As we each chose our own paths, we became aware of our differences. We had not yet come to the place where we could see the commonalities beyond the differences. Most of my friends had decided to continue to work within established traditions to transform them. Some of my closest friends and most admired colleagues had expressed serious reservations about Goddess religion and spirituality rooted in nature. Male theologians sympathetic to feminism drew the line at the Goddess. I felt profoundly isolated. While I had expected criticism from male colleagues, I had not expected it from other feminists. I felt I could not continue to write in face of their criticism. I stopped writing.

As I think about what happened at Eleusis, I realize that I had allowed myself to succumb to the illusion that I was powerless.[6] I had discounted the many women who had drawn strength from my work. I had denied the power of my own experiences, the power I had drawn from the earth, from the Goddesses. Later that summer I wrote in my journal: "I chose to view myself as a victim. I need to recognize that I have made choices, that the experiences I have had and the thinking I have done are powerful. I must understand that if I challenge the traditions, I will meet opposition. I must recognize that my thinking is not only my thinking, that if it is true, it comes from a source much larger than myself. I have drawn from the well

258

of women's wisdom, from the earth, from the power I call Goddess. I am only one voice among many. When we disagree it is not entirely personal. If what I write contains truth, it will be heard. All I can do is to be faithful to the piece of vision and truth that I know because I have experienced it deeply within myself. The rest is not up to me." Since that time I have claimed my power and begun to write more freely, more boldly, and in a way that is more clearly connected to the sources of my vision. I worry much less about what others think. I have gained, what Aloudres, the Haitian priestess who initiated my friend Karen Brown, promised her, "plenty confidence in myself."[7]

Notes

1. See George Mylonos, *Eleusis and the Eleusinian Mysteries* (Princeton: Princeton University Press, 1961), 41; Mircea Eliade, *A History of Religious Ideas*, Vol. 1, trans. Willard Trask (Chicago: University of Chicago Press, 1978), 290–301.

2. Mara Keller, "The Mysteries of Demeter and Persephone," unpublished; Sarah Pomeroy, *Goddesses, Whores, Wives, and Slaves* (New York: Schocken Books, 1975), 77–78.

3. Vincent Scully, *The Earth, the Temple, and the Gods*, rev. ed. (New Haven: Yale University Press, 1962).

4. Charlene Spretnak, *Lost Goddesses of Early Greece* (Boston: Beacon Press, 1978), 105–107.

5. See Zsuzsanna E. Budapest, "Self-Blessing Ritual," in *Womanspirit Rising*, ed. Carol P. Christ and Judith Plaskow (New York: Harper & Row, 1979), 269–2.

6. This was particularly ironic given that I had written about Margaret Atwood's phrase, "This above all, to refuse to be a victim . . . give up the old belief that I am powerless," and had even taken it as a personal motto; see *Diving Deep and Surfacing*, 49.

7. Karen Brown, "'Plenty Confidence in Myself': The Initiation of a White Woman Scholar into Haitian Vodou," *Journal of Feminist Studies in Religion 3*, no. 1 (1987), 67–76.

Also by Diane Stein:

Casting the Circle
A Women's Book of Ritual

All Women Are Healers
A Comprehensive Guide to Natural Healing